THE

COCKTAIL ATLAS

AROUND THE WORLD IN 200+ DRINKS

CHRIS VOLA

UNION
SQUARE
& CO.

NEW YORK

UNION
SQUARE
& CO.
NEW YORK

ISBN 978-1-4549-5240-4
ISBN 978-1-4549-5241-1 (e-book)

Library of Congress Control Number: 2024936604

For information about custom editions, special sales, and premium purchases, please contact specialsales@unionsquareandco.com.

Printed in India

2 4 6 8 10 9 7 5 3 1

unionsquareandco.com

Editor: Caitlin Leffel
Cover design: Patrick Sullivan
Interior design: Gavin Motnyk
Illustrator: Zoë Barker
Illustration, page iii: Shutterstock.com: Intellson (globe)
Project Editor: Ivy McFadden
Production Manager: Kevin Iwano
Copy Editor: Donna Wright

FOR ANY FELLOW TRAVELER WHO BELIEVES THAT THE BEST
WAY TO EXPERIENCE THE WORLD IS BY TASTING IT

CONTENTS

NORTH AMERICA

OCEANIA

SOUTH AMERICA

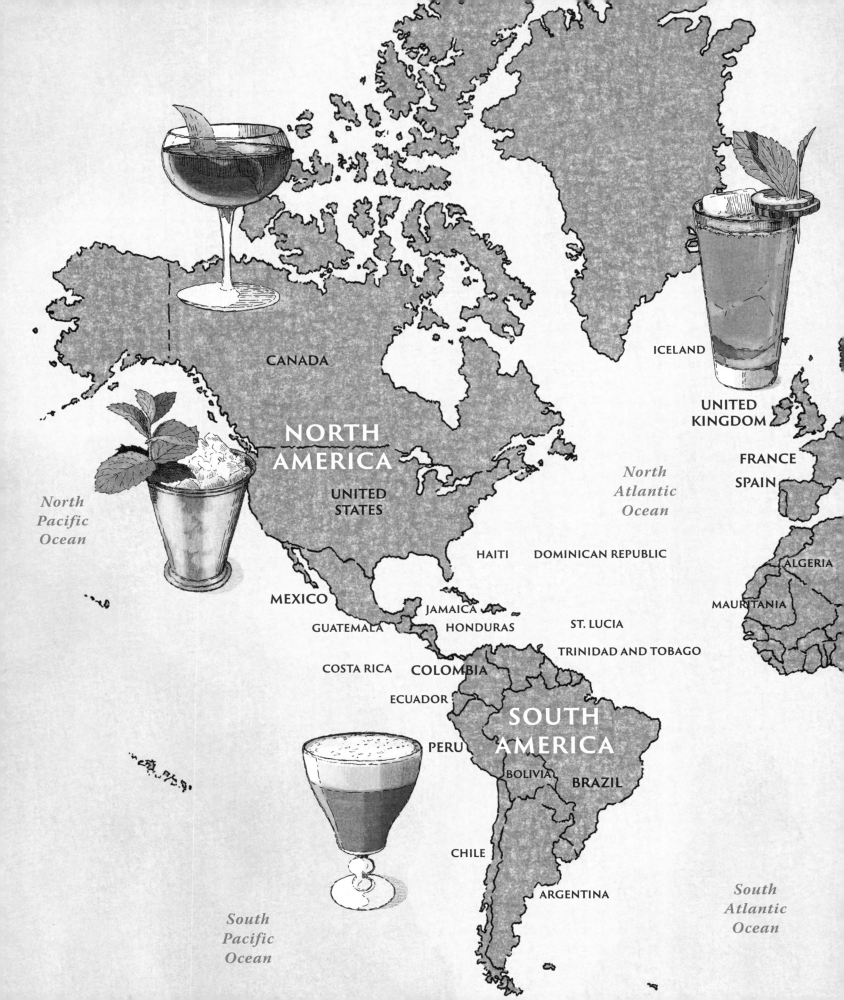

NORTH AMERICA

CANADA

UNITED STATES

North Pacific Ocean

MEXICO

GUATEMALA

COSTA RICA

HAITI   DOMINICAN REPUBLIC

JAMAICA   HONDURAS

ST. LUCIA

TRINIDAD AND TOBAGO

COLOMBIA

ECUADOR

PERU

SOUTH AMERICA

BOLIVIA   BRAZIL

CHILE

ARGENTINA

North Atlantic Ocean

ICELAND

UNITED KINGDOM

FRANCE

SPAIN

ALGERIA

MAURITANIA

South Atlantic Ocean

South Pacific Ocean

Arctic Ocean

FINLAND

RUSSIA

EUROPE

KAZAKHSTAN

MONGOLIA

CHINA

ASIA

JAPAN

Pacific
Ocean

SOUTH
KOREA

EGYPT

INDIA

SUDAN

THAILAND

AFRICA

SRI LANKA

PAPUA
NEW GUINEA

MADAGASCAR

Indian
Ocean

OCEANIA

AUSTRALIA

SOUTH
AFRICA

Southern
Ocean

NEW ZEALAND

INTRODUCTION

For countless budding globetrotters, especially those born before the digital age, their first glimpses of a wider world came from perusing the pages of an atlas. Throughout the centuries, these impressive collections of maps and charts—named for the mythological Greek Titan who was condemned to hold up the heavens for eternity—have been absorbed with wonder, sparking love affairs with geography and allowing bookworms to savor exotic tales of distant lands and legendary creatures from the safety of their favorite reading perches. And while the classic world atlas—like a research trip to the library—may be somewhat of a relic, the format lives on in numerous recent works that ingeniously use the atlas template to navigate any number of topics, from anatomy and ghosts to comic books and *Star Wars*.

As an atlas-obsessed kid myself, I spent entire days memorizing the names of far-off jungles and mountain ranges, following the paths of sinuous rivers and trade routes, tracing centuries of fluctuating geopolitical boundaries, and dreaming of the day when I'd be able to take in all of it firsthand. And while my travel bucket list is continually expanding, I've been fortunate enough to do a fair amount of journeying in the past two decades, immersing myself in surreal landscapes and far-flung cultures from the High Arctic to Kathmandu.

Wherever I've been, one consistent rule seems to be that if you're looking to discover a slice of a place's true soul, it's best to head to wherever locals gather for refreshment, whether in the form of a bustling pub or café, a colorful seaside shack, or a tranquil trailside hut. Sampling dishes and spirits particular to a region, served by the people who grew up with, and in some cases even cultivated, them can offer unparalleled insight into a community's history, values, and traditions, if you choose to fully open your ears—and taste buds. And it's nearly impossible to beat the kind of camaraderie that occurs while sharing a tasty, locally inspired beverage (or three).

Combining my more than fifteen years of experience in the spirits industry and my lifelong love of travel, geography, and always finding the best seat at the bar, I humbly offer this small contribution to the atlas catalogue, a world tour of my favorite drink recipes inspired by countries spanning six continents, and an exploration of the cultures and ingredients that have shaped them. Imbibe like a suave Viking with a Gimlet variation using Brennivín—or Icelandic schnapps—from that country's poshest bar (see page 165). Planning a trip to Trinidad and Tobago? Get in the mood with a tropically inspired, rum-forward Queen's Park Swizzle (page 233). Or taste history in a glass with well-traveled libations like the Suffering Bastard (page 30), a gingery, fizzy thirst quencher that features ingredients from the United States and United Kingdom, was created in Egypt, and has been cited as a contributing factor to the victory of the Allied Forces in World War II. This book contains some of the most highly regarded and oldest classic cocktails, interesting takes on international standbys like the Negroni and the Caipirinha, pioneering concoctions from globally recognized watering holes and innovative bartenders like Uganda's Fred Kubasu and Sweden's Maria Hallhagen, as well as a few dozen of my own creations. For places like the Middle East and parts of Africa where alcohol is scarce or even prohibited, I've attempted to incorporate popular regional flavors as authentically as possible—backed by a boozy kick, of course. With 195 countries and dozens of unique national spirits represented—as well as several lovingly detailed maps for all the cartophiles out there—even the most seasoned booze traveler should expect a few welcome surprises and an arsenal of fun facts to utterly dominate the bar trivia scene.

Atlas readers, according to famed sixteenth-century cartographer Gerardus Mercator, "shall straight away behold the special gifts and peculiar excellence of every country." And as you, intrepid reader of *The Cocktail Atlas*, will discover, the best gifts are often of the liquid variety!

Trinidad and Tobago / Queen's Park Swizzle (page 233)

BARWARE AND GLASSWARE

If you're trying to travel the world via your home bar, you might be concerned about all the gear you're going to need. But it's not hard to travel with the following essentials, most of which can be stowed snugly in any carry-on.

BARWARE

BARSPOONS: There are practically as many barspoons out there as there are countries, but you only need two: a thin, long-handled spoon with a teardrop-shaped bowl for stirring and a sturdier, wider spoon for cracking and shaping ice. If appearances aren't a concern, a long chopstick (or a dawa stick if you're in Kenya) also works great in a pinch.

HAWTHORNE STRAINER: Use a Hawthorne strainer for stirred and shaken drinks. This flat-topped favorite of bartenders around the globe has a coiled wire around the edge that fits snugly into any glass or shaker.

ICE MOLDS: Unless you're in a place like Iceland with a glacier in your backyard, you're going to need to create your own big, sexy blocks of ice. Invest in a couple of silicone ice cube molds, as well as ones that form rectangular blocks called Collins spears, which are ideal for tall drinks.

JIGGER: Wherever you're crafting cocktails, accuracy is fundamental. Use a jigger (or jiggers) with 2-ounce, 1-ounce, ¾-ounce, and ½-ounce markings. In instances where a drink calls for a measurement that falls in between the markings, use your best judgment. For example, when measuring ⅜ ounce of an ingredient, make sure that the liquid gets as close as possible to the ½-ounce mark without touching or going over it.

MIXING GLASS: A pint glass is perfectly fine, but if you're looking to splurge on a professional mixing glass, choose a sturdy one that can hold at least 2 cups of ice and hooch.

MUDDLER: Try to avoid wooden muddlers and those with perforated ends, as they tend to be less durable and harder to clean. Heavy, smooth, plastic muddlers work best—and probably should go in your checked baggage to avoid any awkward weapons-related conversations with airport security.

PEELER: Any inexpensive Y-shaped peeler will work nicely. It offers more control than a straight vegetable peeler—or, say, a traditional hunting knife from Burundi's Hutu tribe—and more control means less potential for finger carnage.

SHAKERS: Busy bartenders tend to opt for a Boston shaker set (two metal tumblers of different sizes that fit together) due to their larger capacity and efficiency in high-volume situations. But in places like Japan, where attention to detail is prized above speed, and anywhere you aren't churning out hundreds of cocktails a night—as in, your kitchen—it's perfectly fine to use a classic three-piece shaker (the kind with a built-in strainer).

GLASSWARE

CHAMPAGNE FLUTE: Another stemmed glass, the Champagne flute has a slender, elongated bowl and is used for elegant drinks comprised mostly of Champagne and other sparkling wines like those found throughout Europe.

COLLINS/TALL GLASS: Larger glassware comes in a variety of styles. The most common of these is a cylindrical tumbler called a Collins glass. For the purposes of this book, the Collins glass can be used for any tall drink requiring ice and club soda, like Namibia's Rock Shandy (page 59), or one that requires lots of crushed ice, like many of the tropically inspired concoctions from the Caribbean and Pacific Islands. However, a standard kitchen water glass or pint glass will work just fine.

COUPE: Alleged to have been inspired by a mold of the breast of France's Marie-Antoinette, this classic stemmed cocktail glass is still used for most drinks served without ice, such as a daiquiri or Last Word (page 239). The longtime bartender favorite should have a bowl that can hold at least 5 fluid ounces.

FIZZ GLASS: A fizz glass is basically just a smaller Collins glass, traditionally used to serve drinks like a Gin Fizz.

JULEP CUP: A descendant of the silver vessels that arose in the American South in the eighteenth and nineteenth centuries, today's julep cups are more commonly made of stainless steel or copper. All three metals are great at keeping drinks like the Mint Julep colder for longer by retaining the temperature of the ice.

MUG: Imbibers on every continent have used a wide variety of mugs to hold their beverages of choice. For heated drinks like the Himalayan Hot Toddy (page 113) and Irish Coffee (page 166), you'll want a hardy ceramic mug with a handle to prevent scalding or a heat-safe glass mug that won't shatter when filled with hot liquid. If you're one of the billions who regularly consumes coffee or tea, chances are you'll be well-stocked already.

ROCKS GLASS: Also referred to as an old-fashioned glass or a lowball glass, this short and stout tumbler is used for spirit-forward drinks served with ice, or "on the rocks." Rocks glasses typically hold between 6 and 10 fluid ounces.

DOUBLE ROCKS GLASS: This slightly roomier tumbler usually holds between 12 and 16 fluid ounces and is ideal for both higher-volume stirred drinks as well as any shaken, citrusy cocktail that requires ice, such as Jamaica's Soursop Margarita (page 223).

WINEGLASS: An attractive option for fizzy, spritz-style drinks, this household staple, depending on its size, can also be used in place of a coupe, Champagne flute, or Collins glass when needed.

SYRUPS

Wherever your journeys may take you, you'll find so-called health-conscious drinkers bemoaning the mere mention of sugar. Nevertheless, sweet elements are crucial for creating perfectly balanced drinks. The following easy-to-make syrups are used frequently in the cocktails in this book.

Bissap Syrup
Yield varies

1⅓ cups superfine sugar
1⅓ cups water
3 (35-gram) hibiscus tea bags
2 teaspoons finely grated fresh ginger
1 teaspoon orange blossom water
Small handful of mint leaves

Combine the sugar and water in a small saucepan and bring to a simmer over high heat, stirring until the sugar has completely dissolved. Remove from the heat and add the tea bags. Steep for 10 minutes, then remove and discard the tea bags. Stir the ginger and orange blossom water into the hibiscus syrup and steep for 5 minutes. Strain the syrup through a fine-mesh sieve into a glass measuring cup and let cool to room temperature, about 20 minutes. Pour into an airtight glass container, cover, and store in the refrigerator for up to 1 week.

Cinnamon Syrup
Yield varies

1 cup superfine sugar
1 cup water
3 cinnamon sticks, crushed

Combine the sugar, water, and cinnamon sticks in a medium saucepan and bring to a boil over medium heat, stirring until the sugar has completely dissolved. Reduce the heat to low and simmer for 2 minutes, then remove from the heat. Strain through a fine-mesh sieve into an airtight glass container. Cover and store in the refrigerator for up to 1 month.

Ginger Syrup

Yield varies

1 part superfine sugar
1 part fresh ginger juice (see Note)

Combine the sugar and ginger juice in a nonreactive airtight container and stir until the sugar has completely dissolved. Cover and store in the refrigerator for up to 5 days.

NOTE: To make ginger juice, simply peel and grate fresh ginger, then squeeze the pulp by hand to release the juice.

Honey Syrup

Yield varies

1 part water
3 parts honey

In a small saucepan, bring the water to a simmer over medium heat; do not allow it to boil. Combine the honey and hot water in a heat-safe airtight container and stir until well blended. Cover and store in the refrigerator for up to 5 days.

Pomegranate Syrup

Yield varies

4 parts simple syrup (see below)
1 part pomegranate juice concentrate, such as FruitFast

Combine the simple syrup and pomegranate juice concentrate in an airtight container and stir until well blended. Cover and store in the refrigerator for up to 1 week.

Simple Syrup

Yield varies

1 part superfine sugar
1 part water

Combine the sugar and water in an airtight container and stir until the sugar has dissolved. Cover and store in the refrigerator for up to 5 days.

NOTE: For Demerara syrup, replace the superfine sugar with Demerara sugar.

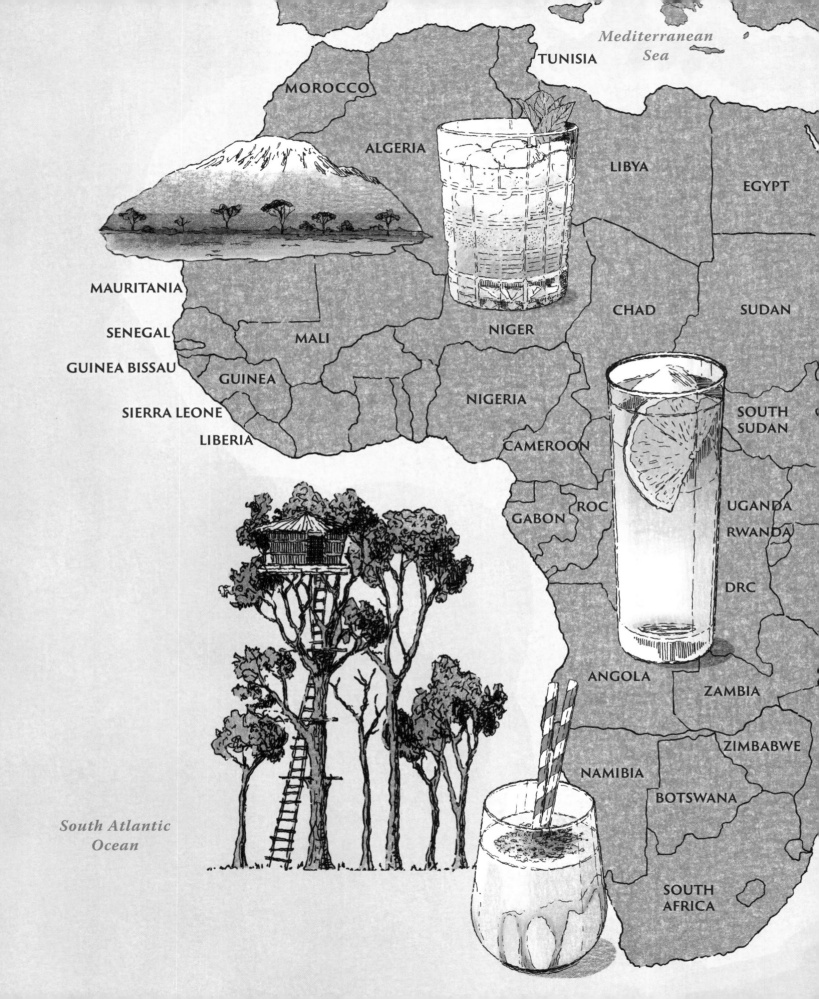

MOROCCO

TUNISIA

Mediterranean Sea

ALGERIA

LIBYA

EGYPT

MAURITANIA

CHAD

SUDAN

SENEGAL

MALI

NIGER

GUINEA BISSAU

GUINEA

NIGERIA

SOUTH SUDAN

SIERRA LEONE

LIBERIA

CAMEROON

GABON

ROC

UGANDA

RWANDA

DRC

ANGOLA

ZAMBIA

ZIMBABWE

NAMIBIA

BOTSWANA

South Atlantic Ocean

SOUTH AFRICA

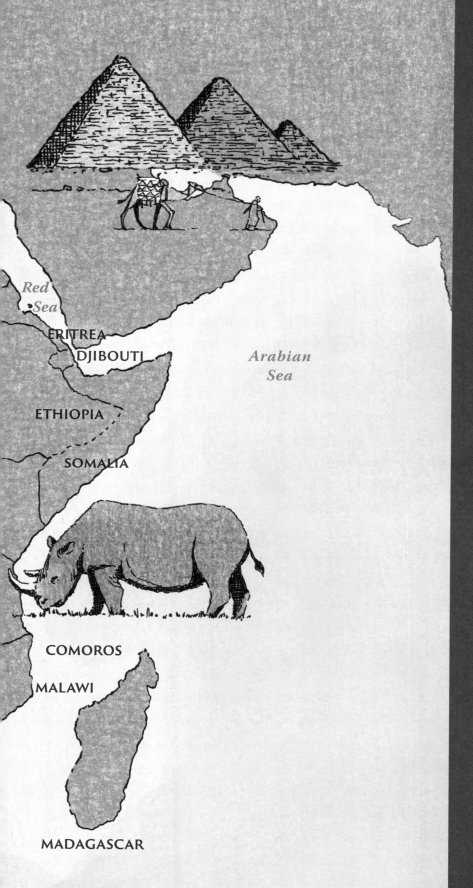

Red
Sea

ERITREA

DJIBOUTI

Arabian
Sea

ETHIOPIA

SOMALIA

COMOROS

MALAWI

MADAGASCAR

AFRICA

ALGERIA

Algeria is a land of vastness. Spanning from the balmy shores of the Mediterranean to some of the most forsaken stretches of the Sahara Desert, it's the biggest country in Africa and tenth largest in the world by area. And even with a sizable population of 44 million citizens—about 90 percent of them residing near the fertile coastline—you'd be hard-pressed to find anyone looking to indulge in a cordial or two. Alcohol is illegal to consume in public, and despite some local palm wine production and beer and wine available at some hotels and restaurants, it's simply not a part of the culture. That's because, like its neighboring countries in the Maghreb region, Algeria has been governed by conservative Muslim regimes for most of the past twelve centuries.

Except for a 132-year period starting in 1830, when France invaded capital city Algiers and decided to stay. It's hard to overstate the negative ramifications of colonialism, but it allowed French soldier and boozy alchemist Gaëtan Picon to familiarize himself with local herbs like gentian and cinchona while stationed in the Algerian countryside. He used these to create Amer Picon, a vegetal, bittersweet aperitif that quickly became a popular tonic for French tipplers both at home and abroad. It was a particular favorite of nineteenth-century Basque immigrants to the United States, who are credited with the earliest recipes for the Picon Punch, an intensely zesty yet refreshing blend of Amer Picon, brandy, grenadine, and soda. Since Amer Picon is no longer commercially available in the United States, you may have to perform some alchemy of your own to re-create its distinct taste (see the recipe opposite), but it's worth it to experience a moment of Algerian history and the unique flavors of its landscape.

IN MOST OF THE UNITED STATES, Amer Picon has become a virtually unknown ingredient to all but the most esoterically minded bartenders. But, oddly enough, Picon Punch is still considered the unofficial drink of Nevada, due to the state's large population of Basque immigrants.

Picon Punch

Makes 1 drink

1½ ounces Amer Picon (or homemade substitute; recipe follows)

¼ ounce grenadine

Club soda, to top

½ ounce brandy

1 long lemon twist, for garnish

Pour the Amer Picon and grenadine into a tall glass filled with ice. Top with club soda, leaving a little room at the top of the glass. Float the brandy on top by pouring it over the back of a spoon into the glass. Place the lemon twist in the glass beside the ice.

Amer Picon Substitute

Yield varies

2 parts Amaro Ramazzotti

2 parts dry curaçao

1 part gentian liqueur, such as Suze

Combine all the ingredients in an airtight container. Cover and store in the refrigerator for up to 1 month.

ANGOLA

With a relatively stable government and a swiftly growing economy due to the largest oil reserves in sub-Saharan Africa, Angola is forging a unique identity as a major force on the world stage. But like much of the continent, the birthplace of dreadlocks and the home of the majestic and critically endangered giant sable antelope is still influenced by its colonial past, when it was ruled by Portugal from the fifteenth century all the way until 1975. In addition to the pervasiveness of the Portuguese language and Christianity, Portugal's influence here extends to Angolan cuisine, particularly in spicy seafood and meat dishes that create a fusion among local ingredients and non-natives like onion, garlic, and chiles.

Both of Angola's most popular drinks, however, are strictly African affairs. Kissangua, a traditional sweet and starchy nonalcoholic cooler, has been made from local maize flour for centuries, and the country's preferred tipple, creamy Amarula liqueur, comes from nearby South Africa, where its one-of-a-kind flavor is provided by the fruit of the indigenous marula tree. Even before Amarula's recent increase in global popularity, Angolans were importing it by the truckload. On its own or served over ice, the nutty, caramelly mélange is an exemplary after-dinner treat. But when combined with vanilla ice cream and diced chiles, it anchors a beautifully complex dessert beverage with enough heat to make even the most spice-immune Angolan blush.

Fiery Dusk
Makes 1 drink

3 ounces Amarula

1 scoop vanilla ice cream

1 teaspoon finely chopped chile (preferably cayenne)

1 vanilla bean, for garnish

1 whole cayenne pepper, for garnish

Combine the Amarula, ice cream, and chopped chile in an ice-filled shaker or a blender. Shake vigorously or blend and then pour into a double rocks glass over ice. Place the vanilla bean and the whole cayenne pepper in the glass.

Angola / Fiery Dusk (page 9)

BENIN

One of the only positive things about conflict is that it tends to breed innovation, as lovers of Benin's national spirit, Sodabi, can attest. The palm-sap-based liquor was created by Bonou Kiti Sodabi, who, as a young man, was forced to fight for France during World War I. On his journeys through the European countryside, Sodabi studied various distillation techniques and, after the armistice, applied these methodologies to the lightly alcoholic palm wines of his homeland. The resulting self-named hooch was an overwhelming success, spreading to the farthest corners of Benin, where it's an important part of weddings, baptisms, and funerals. It's also a popular aperitif or digestif as well as a sign of good faith and camaraderie at business negotiations.

When those deals close—or whenever else they feel like it—the Beninese like to incorporate the intensely floral, nutty, and peppery liquor (which also comes in several flavored versions) into a range of fruity, spicy, and fragrant cocktails. The Caméléon, a signature libation from the country's major distiller, Tambour, beautifully checks off all three flavor boxes. Just like a chameleon constantly changing its colors, the citrusy sipper starts with a mango-forward, tropically inclined nose that's enhanced by Sodabi's notes of plantain and woodiness, then follows that up with an eye-opening dose of hot-pepper heat for a finish as big as the ego of a man with the audacity to name an entire category of spirit after himself.

BENIN'S LEGAL DRINKING age of twenty stems from the ancient belief that consumption of palm wine, or "liquor of the gods," by minors is highly displeasing to the local deities and therefore very bad luck.

Caméléon

Makes 1 drink

Chili powder, for rimming the glass

Fine salt, for rimming the glass

1 lime wedge, for rimming the glass

1½ ounces mango juice

1 ounce Tambour Original White Sodabi (if unavailable, use white rum)

1 ounce Cointreau

½ ounce fresh orange juice

½ ounce fresh lime juice

Combine equal parts chili powder and salt on a small plate. Run the lime wedge around the rim of a coupe, then dip the rim into the salt mix to coat; set aside. Combine the mango juice, sodabi, Cointreau, orange juice, and lime juice in an ice-filled shaker. Shake vigorously and then strain into the prepared coupe.

BOTSWANA

Several of Africa's nicknames—"the Motherland," "the Cradle of Civilization"—refer to the continent being the birthplace of our species. According to archaeologists, Botswana might have been the hand that rocked that cradle. Evidence of modern humans living in the Southern African nation goes back more than 200,000 years, when we were just as likely to hunt Botswanan fauna as be eaten by it. Today, those lions, elephants, hippos, rhinos, wildebeests, and dozens of other large mammals are no longer food for the table, but fodder for photo ops on safaris, which account for much of the country's tourism revenue.

In addition to sampling Botswana's traditional sorghum and millet beers, guests on tour with the uber-swanky Great Plains Conservation safari group are treated to a full menu of signature cocktails. The most versatile of these, Zarafa's Cinnamon Amarula Iced Coffee—named after the company's popular Zarafa campsite—is a perfectly caffeinated pick-me-up for getting the day started or cooling down after a day spent upping your social media cred on the hot savanna. Attributed to chef Lungile Mbangi, this super-refreshing recipe combines the region's favorite liqueur, nutty and citrusy Amarula, with copious quantities of cinnamon, milk, and coffee to give you all the energy you need in the highly unlikely chance your jeep breaks down and you must, like your ancestors, flee a pack of hungry predators on foot.

Zarafa's Cinnamon Amarula Iced Coffee

Makes 1 drink

1 heaping tablespoon medium-ground roast coffee

5 ounces boiling water

1 cinnamon stick

1 ounce Amarula

8 ounces whole milk

Pinch of freshly ground cinnamon, for garnish

Use a coffee plunger to steep the ground coffee in the boiling water for 5 minutes, then press the plunger down completely and pour the coffee into a container. Drop the cinnamon stick into the coffee and refrigerate for 30 minutes. Discard the cinnamon stick, then mix the Amarula into the coffee and pour into a double rocks glass.

Bring the milk to a boil in a small saucepan, then pour into a clean coffee plunger. Vigorously push the plunger up and down to froth the milk. Add ice to the double rocks glass and spoon some milk foam over the ice. Sprinkle with the cinnamon.

IN THE 1890S, Botswana was one of the first countries to introduce a version of nationwide prohibition, when King Khama III of what was then known as Bechuanaland banned alcohol on tribal lands to combat exploitation by invading British colonizers.

BURKINA FASO

A combination of words from the Mossi and Dyula dialects, Burkina Faso roughly translates to "Land of Incorruptible People." It's a fitting name, given that it's hard to be corrupted when you might not be able to understand many of the people around you. This landlocked country in the heart of West Africa is home to sixty indigenous languages and even more ethnic groups, with the Mossi being by far the most numerous, at about 52 percent of the total population. Couple that linguistic divergence with Burkina Faso's widely varied topography, which shifts dramatically from grassy plateaus to river valleys to dense forests, with wild climatic shifts between the rainy and dry seasons, and this is a place of vast diversity.

The one exception is the widespread use of French as the language of government, education, and business—a vestige of the days when the country, once known as the Upper Volta Colony, was part of France's vast territorial holdings. And while Burkina Faso has spent decades developing its own distinct identity, its people still have a great fondness for French pastis, the absinthe-like liqueur that's been delighting licorice lovers since the early 1900s. Combining that anise-forward bouquet with the heavy pineapple vibes of Zoom Koom, Burkina Faso's most popular traditional beverage, the Pastis Ananas is a delicately herbaceous, smoothly tropical, slow-sipping treat with a unique profile that transcends continents and cultures. And that sounds great in just about any language.

Pastis Ananas

Makes 1 drink

1½ ounces pastis

¾ ounce pineapple syrup (recipe follows)

½ ounce fresh lime juice

1½ ounces mineral water

Combine the pastis, pineapple syrup, and lime juice in an ice-filled shaker. Shake gently and then strain into a double rocks glass over ice. Top with the mineral water.

Pineapple Syrup

Makes about ½ cup

¼ cup sugar

1 cup water

½ pineapple, rind removed, cut into small cubes

Combine the sugar and water in a small saucepan and bring to a boil over high heat. Add the pineapple, reduce the heat to medium, and cook for 20 minutes. Strain the syrup through a fine-mesh sieve into an airtight container and let cool. Cover and refrigerate for up to 7 days.

BURUNDI

Though it's perhaps best known today for being the poorest country in the world, Burundi is far more than just an unfortunate economic statistic. Gaining independence from Belgium in 1962, this mostly rural, landlocked East African republic contains several nature reserves and unspoiled national parks, produces some of the best quality tea and coffee in the region, and, according to its few visitors, is home to some of the most hospitable folks around, most of whom belong to the Hutu, Tutsi, and Twa ethnic groups. Burundians are also known for their many local proverbs—"You cannot hide the smoke of the hut you set on fire," "If you are dancing with your rivals, don't close your eyes"—that impart universal truths in the guise of daily life.

When it's time for a celebration, these part-time philosophers like to break out the urwagwa, a home-brewed beer made from bananas or plantains and reserved for special occasions or as part of a big meal. But if you're not in the country, good luck getting your hands on any. Instead, mix yourself an African Queen, named for the classic Humphrey Bogart and Katharine Hepburn film that takes place in German East Africa, a colonial state comprised of Burundi and nearby countries Rwanda, Tanzania, and Mozambique. This simple, sweet burst of Burundian flavor—bananas and oranges being two of the most important export crops—is lovely for promoting positive vibes, either as a fruity brunch sipper or a low-ABV dessert option. Which is important, because, as another proverb goes, "Where there is love there is no darkness."

African Queen

Makes 1 drink

2½ ounces fresh orange juice

1¼ ounces banana liqueur, such as Wenneker crème de bananes

¾ ounce orange liqueur

Club soda, to top

1 orange slice, for garnish

Combine the orange juice, banana liqueur, and orange liqueur in a shaker. Add 1 or 2 ice pebbles, shake briefly, then pour into an ice-filled Collins glass. Top with club soda. Perch the orange slice on the rim of the glass.

IF YOU GET INVITED to a Burundian urwagwa party, be prepared to share. The country's native hooch is almost always served communally in large jugs, with every drinker providing their own straw.

CABO VERDE

Cabo Verde is not a major player on the international stage, due to its small size, lack of natural resources, and remote location several hundred miles off the coast of West Africa. Yet this ten-island archipelago might just have the best official motto of any country in the world: "No stress." With a stable and growing economy, a lovely tropical climate, access to unspoiled beaches, vibrant music and culinary scenes, and a famously slow pace of life, it's easy to see why Cabo Verdeans are the foremost experts in the fine art of relaxation.

When they want to add a little liquid refreshment to their leisure time, most locals prefer grogue (also called grogu or grogo), a dry, subtly flavored sugarcane-based spirit in the aguardente family that's been manufactured in Cabo Verde since the formerly uninhabited islands were discovered by Genoese and Portuguese navigators in the mid-1400s. Traditionally produced using a trapiche, a mill made of wooden rollers used to extract the juice from the cane, grogue was originally—and still is, occasionally—infused with herbs and consumed as medicine. More commonly, however, it forms the basis of a wide range of Cabo Verdean cocktails called ponches. One of these, Ponche de Coco, is particularly popular in areas of the United States like southern New England where there are sizable populations of Cabo Verdean immigrants. This smooth, sweet, and frothy blend of grogue, coconut milk, and condensed milk takes a bit of time and effort to whip up, but if you're in the mood to unwind, it doesn't get much tastier.

Ponche de Coco

Serves 8 to 10

½ cup unsweetened coconut flakes, plus more if needed
1 cup sugar
1 cup water
2 (14-ounce) cans sweetened condensed milk
2 (13.5-ounce) cans unsweetened full-fat coconut milk
18 ounces grogue (if unavailable, use white rum)

Place the coconut flakes in the center of a small piece of cheesecloth. Tie the cloth into a small pouch and place it in a small saucepan. Add the sugar and water and bring to a simmer over medium heat, stirring continuously. Simmer, stirring occasionally, for 5 to 10 minutes, then remove from the heat and let cool.

Empty the cans of condensed milk and coconut milk into a blender, then add the grogue. Place the cheesecloth pouch in a fine-mesh strainer and hold the strainer over the blender. Pour the cooled syrup from the saucepan through the cheesecloth pouch into the blender; discard the coconut (or add half to the blender for some extra texture). Blend on high speed for 1 minute. Pour the ponche into a large bottle or pitcher and refrigerate for at least 2 hours before serving. Serve chilled in mugs or over ice, garnished with a few toasted coconut flakes, if desired.

DESPITE BEING one of the oldest continuously distilled sugarcane-based spirits, grogue was only officially legalized in 1900, ostensibly because of the Portuguese government's concern over its potential health risks. In reality, the centuries-long ban was probably due to the colonizers' inability to properly tax the Cabo Verdean farmers responsible for producing the homegrown spirit.

CAMEROON

Governed in succession by the Bantu, Portuguese, Dutch, Germans, French, and British, Cameroonians long had to deal with regime changes. That is, until recently. Current president Paul Biya has held that office since 1982—after spending seven years as prime minister—making him the longest-serving non-royal national leader in the world. During his time in power, Cameroon has become known as "Africa in miniature" for the exceptional diversity of its culture and geography, which ranges from chilled-out beaches to belching volcanoes to the mineral-rich Korup National Park, the oldest and healthiest forest on the continent. Wherever you find yourself in Cameroon, alcohol is blessedly easy to come by, and, keeping things on-brand, there's a massive variety from which to sip.

Odontol, a palm wine prized for its potency and the ease with which it can be brewed, is the preferred beverage of subsistence farmers living in the mostly rural, inland areas. But in coastal cities that are perfectly positioned along international shipping lanes, there's a smorgasbord of spirits waiting to be conquered. Two longtime Cameroonian favorites are gin and cognac, which also form the dual—and some might say, dueling—bases of the Cameroon's Kick. A play on the Prohibition-era Cameron's Kick, its spirits may seem contradictory at first, but they make excellent bedfellows with nutty orgeat and fresh citrus, with added depth coming from a touch of pastis and Angostura bitters. A cavalcade of time-tested flavors that, like President Biya, won't be going out of style anytime soon.

Cameroon's Kick

Makes 1 drink

1 ounce cognac

1 ounce gin

¾ ounce fresh lemon juice

¾ ounce orgeat

2 dashes Angostura bitters

1 dash pastis

Combine all the ingredients in an ice-filled shaker. Shake vigorously and then strain into a coupe.

Cameroon / Cameroon's Kick (page 17)

CENTRAL AFRICAN REPUBLIC

While the Central African Republic doesn't have the most interesting name, it's certainly an accurate one. The most landlocked country on the continent—one of its regions, an uninhabited forest near the borders with South Sudan and the Democratic Republic of the Congo, is the farthest point from any African coast—this lightly populated stretch of savanna and jungle found itself smack dab in the center of a nineteenth-century European land grab for natural resources, becoming a colony of France until 1960. Since then, as in many post-colonial states, the country's various tribes and ethnicities have, for better or worse, tried to forge a unique identity while remaining linguistically, politically, and culturally connected to its former occupiers.

The French may have left behind a love of grape-based booze, but ancient Central Africans were fermenting their own fruity beverages for thousands of years before European contact, mostly using bananas, a practice that continues in modern times. Thanks to the relatively recent inclusion of a specific yeast during the fermentation process, today's banana wines are sweet, sparkling, and much smoother than their beer-like predecessors. They're also produced on a small scale, meaning that unless you happen to be traveling in Africa, you probably won't be able to get your hands on an authentic bottle of the stuff. But you can still enjoy the flavors of both the Central African Republic's francophone legacy and its native plant life with a Banana Cognac from New York bartender Zachary Gelnaw-Rubin. Its name might be a bit utilitarian but, like the Central African Republic, this brandy sipper's complex bouquet is more than meets the eye.

Banana Cognac

Makes 1 drink

2 ounces cognac

½ ounce banana liqueur

2 dashes chocolate bitters

1 orange twist, for garnish

Combine the cognac, banana liqueur, and bitters in a rocks glass. Add ice and stir with a long-handled spoon for 5 or 6 seconds. Place the orange twist in the glass beside the ice.

Central African Republic / Banana Cognac (page 19)

CHAD

Even though it was named after the massive freshwater lake that dominates the country's southern lowlands, Chad is about as far as it gets from being a wet place. The largest landlocked country in Africa, its scorching geography is dominated by the Sahara Desert and the only slightly less arid Sahel region. And it's only getting drier. Lake Chad, the seventeenth largest in the world, shrank more than 95 percent from 1963 to 1998, though it's seen some significant growth in recent years. Which is great news for the 30 million people who depend on its water.

If the thought of near-constant drought is enough to give you dry mouth, you'd best fix yourself Chad's national beverage, Jus de Fruit, a delightful, smoothie-esque combination of locally available fruits and milk that's served over ice and topped off with a hint of nutmeg and cardamom. Inspired by that cream-and-fruit-based template—as well as Lake Chad's previous incarnation, Lake Mega-Chad, which, 10,000 years ago, contained more water than all the North American Great Lakes, combined—the Mega-Chad Colada floods the taste buds with a massive infusion of sweet and savory flavor and a rich, silky texture that is sure to enthuse piña colada connoisseurs. In Chad, Jus de Fruit vendors use whatever in-season juices they can find. But if you're lucky enough to live where mango, papaya, spiced rum, and cognac are readily available year-round, you'll never have to worry about being parched (or suffer from a bored palate).

Mega-Chad Colada
Makes 1 drink

1½ ounces spiced rum, such as Chairman's Reserve

1 ounce papaya juice

1 ounce mango nectar

½ ounce cognac

½ ounce heavy cream

2 lime wedges

Crushed ice

Combine the rum, papaya juice, mango nectar, cognac, cream, and 1 lime wedge in a shaker. Gently muddle and pour into a tall glass. Fill the glass two-thirds of the way with crushed ice. Add a straw and top with more crushed ice. Perch the remaining lime wedge on the rim of the glass.

COMOROS

Situated in the Indian Ocean off the east coast of Southeastern Africa between Mozambique and Madagascar, Comoros is one of the continent's least-visited countries. Which probably has to do with its remote location and the fact that many people simply haven't heard of the tiny island nation. It's certainly not the smell. Known as the Perfume Isles, the former French protectorate's biggest exports include fragrant spices like vanilla, cloves, and cinnamon; it's the world's largest producer of ylang-ylang, which gives Chanel N°5 its iconic scent. The local cooking is just as aromatic—a fusion of classic French and Arab dishes fused with traditional East African ingredients like coconut milk, plantains, and cassava.

But don't bother looking for a digestif to soothe the belly after a big meal. The islands, with an overwhelmingly Sunni Muslim population, are notoriously bereft of booze, even in many beachside resorts. The preferred palate cleansers come from the juices of local fruits like jackfruit, papaya, and mango, the latter adding a kick of tangy sweetness to the Indian Ocean Swizzle. The ambrosial refresher features a dual French base of cognac and yellow Chartreuse supplemented by allspice and basil, which is also produced on the archipelago and exported as an oil. You may not have the means or the time for a Comoran excursion, but you can harness its flavors and fragrances every time you fix one of these tiki-fied tonics.

Indian Ocean Swizzle

Makes 1 drink

1½ ounces mango juice

½ ounce fresh lime juice

1 ounce cognac

1 ounce yellow Chartreuse

½ ounce allspice dram, such as St. Elizabeth

2 dashes Angostura bitters

3 or 4 basil leaves, plus 1 sprig for garnish

Combine the mango juice, lime juice, cognac, Chartreuse, allspice dram, bitters, and basil leaves in a shaker. Gently muddle and pour into a tall glass. Fill the glass two-thirds of the way with crushed ice and add a straw. Top with more crushed ice. Garnish with the basil sprig.

REPUBLIC OF THE CONGO

To outsiders of yesteryear like Joseph Conrad and Henry Morton Stanley, the mouth of the Congo River represented the gateway into the unknown, the starting point of a journey into an unfathomable, treacherous wilderness that stretched the limits of their imaginations. For modern residents of the Republic of the Congo, many of whose ancestors have lived in the still-densely jungled region of Central Africa for thousands of years, that sense of mysticism regarding the continent's most powerful river is somewhat diminished, but that doesn't mean it isn't important. In addition to being a massive generator of hydroelectric power, it's a watering hole for endangered species like the western lowland gorilla and okapi and a component of lotoko, the local maize or cassava-based moonshine that averages a flaming 50% ABV.

According to the few tourists who get to experience the mighty Congo up close, it's nearly impossible not to be emotionally moved by the vast waterway and the gorgeous yet highly inhospitable landscape that surrounds it. That's the case with British bartender Marc Dietrich, whose Congo Blue cocktail is alleged to have been inspired by the glory of the Congo sunset. First served at London's Atlantic Bar & Grill, the citrusy, grassy sour riff has an excellent fruity bouquet thanks to an invigorating and delicate mixture of apple juice, melon liqueur, and blackberry liqueur. And while the drink's actual hue is more green than blue, there's no color that can't be found among the Congo's impossibly vast collection of flora and fauna.

Congo Blue
Makes 1 drink

1¼ ounces bison-grass vodka, such as Żubrówka

1 ounce unsweetened apple juice

½ ounce green melon liqueur, such as Midori

¼ ounce fresh lemon juice

1 barspoon blackberry liqueur, such as Giffard Crème de Mûre

1 strip of lemon peel

Combine the vodka, apple juice, melon liqueur, lemon juice, and blackberry liqueur in an ice-filled shaker. Shake vigorously and then strain into a coupe. Express the oils from the lemon peel over the rim of the glass and discard the peel.

CÔTE D'IVOIRE

The origins of Côte d'Ivoire stretch back to the 1400s, when Portuguese navigators described various regions of Africa by the most valuable resources each offered, and when the ivory trade was beginning its heyday on the continent's northwest shores. The tusk business was in decline by the time French colonizers permanently settled in the area a few centuries later, but the country's name (which translates to "Ivory Coast") remains. The French language and French cultural and culinary influences are also still prevalent in the current independent republic, mingling with ancient traditions like ancestor worship, which is the primary spiritual practice for most of the population. Religious festivals are rowdy affairs, punctuated by dances, feasts, and beer, which accounts for more than 90 percent of the country's alcohol sales.

When Ivorians want non-boozy refreshment, they spice things up with ginger beer, by far the most popular beverage in the country, often accompanied by homegrown ingredients like fruit. Ginger and passion fruit are also two major flavors in the Ivory Rose, whose base spirit, cognac, is widely available in Côte d'Ivoire, along with other French exports like pastis and Armagnac. A riff on the Finding Rose from Lucinda Sterling, proprietor of Brooklyn's Seaborne, it's a fruity and citrusy liquid antidote for when the days get balmier than a West African summer. And, unlike the ivory trade—which has thankfully been virtually eliminated in Côte d'Ivoire—it's 100% cruelty-free.

Ivory Rose

Makes 1 drink

2 ounces cognac

½ ounce fresh lemon juice

½ ounce passion fruit syrup, such as Liber & Co. Tropical Passionfruit Syrup

¼ ounce honey syrup (page 5)

¼ ounce ginger syrup (page 5)

Club soda, to splash

1 piece candied ginger, for garnish

Combine the cognac, lemon juice, passion fruit syrup, honey syrup, and ginger syrup in an ice-filled shaker. Shake vigorously and then strain into a double rocks glass over ice. Splash the club soda on top. Skewer the piece of candied ginger with toothpicks and perch it on the rim of the glass.

DEMOCRATIC REPUBLIC OF THE CONGO

The prefix *mega-* is prone to overuse, but when discussing the Democratic Republic of the Congo (DRC), it's a more than accurate descriptor. With 10,000 plant species, 400 mammal species, and 1,000 bird species, the DRC is one of 17 mega-diverse countries that contain an astounding percentage of the planet's biodiversity. It's also notable for being the largest francophone country by both area and population, and its capital, Kinshasa, is by far the biggest French-speaking city in the world, with more than 11 million residents. Much of the cuisine also skews French (or Franco-Belgian, as the DRC was a Belgian colony until 1960), while incorporating elements from the more than 200 ethnic groups like the Mongo, Kongo, and Mangbetu-Azande that call the vast country home.

Like most of Central Africa, beer and palm wine are the boozy staples in both rural and urban areas, though cognac and rum are also quite popular and are usually served with a creamy and/or choco-laty twist. Local drinks in this vein include the Lumumba, a deliciously minimalist brandy-and-cocoa enticer that's named after Patrice Lumumba, the country's first president, and has also become a hit in places like Denmark, Germany, and Switzerland. The European version is usually warmed up, while the Congolese prefer theirs mixed over ice or blended to savory and sweet perfection for cooling off in the jungle heat. Either way, it's the ideal hot (or cold) chocolate to satisfy both your boozy desires and mega-chocoholic inner child.

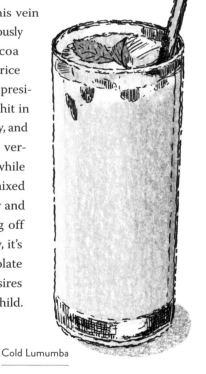

Cold Lumumba

Cold Lumumba
Makes 1 drink

6 ounces chocolate milk

2 ounces cognac

Crushed ice (optional)

1 chocolate mint sprig, for garnish

Combine the chocolate milk and cognac in a shaker. Pour into a tall glass filled two-thirds of the way with crushed or cubed ice. Top with more ice and garnish with the chocolate mint.

Hot Lumumba
Makes 1 drink

4 ounces Homemade Hot Chocolate (recipe follows)

2 ounces cognac

Whipped cream, for serving

Combine the hot chocolate and cognac in a mug. Float some whipped cream on top.

Homemade Hot Chocolate
Makes about 1 cup

1 cup whole milk

1½ teaspoons brown sugar

2 ounces dark chocolate, finely chopped

1 tablespoon heavy cream

Pinch of freshly ground cinnamon

In a small saucepan, heat the milk over medium heat for 3 to 4 minutes. Add the brown sugar and stir until completely dissolved. Stir in the chocolate until completely melted. Remove from the heat and stir in the cream and cinnamon. Use immediately.

DEMOCRATIC REPUBLIC OF THE CONGO'S local grain- and root-based moonshine is often referred to as *pétrole* (French for "oil"), both because of its 100-plus-proof potency and because it's produced in crude stills made from discarded oil drums.

DJIBOUTI

Besides having one of the most fun names to say, Djibouti has a much greater importance to Northeastern Africa and the Middle East than its slight size would otherwise imply. Situated along the Bab el-Mandeb Strait, which separates the Red Sea from the Gulf of Aden, the country's strategically located capital, Djibouti City, features a modern deepwater port, hosts a French naval base, and is a major commercial hub and ship refueling center.

Djiboutian cuisine is nearly as fascinating as the country itself, a distinctive fusion of Somali, French, Yemeni, and Ethiopian fixings, with lots of South Asian influences mixed in, making it abundantly easy for visitors to tantalize their taste buds and fill their bellies. Post-meal digestifs, however, are harder to come by in this conservative Muslim republic.

Djiboutians do enjoy a wide range of mocktails, which are often smoothies made from locally produced fruit and vegetable juices. Like their neighbors throughout the Horn of Africa, they're also quite fond of coffee, which plays a large role in daily life. The caffeinated brew is also the biggest flavor in the Horn of Africa cocktail, an indulgent, well-balanced take on the Espresso Martini and White Russian that features regionally prevalent ingredients like goat's milk alongside vodka from France, whose language is widely spoken in Djibouti's burgeoning cities and shipyards.

Horn of Africa

Makes 1 drink

1½ ounces French vodka, such as Grey Goose

1½ ounces cold-brew coffee liqueur, such as Mr. Black

1 barspoon cane syrup

1 ounce goat's milk

Combine the vodka, coffee liqueur, and cane syrup in a double rocks glass. Add ice, stir briefly, and top with the goat's milk.

EGYPT

Ancient Egyptians were ahead of their time in countless ways, not least of which being their love for fermented beverages. Recent archaeological evidence suggests that breweries were operating along the Nile River as early as 5800 BCE, more than twenty centuries before the invention of hieroglyphics. Today's Egyptians—most of whom identify as Sunni Muslim—don't share the same appreciation for beer, or alcohol in general. Yet only a few decades ago, an unlikely cocktail invented in their country allegedly changed the course of World War II—and human history as we know it.

By 1941, the British forces in North Africa had suffered several catastrophic defeats to the Nazis and were in danger of losing their vital foothold on the continent, particularly the Suez Canal. Morale was low and hangovers were abysmal, given that the troops were forced to drown their sorrows with whatever vile swill they could get their hands on. At the request of a desperate officer, legendary Egyptian barkeep Joe Scialom of Cairo's Shepheard's Hotel devised a revitalizing remedy consisting of equal parts bourbon, gin, and lime juice (some of the few ingredients that were readily available at the time), topped off with a few dashes of stomach-soothing bitters and ginger beer. Scialom's concoction—the Suffering Bastard—was so successful that by 1942, gallons of it were being shipped to the front lines.

The newly energetic Brits started winning battle after battle and eventually forced the Nazis out of Africa, with many soldiers crediting their favorite morning-after tonic for turning the tide. And while this satisfyingly crisp, citrus-infused blend of two normally opposing spirits is more likely to encourage a hangover than prevent one, it's still a powerful example of the good things that can happen when ingenuity meets necessity.

Suffering Bastard

Makes 1 drink

1 ounce bourbon

1 ounce London dry gin

1 ounce fresh lime juice

½ ounce ginger syrup (page 5)

½ ounce simple syrup (page 5)

2 dashes Angostura bitters

Club soda, to top

1 piece candied ginger, for garnish

Combine the bourbon, gin, lime juice, ginger syrup, simple syrup, and bitters in a shaker. Add 1 or 2 ice pebbles, shake briefly, and pour into a tall glass filled with ice. Top with club soda. Skewer the piece of candied ginger with toothpicks and perch it on the rim of the glass.

ANCIENT EGYPTIANS PRODUCED at least twenty-four varieties of wine and seventeen types of beer, all of which were blessed and presented as offerings to gods like Shesmu, the protector of wine cellars, whose identifying hieroglyph was a wine press. Alcoholic beverages during this time were used in all aspects of daily life as well as in the afterlife, as evidenced by the numerous remains of booze-filled jars that have been found stored in tombs.

EQUATORIAL GUINEA

When it rains it pours, especially in the Equatoguinean town of Ureca. The remote jungle village is one of the wettest places in the world, getting dumped on to the tune of 411 inches of rain per year. Major precipitation is a factor throughout the rest of the small Spanish-speaking country, but in recent years, a different liquid has been a more frequent topic of conversation. That would be oil, which accounts for 90 percent of Equatorial Guinea's exports, though only a small percentage of the population sees any real benefit from the precious commodity.

When average citizens want to raise their spirits after lambasting their country's crooked politicians or getting caught in a thunderstorm, they grab a bottle of malamba, a fermented beverage that's been popular in pockets of West Africa since the colonial era. Like Latin American guarapo, it's made with sugarcane that's been crushed and its juice left to sit for at least two weeks, often infused with bark from the bitter kola plant to speed up the fermentation process.

Even if you can't procure any of that equatorial homebrew, you can still get your sugar-based booze fix and explore some of Equatorial Guinea's most vibrant flavors with the Mango Tango. A staple of tiki tomfoolery since at least the 1940s, it's named for the dance that evolved in fellow former Spanish colonies Argentina and Uruguay, as well as one of the most popular traditional Equatoguinean ingredients. This seductive intertwining of coconut rum, mango, and lime is a can't-miss for fans of fruity, warm-weather smoothies and, like residents of Africa's pluvial capital, getting caught in the rain.

Mango Tango
Makes 1 drink

2 ounces coconut rum

2 ounces fresh mango juice or mango nectar

½ ounce fresh lime juice

½ ounce simple syrup (page 5)

2 dashes Angostura bitters

1 mango slice, for garnish

1 mint sprig, for garnish

Combine the rum, mango juice, lime juice, simple syrup, and bitters in an ice-filled shaker. Shake vigorously and then strain into a double rocks glass over ice. Perch the mango slice and mint sprig on the rim of the glass.

ERITREA

If you don't know very much—or anything—about Eritrea, you're not alone. Since achieving independence from neighboring Ethiopia in 1993, the secretive totalitarian state has been governed by a single president, Isaias Afwerki, who controls every aspect of the local media and doesn't take kindly to foreign journalists, to say the least. But what we do know about this historically and culturally compelling slice of the Horn of Africa makes it worthy of a second glance. A former colony of both Italy and the United Kingdom, its 600-mile Red Sea coastline has long made the country a melting pot of religions, ethnicities, and cooking traditions, where the art deco architecture of its modernist capital Asmara borders centuries-old camel markets, lively port towns, and miles of agricultural greenery.

Whether farming the countryside or toiling in the city, Eritreans make coffee breaks a mandatory part of daily life. These social, java-related "ceremonies" feature a complex set of rituals regarding everything from how to properly roast the coffee beans to who is allowed to pour sugar in the brew. And while the Asmara con Caffè cocktail might be foreign to coffee traditionalists—as this is the first time it's appeared in print anywhere—this boozy blend should make Eritreans feel right at home. With plenty of their favorite caffeinated juice, the flavor of bananas (their country's largest fruit export), and two Italian liqueurs, the resulting mixture manages to be fruity, nutty, energizing, and herbaceous at the same time. Melting pot, indeed.

Asmara con Caffè

Makes 1 drink

¾ ounce coffee liqueur

¾ ounce banana liqueur

¾ ounce Amaro Averna

¾ ounce Cynar

Pinch of sea salt

1 orange twist, for garnish

Combine the coffee liqueur, banana liqueur, amaro, Cynar, and salt in an ice-filled mixing glass. Stir with a long-handled spoon for 25 to 30 seconds and then strain into a coupe. Place the orange twist in the glass.

Eritrea / Asmara con Caffè (page 33)

ESWATINI

Eswatini—formerly the Kingdom of Swaziland until 2018—is one of Africa's smallest and most mysterious countries. It's also one of the most fascinating. As the continent's only remaining absolute monarchy, political power rests in the hands of King Mswati III, who rules according to his every wish (including changing his country's name without prior notice or public approval) and has fifteen wives, an eye-popping number that nevertheless pales in comparison to the seventy brides of his father, Sobhuza II. Mswati and the rest of the prodigious royal family preside over Eswatini's spectacular cultural festivals that feature traditional dances, rituals, and marriage negotiations that often involve the transfer of cows, with some princesses demanding herds of up to 300 heads before they'll get hitched.

Things aren't all traditional here, however, as the quickly developing nation has lately embraced a faster way of life, where modern innovations like supermarkets, biomedical research facilities, and cocktail dens are becoming more and more common sights. The earliest Eswatini-inspired drink, however, hails from a much earlier time, when a recipe for the Swazi Freeze first appeared in Harry Craddock's *Savoy Cocktail Book* (1930). This dry and slightly fruity three-ingredient Reverse Manhattan riff calls for Canadian whisky, peach liqueur, and Caperitif, a Prohibition-era vermouth infused with botanicals native to both Eswatini and neighboring South Africa that was defunct by the 1960s. While a new version of the fortified wine has experienced a revival in recent years, it's hard to come by outside of Southern Africa, but a blend of six parts white vermouth (such as Dolin Blanc) and one part Amaro Montenegro works in a pinch to simulate Caperitif's herbaceous aromatics.

Swazi Freeze

Makes 1 drink

1½ ounces Caperitif (see headnote)
¾ ounce Canadian rye whisky
1 barspoon peach liqueur

Combine all the ingredients in an ice-filled mixing glass. Stir with a long-handled spoon for 25 to 30 seconds and then strain into a coupe.

BEFORE IT WAS REINTRODUCED in the twenty-first century by Danish mixologist Lars Erik Lyndgaard Schmidt and South African winemaker Adi Badenhorst, Caperitif was one of the most famous examples of what is known as a "ghost ingredient," one that, like a lost film, was known only by description, in recipes, and other forms of early-twentieth-century media.

ETHIOPIA

If marching to the beat of your own drum was a country, Ethiopia would be that place. The only African nation to escape the clutches of colonialism and the birthplace of coffee, this gorgeous land of otherworldly mountain ranges, savannas, and deserts boasts its own alphabet (Ge'ez script), its own system for counting time, a thirteen-month calendar, around eighty indigenous languages, and a unique form of Christianity that's been practiced for millennia. It was also the stomping ground for one of humanity's oldest bipedal ancestors, *Australopithecus afarensis*, made famous by the discovery of the skeleton known as Lucy in 1974.

Not surprisingly, Ethiopia's national drink has been an integral part of this remarkable cultural heritage and vast history for longer than anyone can remember. Tej, a honey wine that's widely consumed at festivals, weddings, and religious occasions, is perhaps the world's oldest alcoholic beverage, one that's still largely produced using traditional fermentation methods. Unlike other meads, which many wine snobs deride as being overly saccharine and unrefined, tej has a relatively dry flavor profile and a pleasantly herbaceous, slightly bitter finish, thanks to the infusion of gesho, a hops-like herb that grows throughout the country. And while mixed drinks aren't a big part of most Ethiopians' imbibing routines, tej-loving expats use the wine as a base in some truly lovely low-ABV cocktails, like the Wildflower Spritz. Adapted from a recipe by Lost Tribes, an American tej brewing company, it's a shimmering, vegetal take on the ubiquitous summertime classic. Tej's herbal complexities embellish Aperol's notes of zesty citrus and vanilla, making this smooth, icy refresher a great standalone pick-me-up, or a cool complement to Ethiopia's notoriously fiery cuisine.

Wildflower Spritz

Makes 1 drink

3 ounces tej

1½ ounces Aperol

1 ounce fresh lemon juice

Club soda, to top

1 lemon twist, for garnish

Combine the tej, Aperol, and lemon juice in an ice-filled shaker. Shake vigorously and strain into a large wineglass filled with ice. Top with club soda. Place the lemon twist in the glass beside the ice.

FOR MANY CENTURIES, tej was only allowed to be consumed by the king of Ethiopia and other members of the ruling class. It was also common for Ethiopia's beekeepers—who still produce the most honey in Africa by far—to pay their annual taxes in tej.

GABON

At first glance, Gabon shares plenty of similarities with its West and Central African neighbors. An ancient coastal trading center and former French colony, it's home to several dozen distinct ethnic groups; a great diversity of wildlife like gorillas, hippos, and whales; and regional food staples like cassava, rice, and yams. However, thanks to a wealth of natural resources in the form of oil, manganese, and timber, Gabon's citizens enjoy a per capita income four times greater than that of most sub-Sarahan African countries. The relatively well-off Gabonese also have a higher-than-average predilection for booze; in many rural areas, it's easier to find a bar than a place to eat.

The local drinks of choice include beer and malamba—mortar-crushed sugarcane juice that's left to ferment for about two weeks—but colonial-era spirits like pastis and Chartreuse are still widely available (and consumed) here due to an economic partnership with France that's remained strong since Gabon's 1960 transition to independence. These powerful liqueurs are often mixed with the juices of equatorial crops like mangos, bananas, coconuts, and pineapples, the latter two making up the fruity and nutty components of bartender Erick Castro's Piña Verde, which first appeared on the menu at San Diego's Polite Provisions in the 2010s. A creamy and effervescent homage to the piña colada, it's also the perfect liquid encapsulation of Gabon's modern bicontinental culture.

Piña Verde

Makes 1 drink

1½ ounces green Chartreuse
1½ ounces pineapple juice
¼ ounce fresh lime juice
¾ ounce coconut syrup, such as Wildly Organic Coconut Syrup
1 dash heavy cream
Crushed ice
Pinch of freshly grated nutmeg, for garnish
1 pineapple leaf, for garnish
1 lime wedge, for garnish

Combine the Chartreuse, pineapple juice, lime juice, coconut syrup, and cream in a shaker. Shake without ice and pour into a tall glass filled two-thirds of the way with crushed ice. Add a straw and top with more crushed ice. Sprinkle with the nutmeg and perch the pineapple leaf between the ice and the rim of the glass. Place the lime wedge on top of the ice.

THE GAMBIA

Situated on both sides of its namesake river and almost completely surrounded by Senegal, the Gambia is the smallest country in mainland Africa, with a total area less than that of Connecticut. That said, the surprisingly biodiverse former British colony has 50 miles of Atlantic coastline, nearly 600 different kinds of birds, and an array of land and water-based wildlife like hippos, crocodiles, and several species of monkeys. What the Gambia is light on its alcohol, which is mostly reserved for tourists in this conservative Islamic nation. Instead, the main forms of refreshment here are ginger beer and attaya, a green tea that's an integral part of social life and has a ritualistic brewing process that can take hours to complete.

If you're one of the millions of tea lovers who are slightly more impatient when it comes to the need for mild caffeination (with a bonus boozy kick), try a Ginger Tea Cocktail, adapted from a recipe by spirits writer and mixologist Colleen Graham. Invigorating and inviting, with a nice ginger-backed zing, it's a great way to experience two of the Gambia's most popular flavors while slowly absorbing cognac's nerve-soothing properties. Like attaya—which comes from two words in the Fula language meaning "don't go"—this luscious sipper is all about taking an extended break from the tempo of daily life with some good buddies to appreciate the little things . . . and get a bit tipsy, of course.

Ginger Tea Cocktail

Makes 1 drink

½ ounce simple syrup (page 5)

3 mint leaves, plus 1 sprig for garnish

3 (1-inch) pieces fresh ginger

2 ounces freshly brewed green tea, chilled

1 ounce cognac

Combine the simple syrup, mint leaves, and ginger in a mixing glass. Muddle thoroughly, then add the tea and cognac and muddle a little more. Strain into a double rocks glass over ice. Garnish with the mint sprig.

GHANA

One of colonialism's many cruelties is the forced eradication of ancient cultural and culinary traditions. Before the arrival of Europeans, Ghana's Anlo-Ewe people brewed a spirit called *kpótomenui* ("something hidden in a coconut mat fence"), which was prized by local tribes for its exceptional strength and smoothness. The conquering British were of a much different opinion, however, declaring kpótomenui to be disagreeably tasting and too potent for indigenous use.

When the liquor was outlawed in 1936—probably due to the British wanting to increase sales of imported gin from England—native Ghanaians began producing the local spirit illegally under its current name, *akpeteshie*, a word that means, loosely, "they are hiding" in the Ga language, referring to the covert methods by which the clear, palm-sap-based firewater had to be produced and consumed.

Today, fully independent Ghana has a relatively egalitarian drinking culture, where akpeteshie and gin are quaffed in equal measure, despite the conflicting histories of both spirits in the West African nation. And while gin's juniper-forward bouquet is a far cry from akpeteshie's sharp, mostly neutral flavor profile, either works well as the base in the Son of a Bee Sting, a slightly floral Penicillin riff that was created by Michael Madrusan at New York's Milk & Honey in 2009. You might have to book a Ghanian vacation to get your hands on a bottle of akpeteshie, but the rest of the drink's ingredients—lemon, ginger, honey, and rose water, are all harvested in Ghana and factor heavily in the local cuisine.

Son of a Bee Sting

Makes 1 drink

2 ounces akpeteshie or gin

¾ ounce fresh lemon juice

⅜ ounce ginger syrup (page 5)

⅜ ounce honey syrup (page 5)

Rose water, in an atomizer

1 piece candied ginger, for garnish

Combine the akpeteshie, lemon juice, ginger syrup, and honey syrup in an ice-filled shaker. Shake vigorously and strain into a double rocks glass over ice. Spritz with the rose water. Skewer the piece of candied ginger with toothpicks and perch it on the rim of the glass.

GHANIAN IMBIBERS often describe the experience of shooting akpeteshie as feeling like a knockout punch. To acknowledge the sensation, you'll often see seasoned drinkers pounding their chests or aggressively blowing out air after taking a shot.

GUINEA

The relatively small West African nation of Guinea only has one UNESCO World Heritage Site, but it's a doozy. The Mount Nimba Strict Forest Reserve is so biodiverse that new plant species are still being discovered regularly, like the tree species *Talbotiella cheekii*, which was unknown to science until 2017 despite reaching a height of 80 feet. It's also the place where, in 2009, chimpanzees were first observed using stone anvils and stone and wooden cleavers to chop fruit into bite-sized portions. Guinea's human gastronomes have been using similar tools for thousands of years to make dishes plentiful in ground manioc, taro, and maize, which is part of a popular corn couscous that's served with curdled milk. Corn is also sometimes used to increase the alcohol content in the country's homemade palm wine and rum-like distillates.

Guinea's significant population of teetotalers—nearly 90 percent of citizens list Islam as their religion—prefer their liquid refreshment a bit juicier and on the spicy side. Dozens of strong, ginger-based soft drinks dominate the market, frequently paired with sweet syrups like bissap, which is derived from a species of hibiscus found throughout Western and Central Africa. Sugarcane, ginger, and bissap also round out a trifecta of explosive flavor in the Mount Nimba Mule, a spicy, ultra-fresh Guinean variation of the Gin-Gin Mule, the widely quaffed modern classic from Pegu Club's Audrey Saunders. Trying one of these fizzy coolers for the first time is almost as exciting as discovering a new species of flora, if you're into that sort of thing.

Mount Nimba Mule

Makes 1 drink

2 ounces light rum

1 ounce fresh lime juice

½ ounce bissap syrup (page 4)

½ ounce ginger syrup (page 5)

5 or 6 mint leaves, plus 1 sprig for garnish

Club soda, to top

1 piece candied ginger, for garnish

Combine the rum, lime juice, bissap syrup, ginger syrup, and mint leaves in an ice-filled shaker. Shake vigorously and then strain into an ice-filled Collins glass. Top with club soda. Skewer the piece of candied ginger with toothpicks and perch it on the rim of the glass. Place the mint sprig in the glass beside the ice.

GUINEA-BISSAU

You don't have to explore Guinea-Bissau's exotic beaches and abundant mangrove swamps, or take in the diverse wildlife roaming the country's mainland and offshore islands, to fully appreciate the flavors of this remote corner of West Africa. Just head down to the corner store and treat yourself to a bag of cashews. Despite its small size, Guinea-Bissau is one of the top five producers of the nutritious nuts, which constitute their largest and most lucrative crop by far.

Cashews are also the signature ingredient in Guinea-Bissau's national liquor, cana de cajeu, a dry, highly potent rum made from the fruit of the nut. Produced locally and enjoyed widely in other nearby former Portuguese colonies like Cabo Verde and São Tomé and Príncipe, it's the preferred beverage at any Bissau-Guinean festivity, occasionally accompanied by a palm wine chaser.

While cana de cajeu is quite difficult to find outside of lusophone (Portuguese-speaking) West Africa, the rum and cashew one-two punch is easy to harness in a creamy Cashew Flip. It does require you to make your own cashew orgeat—based on a recipe that first appeared on Thrillist (as store-bought versions of the earthy sweetener are hard to come by)—but the versatile syrup is well worth the effort, upping the richness in this eggnog-like dessert drink that also benefits from port wine's depth and—most importantly—nuttiness.

Cashew Flip

Makes 1 drink

2 ounces dark rum
¾ ounce Cashew Orgeat (recipe follows)
¾ ounce heavy cream
1 large egg yolk
Pinch of freshly grated nutmeg, for garnish

Combine the rum, orgeat, cream, and egg yolk in a shaker. Shake without ice for 5 or 6 seconds to emulsify the egg yolk, then add ice and shake vigorously. Strain into a sour glass. Garnish with the nutmeg.

Cashew Orgeat

Makes about 1 cup

1 cup raw cashews
1 cup water
1 cup sugar
¼ teaspoon sea salt
¼ cup white rum
2 dashes orange blossom water

Lightly toast the cashews in a small saucepan over low heat until lightly browned, making sure not to burn them. Transfer the toasted cashews to a food processor and pulse a few times to coarsely grind them (do not overprocess the nuts). Whisk the ground cashews with the water and transfer to a jar. Seal the jar and let sit at room temperature overnight, shaking the jar occasionally.

Strain the mixture through a cheesecloth-lined fine-mesh sieve into a small saucepan. Add the sugar and salt and heat over low heat, stirring continuously until both fully dissolve. Remove from the heat and let cool. Add the rum and orange blossom water and whisk for a minute or so to fully incorporate. Store in an airtight container in the refrigerator for up to 1 month.

KENYA

From the majestic slopes of Mount Kilimanjaro to the lush savanna wilderness of the Maasai Mara National Reserve, cocktail-minded Kenyans in need of a sweet and citrusy pick-me-up hold one such refresher in higher regard than all others: the Dawa. A menu mainstay at nearly every safari lodge, restaurant, and hotel bar in the country, the soothing blend of vodka, muddled lime, honey, and brown sugar is a particularly popular option during a sundowner. This equatorial equivalent of happy hour dates to the nineteenth century, when colonialist Brits would break at the end of the day to enjoy the sunset over the African plains with the aid of a malaria-preventing Gin and Tonic, or three.

The Dawa, however, is a much more recent tradition. Created as a spinoff of the cachaça-based Caipirinha with an easier-to-procure base spirit, as well as a nod to Kenya's robust beekeeping industry, it was dreamed up by Kenyan restaurant executive Martin Dunford in 1980 after a trip to Brazil and debuted at Nairobi's the Carnivore restaurant soon after. Samson Kivelenge, the beverage professional credited with naming the concoction—*dawa* means "medicine" in Swahili—still slings rounds to the Carnivore's grateful patrons, who use it to coat their bellies before or after a battle with the restaurant's notoriously massive cuts of game meat. Most Kenyan bartenders, including Kivelenge, prefer to serve their Dawas on the rocks accompanied by a large wooden or plastic "dawa stick," onto which the drink's honey component has been drizzled. Though the honey syrup in the following recipe has been diluted enough that a stirring tool isn't necessary for dissolving purposes, feel free to use pure honey for a more authentic experience at your next happy hour. Or any hour, really.

Dawa

Makes 1 drink

2 ounces vodka

¾ ounce honey syrup (page 5)

5 lime wedges

1 brown sugar cube

1 lime wheel, for garnish

Combine the vodka, honey syrup, lime wedges, and sugar cube in a shaker. Muddle thoroughly and fill the shaker with cracked ice. Shake 4 or 5 times and pour the contents of the shaker in a double rocks glass. Place the lime wheel in the glass beside the ice.

KENYANS ARE NOTORIOUSLY fond of boasting about their boozing abilities, especially during Oktobafest, a month-long festival modeled after the German Oktoberfest sponsored by Tusker, a local beer brand. Highlights include live music performances, soccer games, horse races, and, of course, nonstop drinking contests.

LESOTHO

Judging by Lesotho's many altitude-related nicknames—the Mountain Kingdom, the Kingdom of the Sky, the Roof of Africa, the Switzerland of Africa—you'd expect to find some impressive terrain in this small enclave surrounded by South Africa. And you'd be right. Dominated by the snowcapped Maloti Mountains (which contain the highest peaks in southern Africa and the only two ski areas in the region), the country has an average elevation of more than 7,000 feet and even its lowlands would be considered highlands anywhere else on the continent.

Lesotho is the ancestral home of the Basotho people, who comprise more than 99 percent of the constitutional monarchy's approximately two million subjects, and whose particular love of gin is a legacy of the country's nearly one hundred years as a British Crown colony during the nineteenth and twentieth centuries. Spirit production has taken off in recent years, with several varieties—most notably Senate Premium Gin—being lauded for incorporating local ingredients such as rosehips, which grow wild in the mountains. The annual Gin & Trout Festival attracts numerous international visitors with twelve days of tastings, hiking and fishing expeditions, and musical performances from the biggest Basotho artists.

In addition to distilling and ecotourism, the Lesothan government also encourages growing fruit to lessen the country's dependence on other nations, particularly South Africa. The Basotho Gin, a slight variation of Charles H. Baker Jr.'s classic Invisible Gin, features the flavors of several of these crops—pineapple, peach, lemon—as well as ginger beer, a big-time local favorite. Crisp and refreshing as a cool mountain breeze, this juniper-forward sipper is worth the arduous trek to both the liquor store and the supermarket.

Basotho Gin

Makes 1 drink

1½ ounces dry gin, such as Senate Premium
1 ounce pineapple juice
¾ ounce ginger syrup (page 5)
½ ounce peach liqueur
½ ounce fresh lemon juice
1 dash Angostura bitters
Club soda, to top
1 piece candied ginger, for garnish

Combine the gin, pineapple juice, ginger syrup, peach liqueur, lemon juice, and bitters in a shaker. Add 1 or 2 ice pebbles, shake briefly, and pour into a tall glass filled with ice. Top with club soda. Skewer the piece of candied ginger with toothpicks and perch it on the rim of the glass.

LIBERIA

By the middle of the nineteenth century, the United States had become a world power, pursuing an aggressive policy of expansionism and annexation. Liberia, however, was a fascinating exception to the rule. Founded by the American Colonization Society as a new homeland for recently freed American slaves, the first internationally recognized independent African state was mostly left to its own devices. But America's fingerprints are still all over this West African coastal republic, from its style of government to the predominant use of English to its red-white-and-blue, starred-and-striped flag.

In the past 150 years or so, Liberian culture has diverged from that of its mother country in numerous ways. Like many West Africans, Liberians enjoy eating bush meat like hippopotamus (despite its Ebola-associated risks), brewing several varieties of potent palm wine, and getting their non-alcoholic refreshment in the form of spicy, sweet, and fizzy juice blends. A souped-up take on the country's national drink, ginger beer, the West African Buck features commonly available ingredients—ginger, lime, peppercorns, and pine-apple juice—as well as American bourbon. It's a truly trans-atlantic treat that's as rare and uplifting as a formerly oppressed group seizing the opportunity to forge a new identity on their own terms.

West African Buck

Makes 1 drink

2 ounces bourbon

1 ounce pineapple juice

½ ounce fresh lime juice

½ ounce ginger syrup (page 5)

½ ounce Peppercorn Syrup (recipe follows)

Club soda, to top

1 piece candied ginger, for garnish

Combine the bourbon, pineapple juice, lime juice, ginger syrup, and peppercorn syrup in a shaker. Add 1 or 2 ice pebbles, shake briefly, and pour into an ice-filled Collins glass. Top with club soda. Skewer the piece of candied ginger with toothpicks and perch it on the rim of the glass.

Peppercorn Syrup

Makes 1 cup

2 tablespoons whole black peppercorns

1 cup water

1 cup superfine sugar

In a small saucepan, toast the peppercorns over medium heat until fragrant, or about 1 minute. Add the water and bring to a simmer. After 10 minutes, reduce the heat to low and add the sugar, stirring until it completely dissolves. Strain the liquid into an airtight container, discard the peppercorns, and let cool. Cover and store in the refrigerator for up to 1 week.

ALCOHOL IN LIBERIA is such an essential part of the local culture that it's usually cheaper to buy a drink than a cup of rice.

LIBYA

To most Westerners, Libya is still closely identified with the decades-long, iron-fisted reign of Colonel Muammar Gaddafi, who was deposed in 2011 during the Arab Spring uprisings. In just the past two centuries, however, the large, sparsely populated Saharan country has also been an outpost of the Ottoman Empire, an Italian colony, an independent kingdom, and, as it is today, a volatile postwar transitory state. No matter who's been running the show, one thing has remained constant in this conservative Muslim nation: it's hard to find a drink. Not that you'd even want to. Getting caught with booze carries extremely harsh penalties, so Libyans who prefer to remain out of jail get their buzzes from coffee, tea, and an enticing array of sugary cookies and biscuits that are famous on both sides of the Mediterranean Sea.

One of the most common ingredients in Libyan desserts—and North African cuisine in general—is the almond, which grows abundantly in a few fertile areas along the country's 1,099-mile coastline. It's also, unsurprisingly, a predominant flavor in the Burnt Almond Cocktail, thanks to amaretto liqueur from Libya's nautical neighbor Italy. A slightly more complex White Russian riff based on a recipe by Colleen Graham, this adult milkshake packs a creamy, caffeinated punch with plentiful nutty vibes to satiate any sweet tooth. A nightcap worthy of 1,001 nights, Arabian or otherwise.

Burnt Almond Cocktail

Makes 1 drink

1 ounce vodka

1 ounce amaretto liqueur

1 ounce coffee liqueur

Splash of heavy cream, or more to taste

Combine all the ingredients in a shaker. Add 1 or 2 ice pebbles, shake briefly, and strain into a double rocks glass over ice.

MADAGASCAR

Many isolated countries boast unique flora and fauna. But when we're talking endemic species, nowhere else can compete with the sheer diversity of spectacular oddities found only in Madagascar, including all its famous wild-eyed lemurs, half of its birds, and the vast majority of its reptiles and amphibians. Humans and agriculture, on the other hand, are relatively recent imports to Africa's largest island. And while most of its signature crops are non-native, Madagascar's vanilla, rice, sugarcane, coffee, and bananas are all highly sought-after due to their exceptional quality. The country's rums, though not as well-known globally, are also a huge point of pride for the locals, with restaurateurs infusing their bottles with a variety of ingredients like ginger, mango, lychee, and licorice.

Outside of the hotel and resort scene, cocktails aren't really a prominent part of Madagascan life, yet the island's homegrown flavors are ripe for boozy collaboration. Such as can be found in the Muddy Madagascar, a creamy, delicately layered, and more complex White Russian–style dessert beverage. Backed by equal parts aged rum (Madagascan if you can find it, though any decent rum will work fine) and coffee liqueur, the drink takes a slightly fruity twist with the inclusion of banana liqueur, packs an aromatic punch from vanilla liqueur that's made using an extract of beans grown on Madagascar, and finishes with a hint of sea salt as a briny ode to the country's approximately 3,000 miles of coastline.

Muddy Madagascar

Makes 1 drink

1 ounce Madagascan aged rum, such as Dzama 6 year

1 ounce Caffé Lolita or comparable coffee liqueur

½ ounce banana liqueur

½ ounce vanilla liqueur, such as Giffard Vanille de Madagascar

½ ounce heavy cream

Pinch of sea salt

Combine all the ingredients in an ice-filled shaker. Shake vigorously and strain into a double rocks glass over ice.

MALAWI

Malawi is often called "the Warm Heart of Africa," which can be a bit misleading if taken literally. The rugged, mostly rural, and landlocked country has a moderate climate thanks to an average elevation of more than 2,500 feet above sea level, and it's nowhere near the geographic center of the continent. Instead, the nickname refers to the friendliness of its people, who represent a diverse array of ethnicities, language groups, and religions.

Regardless of their backgrounds, famously hospitable Malawians like to welcome their guests with a glass of thobwa, a sweet fermented maize-based beverage that's brewed year-round in every city and village. Available in both nonalcoholic and slightly boozy varieties, the chilled, grainy mixture is a daily refresher during the hotter months and an easily chugged favorite at raucous Malawian weddings and other celebratory events, where it's served in traditional clay pots.

Chances are you don't have the time (or desire) to grow corn, painstakingly harvest it, turn it into flour, and utilize age-old Malawian methods of boiling and fermentation to make thobwa. But you can still achieve a maize-backed buzz with a Malawi Jackal. It's a souped-up take on the Malawi Shandy, a nonalcoholic blend of popular southeastern African ingredients like citrus, ginger, and lemon-lime soda that's sold at Mugg & Bean, a coffee-themed restaurant chain with locations throughout the region. Named for one of Malawi's sneakiest carnivores, this outstandingly crisp, sweet-and-sour pick-me-up will have you scavenging your local liquor store for another bottle of corn whiskey sooner than you might expect.

Malawi Jackal

Makes 1 drink

2 ounces corn whiskey, such as Mellow Corn

¾ ounce ginger syrup (page 5)

½ ounce fresh lemon juice

½ ounce fresh orange juice

4 dashes Angostura bitters

Lemon-lime soda, to top

1 piece candied ginger, for garnish

1 thin orange slice, for garnish

Combine the whiskey, ginger syrup, lemon juice, and orange juice in a shaker. Add 1 or 2 ice pebbles, shake briefly, and pour into a tall glass filled with ice. Add the bitters and top with lemon-lime soda. Skewer the piece of candied ginger and the orange slice with toothpicks and perch them on the rim of the glass.

NOTE: For a drier drink, top with equal parts lemon-lime soda and club soda.

MALI

With most of its geography dominated by the terrifyingly hot and barren Sahara Desert, as well as an only slightly less imposing area of semiarid steppeland, Mali seems like the kind of place where you'd want to always keep an icy libation close by. Except that this landlocked country—the former center of the legendary Mali Empire, whose greatest ruler, Mansa Musa, is often described as the richest person in history—has been a pillar of strict Islamic values for more than a thousand years. That's not to say that booze is expressly forbidden to tourists. However, most Malians would rather have their guests partake in glasses of tea, fresh-squeezed fruit juices, or djablani, a popular cold beverage consisting of ginger, lemon, and mint.

One of the most prized local ingredients is the tamarind fruit, whose tangy nectar is consumed widely in both refreshing drinks and vegetal syrups that are used to break fasts during Ramadan and fight dysentery. Lara Lee at *Food & Wine* has a fabulous recipe for a tamarind cocktail base, a syrup combining the fruit with aromatic lemongrass, spicy ginger, coconut sugar, and makrut lime leaves, whose tangy flavor highlights curries and similar dishes around the world. Unforgettably rich and zippy, it makes a great modifier in cocktails like the Tamarind Cooler, based on one of Lee's recipes in the same magazine. The ice-blasted trifecta of tequila, tamarind, and club soda (with a touch more citrus for added tartness) is guaranteed to beat—or drink—the hottest desert heat into a cool oblivion.

MALI'S NATIONAL (nonalcoholic) drink is sweet tea, which is traditionally offered to guests in three servings from the same pot. The first cup is said to be *âpre comme la vie* (French for "bitter [or harsh] as life"), the second is *doux comme l'amour* ("sweet as love"), and the third is *suave comme la mort* ("smooth [or soft] as death").

Tamarind Cooler

Makes 1 drink

2 ounces tequila

1 ounce Tamarind Cocktail Base (recipe follows)

¼ ounce fresh lime juice

Club soda, to top

1 lime wedge, for garnish

Combine the tequila, tamarind cocktail base, and lime juice in a shaker. Add 1 or 2 ice pebbles, shake briefly, and pour into an ice-filled Collins glass. Top with club soda. Perch the lime wedge on the rim of the glass.

Tamarind Cocktail Base

Makes ⅔ cup

1 (2½-ounce) block seedless tamarind

1 medium (about 10-inch-long) lemongrass stalk

1 (1-inch) piece fresh ginger, peeled, cut crosswise into ¼-inch-thick slices, and smashed

¼ cup plus 2 tablespoons coconut sugar or packed light brown sugar

4 makrut lime leaves, torn in half

Place the tamarind block in a medium bowl and add water to cover. Soak for 10 minutes. Drain and tear into roughly 1-inch pieces.

Trim the top 2 inches from the lemongrass stalk, leaving the root end attached. Halve the stalk lengthwise, then hit it firmly using the back of a chef's knife until bruised, 6 to 8 times. Combine the lemongrass, ⅓ cup water, and ginger in a medium saucepan. Bring to a boil over medium heat, then remove from the heat. Add the coconut sugar, tamarind, and makrut lime leaves. Using a whisk or fork, break up the tamarind as much as possible. Let stand for 30 minutes.

Pour the mixture through a fine-mesh sieve into a blender. Discard the lemongrass and lime leaves and add the tamarind and ginger from the strainer to the blender. Blend until smooth, about 25 seconds. Strain through a fine-mesh sieve into a medium bowl, pressing on the solids with the back of a spoon to extract as much liquid as possible. Scrape the pulp into the bowl as well. Discard the remaining solids. Store in an airtight container in the refrigerator for up to 1 week.

MAURITANIA

Named after the ancient Berber kingdom of Mauretania, which existed until the seventh century CE, most of modern Mauritania still looks the same as when that nomadic group ran the show. As in, miles of sweltering sand, often with no end in sight. Two-thirds of this large coastal nation's total area is covered by inhospitable Saharan dunes and wind-burned plateaus, leaving its approximately 4.6 million thirsty citizens to find refreshment any way they can. Traditionally, that's been the role of jus de bouye, a drink derived from the fruit of the baobab tree, which is prominent in the country's slightly less arid southern regions. With a mildly buttery and acidic flavor that's described as being a bit less sweet than apple, pear, or apricot juice, the nectar is high in vitamin C, potassium, and phosphorus, a blessing in a place where nutrient-rich food sources are as scarce as a rainstorm.

Like many North Africans, Mauritanians are also quite fond of imported green tea, which is served after most meals and is poured from a height to create froth. That marriage of grassy, vegetal tang and foamy mouthfeel defines the Green Tea Sour, a mildly caffeinated riff on the classic Gin Sour. You won't find any gin infused with green tea in Mauritania—or probably any gin for that matter, as alcohol is totally forbidden for both tourists and locals in the Islamic republic—but the fragrant, stimulating blend is easy to make in less prohibitive locales, and far easier to quaff when combined with bright citrus, bitters, and just the right amount of sweetness.

Green Tea Sour

Makes 1 drink

2 ounces gin

¾ teaspoon loose green tea leaves

¾ ounce fresh lemon juice

¾ ounce simple syrup (page 5)

2 dashes Peychaud's bitters

1 egg white

Pour the gin into a small bowl or mug and add the green tea. Let stand for 1 hour, then strain the infused gin through a fine-mesh sieve into a mason jar and chill in the refrigerator for a few minutes. Pour the infused gin into a shaker and add the lemon juice, simple syrup, bitters, and egg white. Shake without ice for 5 or 6 seconds to emulsify the egg white, then add ice and shake vigorously. Strain into a double rocks glass over ice.

MAURITIUS

Located about 700 miles east of Madagascar in the Indian Ocean, the island nation of Mauritius is prized by travelers for its highly photogenic beaches, lagoons, and waterfalls, as well as the hiking trails that crisscross its mountainous, rainforest-filled interior. And while the country today boasts 600 species of plants and animals, its most famous resident was the dodo, an endearingly goofy, flightless bird that was unfortunately eradicated by 1681. Far from extinct, however, are Mauritius's vast sugarcane fields that comprise around 50 percent of the country's arable land and account for a sizable chunk of its export revenues. In recent years, that prolific crop has also given rise to a burgeoning spirits industry dominated by Starr, a field-to-bottle, single-estate rum that's distilled, oak-aged, blended, and bottled locally.

When introducing the spirit to American rum enthusiasts in the mid-2000s, Starr CEO Jeffrey Zarnow would often suggest using it as the base in his favorite cocktail, the Rumble. A riff on a version of the classic Bramble, its simple and straightforward ingredients—lemon, sugar, and muddled blackberries—work nicely with the light molasses rum's cherry and cardamom base and hints of citrus, nutmeg, and vanilla. If a trip to pristine Mauritius isn't on your bucket list, it's still worth trying one of these sweet-and-sour blasts of refreshment as they're the most authentic way to experience the character of this captivating nation—unless you're planning a *Jurassic Park*–style resurrection of the dodo, of course.

Starr Rumble

Makes 1 drink

2 ounces Starr Ultra Superior Light Rum

¾ ounce fresh lemon juice

¾ ounce simple syrup (page 5)

4 blackberries

Crushed ice

Combine the rum, lemon juice, and simple syrup in a shaker. In a double old-fashioned glass, muddle 3 blackberries, then fill the glass two-thirds of the way with crushed ice. Add the contents of the shaker and top with crushed ice. Top with the remaining blackberry.

Mauritius / Starr Rumble (page 55)

MOROCCO

Many countries, especially those situated near continental borders, have been described as "cultural crossroads." Few, if any, are as historically, ethnically, or culinarily diverse as the Kingdom of Morocco, which lies just seven nautical miles south of Spain across the Strait of Gibraltar. Home of northwestern Africa's indigenous Berber people, it's also played host to Romans, Arabs, French and Spanish imperialists, and exiled Jews, among many others. Today, all that traffic has created a fascinating convergence of languages, art, and architectural styles, and an embarrassment of to-die-for dishes that blend Arabian, Andalusian, and western European ingredients, as well as homegrown delicacies like saffron, mint, and olives.

Whether enjoying a day of Mediterranean sunbathing, hiking the snowcapped peaks of the iconic Atlas Mountains, or trekking camelback across the Sahara Desert, you're likely to find refreshment in a cup of mint tea, which has been a central component of North Africa's social life for centuries. If you're luckier, you might be offered some mahia, an anise-tinged fruit brandy made by the local Jewish community. Or, like a true adventurer, you could take matters into your own hands, whip up a Moroccan Mojito, and explore both beverages' traditional flavors. Savory, mildly sweet, and summery, its complex backbone of brandy, tea, cardamom, and rose water is embellished gorgeously by enough bright, citrusy, and minty undertones to appease even the most stringent mojito fundamentalists. An aromatic and energizing mashup that's as unique as the land that inspired it.

FOR A COUNTRY that's mostly desert, and where drinking alcohol is shunned by much of the population, Morocco produces what many consider to be the finest wines in the Arab region. One brand, Boulaouane, has been one of the best-selling foreign wines in France since the 2000s.

Moroccan Mojito

Makes 1 drink

1½ ounces brandy

1 ounce brewed black tea

1 ounce fresh lime juice

¾ ounce Cardamom Syrup (recipe follows)

½ ounce aged rum

Small handful of mint leaves, plus 1 sprig for garnish

1 brown sugar cube

Crushed ice

Combine the brandy, tea, lime juice, cardamom syrup, rum, mint leaves, and sugar cube in a shaker. Muddle gently and then pour into a tall glass. Fill the glass two-thirds of the way with crushed ice. Add a straw and top with more crushed ice. Garnish with the mint sprig.

Cardamom Syrup

Makes about 1 cup

1 cup water

¼ cup green cardamom pods

1 cup sugar

Combine the water and cardamom pods in a medium saucepan and bring to a boil. Add the sugar and stir until fully dissolved. Reduce the heat to low, cover, and simmer for 10 minutes. Remove from the heat and let cool for a few minutes. Transfer the mixture to an airtight container and refrigerate for 3 days to infuse. Strain the syrup through a fine-mesh sieve, then pour into a lidded bottle. Store in the refrigerator for up to 3 weeks.

MOZAMBIQUE

Depicting a rifle—specifically an AK-47—Mozambique's flag looks a bit intimidating. But instead of advocating violence, it symbolizes defense, vigilance, and the centuries-long struggle for independence from Portugal, which started setting up trading posts along the country's coastline in 1505. Today, Mozambique's citizens—one of the youngest populations in the world with a median age of seventeen—are forging a brand-new identity with rapidly growing food, beverage, and manufacturing industries in one of the fastest developing economies on the African continent. Yet there's still a great deal of Portuguese influence here, from the national language to the presence of spices like chili powder and garlic in many dishes to the consumption of Madeira, the country's most popular beverage.

Produced in a wide variety of both dry and sweet styles, the fortified wine originated in the Madeira Islands—a formerly uninhabited North Atlantic archipelago that was settled by the Portuguese in the early fifteenth century—and were prized for their stability during long sea voyages. Commonly enjoyed as an aperitif or a dessert sipper, or used as a flavor enhancer in cooking, it also can add interesting depth, fruitiness, and nuttiness to cocktails like the Hot in the Shade, which was created by bartender Dan Greenbaum at New York's Diamond Reef in 2017. Featuring tropical ingredients invoking Mozambique's long Indian Ocean coastline that's dotted with popular beaches, offshore coral islands, and mangrove-covered Ibo Island with its mysterious colonial-era ruins, the sultry, smoky revelation is known for creating a sunny disposition in drinkers of all stripes.

Hot in the Shade

Makes 1 drink

1½ ounces mezcal

1 ounce pineapple juice

½ ounce fresh lime juice

½ ounce orgeat

Crushed ice

½ ounce Madeira

1 mint sprig, for garnish

Combine the mezcal, pineapple juice, lime juice, and orgeat in a shaker. Pour into a tall glass filled two-thirds of the way with crushed ice. Add a straw. Float the Madeira on top by pouring it over the back of a spoon into the glass. Top with more crushed ice and garnish with the mint sprig.

***

MADEIRA IS INTENTIONALLY exposed to high heat and oxygen during its maturation process, making it one of the world's longest-lasting wines. Vintages that are 200 years or older (and still in excellent condition) are routinely sold at rare wine shops, with the oldest known bottle on the market dating to 1715. Even opened bottles can last for decades if corked properly.

NAMIBIA

For a place that's shockingly short on people, Namibia is still big on fun facts. At twice the size of California, but with only 2.5 million citizens, it's the second least-densely populated country on Earth. It's also home to the world's largest group of free-roaming cheetahs, the largest seal colony, and the largest underwater lake. But perhaps the most impressive feature is the Namib Desert, which, at 55 to 80 million years, is the planet's oldest. Once a death trap for unwitting explorers, it's now a tourist hotspot—literally—where thousands trek each year to experience some of the most impressive sand dunes found on any continent.

After a few hours of dune buggy riding, sandboarding, or avoiding a stampede of a rare herd of desert elephants, you'll want to make like the locals and grab yourself a Rock Shandy. A holdover from the days when much of southern Africa was colonized by the British, this Angostura bitters–infused lemonade is still a wildly popular refresher throughout the region, with drink-slingers in some countries tweaking the recipe by adding ingredients like ginger ale and homemade beer. Namibians generally prefer the cocktail in its simplest form—lemon, sugar, bitters, and club soda—a vitamin C–replenishing, stomach-settling treat to combat the most diabolical climates. Choosing the amount of 90-proof bitters to use is a matter of personal preference, with most imbibers preferring to keep it low-ABV at only a few drops to half a teaspoon. Feel free to ratchet up the herb-and-spice content, but be ready for an exponentially aggressive blast of boozy flavor. Which might be exactly what you need after a close encounter with a wild cheetah.

Rock Shandy

Makes 1 drink

1½ ounces fresh lemon juice

1½ ounces simple syrup (page 5)

Angostura bitters, to taste

Club soda, to top

1 lemon wheel, for garnish

Combine the lemon juice, simple syrup, and bitters in a shaker. Add 1 or 2 ice pebbles, shake briefly, and pour into a tall glass filled with ice. Top with club soda. Place the lemon wheel in the glass beside the ice.

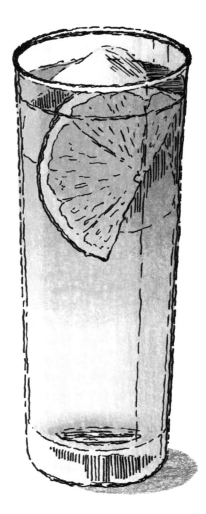

NIGER

Playing with mud is usually considered a childish pastime (or was, in the days before hand-sanitizer-wielding, germophobic parents). In Niger, it's been elevated to an art form, particularly in the Saharan city of Agadez, which has existed as a thriving trading hub since the sixteenth century. Due to a lack of other materials, the buildings here are almost entirely made of mud-bricks packed with straw and gravel and the town's towering Grand Mosque is the tallest mud-built structure in the world.

After Niger's resourceful architects—and the millions of other workers toiling in the dusty, arid conditions—clean up after a long day on the job, their culinary and refreshment options are much more diverse than the singular substance used to construct their homes. West African specialties like hearty rice and vegetable stews, beef and mutton skewers, and palm nut soup are all on the menu, with many cooking methods also derived from France, from whom Niger achieved independence in 1960. After grubbing out, predominantly Muslim Nigeriens wash it all down with tea or juice from the ogbono fruit, or bush mango.

Culturally and geographically close to the Middle East, Niger has also adopted Arab specialties like laban, a drink that's made with water, salted yogurt, and mint and is most popular during the hottest months (which, in the Sahara, means year-round). The Brandy Laban offers a boozy, cara-melly twist to the dessert beverage with French cognac and a bit of rich demerara sugar for some sweet depth. It's just the ticket for getting your mind out of the mud and onto a higher plane of smooth and creamy, spirits-induced bliss.

Brandy Laban

Makes 1 drink

¼ cup (2 ounces) plain full-fat yogurt

2 ounces cold water

1½ ounces cognac

¾ ounce Demerara syrup (see Note, page 5)

¼ teaspoon sea salt

1 mint sprig, for garnish

Combine the yogurt, water, cognac, Demerara syrup, and salt in an ice-filled shaker. Shake vigorously and then strain into a fizz glass. Garnish with the mint sprig.

NIGERIA

With the most citizens of any African country and the continent's most powerful economy, Nigeria's diversity is off the charts. More than 500 languages are spoken by its 250 ethnic groups, who belong to some of the world's largest Christian and Muslim populations, simultaneously. Outside of mega-size cities like Lagos, there's also a wealth of nature, with 550 unique species of mammals and birds, 1,000 species of butterflies, and 4,000 species of plants. The juice from one of the plants, the Raffia palm, is fermented and distilled to make *ògógóró*, or "local gin," a super-potent, inexpensive, and usually homemade liquor that's widely available throughout Nigeria, even in areas where alcohol is technically illegal for religious reasons.

When they need to soothe their throats after a few rounds of fiery òg̀ógóró shots, or if they're simply craving some fruity refreshment to beat the sweltering sub-equatorial heat, Nigerians head to their local bar, restaurant, or roadside stand for an ice-cold Chapman. Created in the 1930s by Sam Alamutu at Lagos's swanky Ikoyi Club, the sweet and fizzy drink is usually made as a punch with orange and lemon-lime sodas, grenadine, and Angostura bitters poured over a mix of sliced fruits and cucumbers. The Chapman Cocktail, adapted from a recipe by Nigerian chef Immaculate Ruému, employs the citrus elements from its nonalcoholic namesake, as well as a pomegranate-based sweetener, muddled cucumbers, and bitters. Ògógóró has only started to be produced commercially within the past few years, in limited batches; if you can't find any, London dry gin (a favorite of affluent Nigerians since the twentieth-century British occupation), works as a lovely base for this flavorful summer sipper with global appeal.

Chapman Cocktail
Makes 1 drink

2 ounces ogógóró or London dry gin

1 ounce fresh orange juice

½ ounce fresh lime juice

½ ounce pomegranate syrup (page 5)

2 dashes Angostura bitters

4 thin cucumber slices

Club soda, to splash

1 lime twist, for garnish

Combine the gin, orange juice, lime juice, pomegranate syrup, bitters, and 3 cucumber slices in an ice-filled shaker. Shake vigorously and then strain into a double rocks glass over ice. Splash with club soda. Place the lime twist and remaining cucumber slice in the glass beside the ice.

IN NIGERIA'S non-Muslim communities, a bride and groom are considered officially married only after each has taken a drink of local palm wine.

RWANDA

The American dairy farmers' "Got Milk?" campaign would've been a giant waste of time and money in Rwanda. The small, densely populated Central African nation is already the most milk-crazy region on the planet, a place where cows are considered a sign of wealth and the most valuable of gifts, and where children are named after the massive mammals and traditional dances emulate bovine movements. First-time visitors looking for a drink in the capital city, Kigali, are often shocked at the number of pub-like establishments that only serve milk, both hot and cold, fermented and fresh, which is no surprise given that Rwandans generally drink 3 liters or more of the stuff every day.

According to a 2021 *New York Times* article, Rwandans love milk for its flavor, nutritional value, and above all, its stress-reducing properties, especially when sipped (or chugged) in a communal setting. For the lactose-intolerant and those looking for a boozier form of socialization, there are plenty of imported whiskey and gin options, domestic beers, and home-brewed banana wines that Rwandans like to chase with—you guessed it—milk. That same fruity and creamy combo is the defining feature of the Bourbon Banana Flip, a tasty dessert beverage from Sam Ross, proprietor of New York's Attaboy. Its milkshake-like mouthfeel and decadently soothing finish will help you achieve the same level of bliss experienced by Rwandans at a milk bar, minus the bottle or three of cow juice.

Bourbon Banana Flip

Makes 1 drink

1½ ounces bourbon

¾ ounce banana liqueur

¾ ounce simple syrup (page 5)

½ ounce heavy cream

1 egg yolk

Pinch of freshly grated nutmeg, for garnish

Combine the bourbon, banana liqueur, simple syrup, cream, and egg yolk in a shaker. Shake without ice for 5 or 6 seconds to emulsify the egg yolk, then add ice and shake vigorously. Strain into a coupe and sprinkle with the nutmeg.

IN THE DAYS of the Kingdom of Rwanda, which existed until the last king was deposed in 1961, the desire for easy access to milk even extended to the royal family. Fresh milk from prized cattle was kept in ornate wooden bottles with conical lids in a special storage area directly adjacent to the king's thatched palace.

SÃO TOMÉ AND PRÍNCIPE

Humans have always been compelled to journey into the unknown. Portuguese sailors in the fourteenth and fifteenth centuries turned that urge into a lifestyle. The first Europeans to thoroughly explore the Atlantic Ocean, they colonized the previously uninhabited Madeira and Azores archipelagos before heading south along the coast of Africa, discovering the lush equatorial islands of São Tomé and Príncipe around 1470. Fully independent since 1975, the second-smallest country in Africa is known for its centuries-old plant and fish–based cuisine, creole language, and love of palm wine, the national drink, which is produced both commercially and at home in just about every village.

The legacy of Portuguese rule remains, however, perhaps most saliently in the vast sugarcane plantations that still dot the landscape of both islands. And wherever there's sugarcane, it's a solid bet that spirits production is happening nearby. In São Tomé and Príncipe, like other former colonies such as Cabo Verde and Madeira, that takes the form of aguardente, which today is often distilled with locally grown crops like vanilla, offering a flavorful introduction to the islands' unique terroir. Those who prefer their "fire water" a bit softened out use it (or other sugarcane-based spirits like rum and cachaça) as the base in Poncha, the country's most popular cocktail, a mouthwatering blend of citrus, honey, and cinnamon—a common spice in São Toméan cooking—that's been enjoyed for centuries, and for good reason.

Poncha

Makes 1 drink

2 ounces aguardente, cachaça, or rum
½ ounce honey syrup (page 5)
¼ ounce cinnamon syrup (page 4)
4 lemon wedges
3 thin orange slices
Pinch of freshly grated cinnamon, for garnish

Combine the aguardente, honey syrup, cinnamon syrup, lemon wedges, and 2 orange slices in a shaker. Muddle, then fill the shaker with cracked ice. Shake 5 or 6 times. Pour the contents of the shaker into a double rocks glass. Perch the remaining orange slice on the rim of the glass and sprinkle with the cinnamon.

IF YOU WANT TO SAMPLE the best of São Tomé and Príncipe's palm wines (*vinho de palma*, or *vim pema* in the local creole), be prepared to go for a hike. The purest, most undiluted versions are made in remote high-altitude forests, decreasing in quality the closer to town you get.

SENEGAL

In the language of the Wolof people—Senegal's largest ethnic group—the word *téranga* means "hospitality," which is more than just an abstract concept to the Senegalese. Known throughout West Africa for their warm, welcoming spirit, they're famous for wasting no time in offering guests chilled glasses of their national drink, bissap. A delicately sweetened, wine-colored juice made from the dried flowers of the roselle plant, a variety of hibiscus that grows just about everywhere in the country—with particularly large concentrations near the capital city of Dakar—it's the ideal tonic for Senegal's hot and humid climate and a source of mutual enjoyment for the country's dozen or so unique tribal entities.

Whatever their heritage, Senegal's predominantly Muslim bissap drinkers prefer their beverages ice-cold and unadulterated, with maybe only a pinch of local spice for an occasional extra kick. But the slightly tart, grapelike nectar is ripe for a little tinkering, as when it's used as the primary flavor component of the Spiked Bissap. Jazzed up with cognac from France—whose language is still the de facto tongue for government and business in the former French colony—a bit of citrus, allspice, and bitters, the smooth and flowery concoction is just as refreshing as the juice by itself, but with a subtle, booze-aided complexity that will make fast friends of hospitable cocktail lovers, wherever they might be found.

Spiked Bissap

Makes 1 drink

2 ounces cognac

¾ ounce fresh lemon juice

¾ ounce bissap syrup (page 4)

2 dashes Angostura bitters

Small handful of mint leaves, plus 1 sprig for garnish

Club soda, to top

Combine the cognac, lemon juice, bissap syrup, bitters, and mint leaves in an ice-filled shaker. Shake vigorously and then strain into an ice-filled Collins glass. Top with club soda. Garnish with the mint sprig.

SEYCHELLES

Though they've only been inhabited for about 500 years, the Seychelles have had a full and varied history where human activities are concerned. The remote and impossibly gorgeous Indian Ocean island chain was an overseas territory of both France and the United Kingdom, served as a longtime hangout for infamous pirates, and is one of Africa's major producers of rum, which was introduced by the British Navy in the late seventeenth century and later distilled locally after the proliferation of sugarcane fields on the islands. Today, cane is crushed and distilled both on a familial level and by globally regarded spirits producers like Takamaka Rum (named after an indigenous species of tree), then blended with local-grown fruit extracts, spices, and island spring water for a uniquely Seychelles taste.

The archipelago has also been mentioned in cocktail circles for the innovative drinks that have begun popping up at the country's many beach bars and resorts, which do a marvelous job of showcasing the islands' eclectic potpourri of flavors and influences. Spearheading this mixological surge is food and beverage writer Flavien Joubert, whose book *Seychelles Magical Cocktails* (2015) features dozens of locally inspired concoctions like the Victoria Fizz. Featuring a highly unusual pairing of pastis and Drambuie—a strong liqueur made from Scotch, heather honey, herbs, and spices—it's a highly herbaceous callback to centuries of French and British cultural influence, with plenty of citrus and bubbles for an unquestionably brisk and breezy island vibe.

Victoria Fizz

Makes 1 drink

2 ounces fresh orange juice

1½ ounces Drambuie

½ ounce pastis

1 barspoon cane syrup

Club soda, to top

1 thin orange slice, for garnish

Combine the orange juice, Drambuie, pastis, and cane syrup in a shaker. Add 1 or 2 ice pebbles, shake briefly, and pour into an ice-filled Collins glass. Top with club soda. Perch the orange slice on the rim of the glass.

SIERRA LEONE

Upon sailing into what is now Sierra Leone's Freetown Peninsula in 1462 during a violent thunderstorm, Portuguese explorer Pedro da Cintra named the area Serra Lyoa, which roughly translates to "roaring mountains" or "lion mountains." Roaring is also an accurate way to describe one's hangover after overconsuming poyo, the country's national drink, which is distilled by villagers from the fermented sap of coconut palms. The longer the sap ferments, the higher the percentage of alcohol in the drink, meaning that freshly tapped poyo is sweet and light, with the potency of a strong beer or glass of wine. But when the sap is left simmering for 12 hours or more, the resulting liquor becomes strong enough to drag you headfirst into the danger zone with little or no warning.

If playing Russian roulette with home-brewed palm hooch isn't your thing, there are plenty of risk-free Sierra Leonean staples that would be a boon to any tropically inclined drink-slinger. Inspired by the year-round flavors of the West African republic, the Guava-Coco Cooler is a roaring rainstorm of guava, coconut, ginger, lime, and bitters, which, when sipped slowly, offers a far less direct route to a destructive hangover (and at the very least a tastier one, if it does happen). In Sierra Leone, they say that poyo was a gift from celestial entities. And while this brisk and breezy tipple has much humbler origins, it might be just what the doctor (or bartender) ordered to elevate your mind from the realm of earthly worries.

IF YOU'RE in Sierra Leone and want to try the low-alcohol version of poyo that's freshly tapped from the tree, be sure to ask for it "from God to man."

Guava-Coco Cooler

Makes 1 drink

1½ ounces aged rum

½ ounce black rum, such as Goslings Black Seal Rum

1½ ounces guava nectar

1 ounce unsweetened full-fat coconut milk

½ ounce fresh lime juice

¼ ounce ginger syrup (page 5)

1 barspoon cane syrup

2 dashes Angostura bitters

1 lime wedge, for garnish

Combine the rums, guava nectar, coconut milk, lime juice, ginger syrup, and cane syrup in an ice-filled shaker. Shake vigorously and then strain into a double rocks glass over ice. Add the bitters and perch the lime wedge on the rim of the glass.

SOMALIA

Sauntering across the deck of a galleon wearing an eye patch, parrot on shoulder. Hoisting a skull-and-crossbones flag and screaming "Arr, matey!" This is how most of us picture pirates, but modern buccaneers, the most infamous being from Somalia (as featured in films like 2013's *Captain Phillips*), are a far cry from Jack Sparrow. Many former fishermen still prowl the longest coastline in mainland Africa, a risky occupation whose popularity in the world's second-poorest country shouldn't come as a surprise. And while Somalia continues to suffer from the fallout of a thirty-plus-year civil war, this arid land of plains, plateaus, and jagged highlands remains a fascinating historical hotbed. Home to numerous Paleolithic cultures, its notable archaeological sites include gravesites boasting the oldest evidence of burial customs in the Horn of Africa, as well as the 5,000-year-old Laas Geel cave complex and its extraordinarily vivid rock art, a relatively recent discovery that never fails to wow the few intrepid tourists who get to check it out each year.

Despite their discrepancies, Somalia's various political factions share a love for both black tea and xawaash, a blend of easy-to-find household spices that's added to everything from meats and stews to fish and coffee. The two are often combined in a steamy, powerful beverage that's supremely savory, slightly sweet, diverse, and delectable enough to enjoy in any season or time of day. Alcohol is explicitly forbidden in Somalia—Islam is the only state-sanctioned religion practiced by more than 99 percent of the population—but you'd do well to add some dark liquor to this pleasantly energizing brew, specifically rum if you're chasing that old-timey (and mostly fictionalized) pirate feeling.

Xawaash Toddy

Makes 1 drink

5 ounces water

2 whole cloves

2 black or green cardamom pods

½ cinnamon stick

Pinch of ground ginger

Pinch of freshly grated nutmeg

Pinch of fenugreek seeds

Pinch of ground coriander

Pinch of ground cumin

Pinch of ground turmeric

Pinch of dried sage

1 tablespoon loose black tea leaves

¾ ounce honey syrup (page 5)

2 ounces brandy, whiskey, or dark rum

1 lemon wedge, for garnish

Combine the water, cloves, cardamom pods, cinnamon stick, ginger, nutmeg, fenugreek, coriander, cumin, turmeric, and sage in a small pot. Bring the water to just below boiling and remove it from the heat. Add the tea leaves and steep for 4 to 5 minutes. Strain through a fine-mesh strainer into a large mug and stir in the honey syrup. Float the brandy on top of the drink by pouring it over the back of a spoon into the mug. Perch the lemon wedge on the rim of the mug.

SOUTH AFRICA

South Africa and superlatives seem to go hand in hand. The continent's most industrialized and most technologically advanced country is home to the oldest discovered human remains, the largest man-made forest, and an insane amount of wildlife, including the planet's largest and smallest mammals (the African elephant and least dwarf shrew, respectively). It's also the location of the longest wine route, Route 62, featuring seventy distinct vineyards, as well as SABMiller, the world's largest brewing company by volume. Meaning, South Africans are known to enjoy a tipple or several. And when they're in the mood for a creamy nightcap, they break out a bottle of Amarula, a liqueur made from the fruit of the marula tree, which only grows in subequatorial Africa and is also a favorite of elephants, who travel miles to feast on the juicy yellow morsels.

With a citrusy, milky, and nutty flavor and a silky texture reminiscent of Kahlua, Amarula is perfect for sipping on its own or over ice. But South Africans like to ratchet up the dessert vibes—and caloric content—with the Don Pedro (or Dom Pedro), a cocktail that's been a popular after-dinner treat since the mid-1980s, when Amarula was officially introduced to the local market. Recipes vary, but the standard ingredients, alongside a healthy dose of Amarula, of course, are vanilla ice cream, an extra shot of heavy cream (because why not?), and half a bar of flaked chocolate, either blended with the rest of the drink or sprinkled on top. Absurdly tasty—if not vegan or fitness-friendly—this diabolically decadent adult milkshake may inspire you to make plans to visit the Southern Hemisphere. If you can get off the couch after finishing one.

When it comes to using local ingredients, South African bartenders aren't solely about the dessert drinks. Eugene Thompson of Johannesburg, the country's most populous city, employs homegrown rooibos tea in his Fynbos, which is named for the unique biome where the rooibos plant, a shrub with a grassy, malty flavor that's prized for its restorative properties, grows. Winner of the 2012 FHM Brandy Cocktail of the Year competition, the gingery, herbaceous concoction also—unsurprisingly—includes brandy, which in recent years has become South Africa's most popular liquor.

Don Pedro

Makes 1 drink

3 ounces Amarula
1½ ounces heavy cream
2 generous scoops vanilla ice cream
½ ounce chocolate, grated

Combine the Amarula, cream, and ice cream in a blender and blend until smooth. Pour into a tall glass. Top with the grated chocolate.

Don Pedro

Fynbos

Makes 1 drink

1½ ounces South African brandy, such as Jonathan Barry XO
    Handcrafted Cape Brandy
1½ ounces brewed rooibos tea
¾ ounce simple syrup (page 5)
½ ounce ginger liqueur, such as Butlers
1 teaspoon honey
1 lemon twist, for garnish

Combine the brandy, rooibos tea, simple syrup, ginger liqueur, and honey in an ice-filled shaker. Shake vigorously and then strain into a coupe. Place the lemon twist in the glass.

SOUTH SUDAN

Breaking up is hard to do. That line, first crooned by Neil Sedaka in the 1960s, rings just as true when applied to twenty-first-century geopolitics. Though it officially declared independence from Sudan in 2011, South Sudan is still engaged in the international relations version of who gets to keep the dog over—what else—oil, as the East African republic contains 75 percent of Sudan's former reserves. That drama, coupled with near-constant civil war, has made it a rocky start for the world's newest internationally recognized country. But the South Sudanese manage to keep their spirits up thanks to a fascinating tradition of oral storytelling and araqi, a homemade liquor made with dates that's officially illegal in the observant Muslim nation, but still plays a big part in the local social life, especially among older men.

Recently, South Sudan's newly independent citizens have also taken inspiration from a somewhat unlikely source: the fictional African nation of Wakanda, a technological utopia ruled by the Marvel Comics superhero Black Panther. And which, according to Marvel Universe world maps, sits directly on much of South Sudan's current territory. It's also the namesake of the date-flavored Wakanda Cocktail. This creamy, caffeinated cooler of unknown origins merges both date liqueur with muddled dates, as well as goat's milk and coffee, two South Sudanese kitchen standbys. Fruity, savory, and exuding positivity, it's a superpowered pick-me-up for when you're trying to build a new nation from scratch, or just need a little extra juice for the weekend.

Wakanda Cocktail

Makes 1 drink

1 ounce date liqueur

1 ounce coffee liqueur, such as Caffé Lolita

1 ounce goat's milk

2 or 3 dates, halved and pitted

Combine all the ingredients in a shaker and muddle thoroughly. Add ice and shake vigorously. Strain into a double rocks glass over ice.

SUDAN

Losing nearly a quarter of a million square miles of territory in 2011 after a decades-long civil war knocked Sudan off the list of the world's top ten biggest countries, though the still-massive Northeast African republic continues to put up big numbers in other statistical categories. Sudan has the most ancient pyramids of any country (and around one hundred more than neighboring Egypt), contains more of the world's longest river, the Nile, than any other country, and it's also involved in the Great Green Wall Initiative, helping to build a 5,000-mile-long wall of trees stretching across Africa that will eventually be the largest living structure on the planet.

Where you won't find Sudan is near the top of any list regarding boozing. According to the World Health Organization, it's the fourteenth-driest country, with residents averaging a measly 0.5 liters of alcohol each year, mostly in the form of araqi, the illicitly made, date-based liquor that's also prevalent in its former South Sudanese territories. Sudan's 41 million Muslims prefer to quench their thirst with hibiscus-flavored teas, juices, and soft drinks that are prized for their velvety red hue, silky texture, and tangy bite. That color and flavor profile is the primary inspiration for the Sudanese Rose, a tea-forward chiller from spirits writer Chris Stanley that first appeared on his *Rookie Libations* blog. Delicate yet complex, airy yet earthy, it's a big-time burst of flavor celebrating a country where largeness is routine.

Sudanese Rose

Makes 1 drink

2 ounces brewed hibiscus tea

1½ ounces rhum agricole

½ ounce Lillet Blanc

¼ ounce Hibiscus Grenadine (recipe follows)

1 lime twist, for garnish

1 food-grade rose petal, for garnish

Combine the hibiscus tea, rhum agricole, Lillet Blanc, and grenadine in an ice-filled mixing glass. Stir with a long-handled spoon for 15 to 20 seconds and then strain into a double rocks glass over ice. Place the lime twist in the glass beside the ice and garnish with the rose petal.

Hibiscus Grenadine

Makes about 1 cup

2 cups sugar

1 cup water

Seeds from 1 pomegranate

¼ cup dried hibiscus flowers

Combine the sugar and water in a small saucepan and bring to a simmer over medium heat, stirring to dissolve the sugar. Add the pomegranate seeds and hibiscus flowers and simmer, stirring occasionally, for 20 minutes. Strain through cheesecloth or a fine-mesh sieve and discard the solids. Store in an airtight container in the refrigerator for up to 1 month.

UNTIL RECENTLY, about 80 percent of inmates in Sudan's only women's prison were there on charges of either prostitution or brewing araqi. That began to change in 2020, when a new law permitting the sale of alcohol to non-Muslims was enacted, providing a legal source of income for thousands of Sudanese distillers, most of whom are female.

TANZANIA

While Tanzania has been inhabited for at least 7,000 years, its national drink has a far shorter history. Yet Konyagi, which has only been legally distilled since the 1970s, has already imbedded itself deeply in the local culture, with many traditions surrounding its consumption. A more sophisticated version of the moonshine that has long been consumed in the East African republic, the clear liquor must be tapped at the base of its bottle several times with one's palm before opening, in order to release the (metaphysical) spirits within and ensure a pleasant drinking experience. After pouring, the bottle is usually left on its side—again, to appease the spirits—until someone is ready for a refill. Most Konyagi bottles have uniquely flattened sides for this purpose.

The etiquette may be set in stone, but there's still a fierce debate as to whether Konyagi is a vodka, gin, or a rum. With a piney, almost medicinal nose, as well as elements of vanilla, mellow citrus, and cardamom, the cane sugar distillate contains elements of all three spirits, but many of those who regularly partake consider it to be something else entirely. Whichever way you choose to classify it, Konyagi makes for a powerful yet unobtrusive base in most fruit-forward refreshers, with the Tanzanian Tonic being one of the best examples. Succulent Tanzanian staples like guava, peach, and pineapple form an excellent contrast to Konyagi's floral bitterness, while doses of citrus and tart pomegranate syrup keep things as nicely balanced as a Konyagi bottle on its side. Remember to placate the spirits before downing a couple of these, because no one likes a supernaturally inflicted hangover.

Tanzanian Tonic
Makes 1 drink

2 ounces Konyagi (if unavailable, use white rum or vodka)

½ ounce pineapple juice

½ ounce fresh orange juice

½ ounce peach nectar

½ ounce guava nectar

¼ ounce fresh lemon juice

¼ ounce pomegranate syrup (page 5)

1 thin orange slice, for garnish

1 brandied cherry, for garnish

Combine the Konyagi, pineapple juice, orange juice, peach nectar, guava nectar, lemon juice, and pomegranate syrup in a blender. Add a few small ice cubes and blend until smooth. Pour into a tall glass. Using toothpicks, perch the orange slice and brandied cherry on the rim of the glass.

THE EFFECTS of drinking Konyagi are said to be different from any other spirit, a hazy, tingly sensation more akin to the "body high" experienced by smokers of certain strains of cannabis. This initially pleasant feeling is blamed for lulling drinkers into a false sense of security that leads to overindulging and famously miserable mornings after.

TOGO

If you have the bad luck of getting sick or hurt in Togo, you may not be rushed to the nearest hospital. Instead, you'll probably be taken by a practitioner of one of the local voodoo-like cults to a fetish market, where they'll obtain the appropriate trinket or sacrificial animal to appease whatever evil being has afflicted you. Unlike most Africans, who have wholeheartedly embraced the Christian and Islamic faiths, the Togolese have mostly stayed true to the animist religion of their ancestors, a belief system where supernatural beings exist in every inanimate object and are the cause of every success or misfortune. And where, judging by the locals' enthusiastic consumption of palm wine and its stronger distillates, alcohol is not only accepted but fully embraced within the culture.

Whether they're performing a rite to appease the spirits, praying for a fertile harvest, or welcoming guests into their homes, Togo's gracious and superstitious citizens always keep a bottle of the local—and usually homemade—hooch close at hand. But when a special occasion calls for something a little fancier, they often will opt for sodabi, the industrially produced palm liquor that's made in neighboring Benin and renowned throughout the region for its subtle nutty and peppery notes and consistent potency. It's the cleanest way to experience the High Priestess, which also includes everyday Togolese flavors like pineapple, bissap, and ginger. It's tempting to go hard on this spicy and fruity, mule-like mind-soother, but down more than a couple and the spirits may bless you with a hangover so extraordinary, no amount of voodoo magic will be able to save you.

High Priestess
Makes 1 drink

2 ounces Tambour Original White Sodabi (if unavailable, use white rum)

¾ ounce ginger syrup (page 5)

½ ounce pineapple juice

½ ounce fresh lime juice

¼ ounce bissap syrup (page 4)

1 thin pineapple slice, for garnish

1 piece candied ginger, for garnish

Combine the sodabi, ginger syrup, pineapple juice, lime juice, and bissap syrup in an ice-filled shaker. Shake vigorously and then strain into a double rocks glass over ice. Place the pineapple slice in the glass beside the ice. Skewer the piece of candied ginger with toothpicks and perch it on the rim of the glass.

TUNISIA

The smallest country in North Africa, Tunisia has, perhaps unexpectedly, played host to some truly big historical moments. The center of the powerful and wealthy Carthaginian Empire, it was the site of Carthage's defeat at the hands of the ancient Romans in 146 BCE, a battle that paved the way for Rome's eventual dominance of the Mediterranean world. Much more recently, Tunisian protesters jumpstarted the region-altering Arab Spring uprisings of the 2010s in response to government corruption and economic inequality.

Spirits lovers might also be surprised that this predominantly Muslim nation—specifically its small yet resilient Jewish community—has been making a highly regarded distilled beverage for hundreds of years. Boukha, which translates to "alcohol vapor" in Judeo-Tunisian Arabic, is a clear, fig-based liquor with complex notes of raisins and local spices. As with most brandies, it's sipped neat, chilled, or as the basis for cocktails like the Monastir, a Brandy Alexander riff named after one of Tunisia's most prominent coastal cities. Fruity, creamy, and chocolaty, it makes for an excellent reward after a rough day trudging across the North African desert, or when life just makes you feel that way.

If you can't get your hands on any boukha, but still find yourself hankering for a taste of the Tunisian terroir, try the Izak (page 74), a zesty and vegetal Whiskey Sour variation from American bartender Nick Checchio. His recipe, which first appeared on Liquor.com, features a harissa syrup made from cinnamon, sugar, and the Tunisian spice blend Izak N.37 from New York City–based spice shop La Boîte. This authentic mix of sweet chiles and cumin serves as the perfect complement to the drink's whiskey, citrus, and hot pepper rim, for a cocktail that's as diversely flavored as Tunisia's long and fascinating history.

Monastir

Makes 1 drink

1½ ounces boukha

1 ounce heavy cream

1 ounce crème de cacao

Combine all the ingredients in an ice-filled shaker. Shake vigorously and then strain into a coupe.

Izak

Makes 1 drink

Aleppo pepper, for rimming the glass

1 lemon wedge, for rimming the glass

1½ ounces bourbon

¾ ounce fresh orange juice

½ ounce fresh lemon juice

½ ounce Harissa Syrup (recipe follows)

¼ ounce Cynar 70 amaro

Spread some Aleppo pepper over a small plate. Run the lemon wedge around the rim of a coupe, then dip the rim into the Aleppo pepper to coat; set aside. Combine the bourbon, orange juice, lemon juice, harissa syrup, and Cynar in an ice-filled shaker. Shake vigorously and then strain into the prepared coupe.

Harissa Syrup

Makes 1 cup

5 cinnamon sticks

1 cup sugar

1 cup water

1 tablespoon La Boîte Izak N.37 harissa-inspired spice blend

Toast the cinnamon sticks in a large saucepan over medium-high heat for 3 to 5 minutes. Add the sugar, water, and spice blend. Heat, stirring, until the sugar has dissolved, then remove from the heat. Remove and discard the cinnamon sticks. Cover and let stand overnight. Strain through a cheesecloth-lined conical strainer. Store in an airtight container in the refrigerator for up to 2 weeks.

UGANDA

Landlocked Uganda has long been famous for being the location of the source of the Nile River and having an astonishing amount of wildlife, even by African standards, including the continent's "Big Five" mammals—the African leopard, African lion, African bush elephant, southern white rhino, and Cape buffalo—as well as the critically endangered mountain gorilla. In recent years, its capital city of Kampala has become, somewhat surprisingly, one of the continent's rising cocktail hotspots, with a plethora of highly rated restaurants and hotel bars dishing out world-class libations and hosting an annual Kampala Cocktail Week that's attended by thousands of drinks nerds and casual liquor lovers alike.

That event is largely fueled by waragi, a robust local gin that's been home-distilled for generations and refined on an industrial scale since the 1960s by a coalition of Ugandan manufacturers. It's best to avoid the homemade hooch, which can contain fatal amounts of ethanol, but when it's made properly in a licensed distillery, the final product is singularly vibrant and tangy, imbued with botanicals like lime peel, cassia bark, and nutmeg. It's also a lovely base in the Queen of Katwe, adapted from a recipe by Fred Kubasu, bartender at the now-shuttered Mythos Greek Taverna and Lounge in Kampala's Makerere neighborhood, whose mixological talents won him the award for Best Cocktail at the 2015 Kampala Cocktail Week. Named after a film depicting life in a local slum, the drink is a fruity and gorgeously composed blend of waragi, pineapple, basil, and Midori, with an agreeably foamy texture and an herbal finish that's perfect as both a start to a night on the town or as a safari nightcap in a star-filled wilderness.

Queen of Katwe

Makes 1 drink

1½ ounces waragi or London dry gin

¾ ounce pineapple juice

¾ ounce fresh lemon juice

¾ ounce simple syrup (page 5)

¼ ounce Midori

2 basil leaves

1 food-grade rose petal, for garnish

Combine the waragi, pineapple juice, lemon juice, simple syrup, Midori, and basil in an ice-filled shaker. Shake vigorously and then strain into a coupe. Garnish with the rose petal.

ZAMBIA

One-third of Zambia's territory is comprised of national parks, showcasing an impressively varying array of natural habitats, geological formations, and incredible wildlife. The landlocked republic, located at the junction of Central, Southern, and East Africa, has a human population that's equally diverse, with 72 languages spoken among an even greater number of ethnic groups. The country's cultural melting pot is centered in and around its capital, Lusaka, one of Africa's fastest developing cities, where well-heeled urbanites can sip quality drinks at restaurants that fuse Western and Asian culinary influences with local favorites like Nile perch and salmon. And where it's equally enjoyable to explore the capital's more rustic enclaves, filled with food stalls offering strictly Zambian treats like dried game, sautéed insects, and Chibuku, a popular beer made with maize and sorghum that's based on traditional recipes.

Regardless of their tribal affiliation or social status, most Zambians have a profound appreciation for mabuyu juice, a cloudy, nutrient-dense concoction made primarily with fruit from the baobab, or mabuyu tree, that's been sipped for its health benefits for centuries. Lately, it's also become a semi-sweet and texturally interesting addition to cocktails like the Mabuyu Sour from Natasha Sandra Sinkala, who manages the Chic Bar Zambia, a bespoke mobile bar service. Her bold, fizzy, and fruity blend of mabuyu, Irish whiskey, and fresh citrus is a powerful tool for unleashing the best summery vibes no matter when you choose to shake one up. It's also a great example of the good that can happen when one combines local tradition, modern techniques, and a pinch of outside influence in a balanced and thoughtful manner.

Mabuyu Sour

Makes 1 drink

2 ounces Irish whiskey, such as Jameson Black Barrel
1 ounce Mabuyu Juice (recipe follows)
½ ounce fresh lime juice
½ ounce simple syrup (page 5)
1 lime wedge, for garnish
1 pineapple slice, for garnish

Combine the whiskey, mabuyu juice, lime juice, and simple syrup in an ice-filled shaker. Shake vigorously and then strain into a double rocks glass over ice. Perch the lime wedge and pineapple slice on the rim of the glass.

Mabuyu Juice

Makes about 2 cups

1 baobab fruit (see Note)
2 cups lukewarm water
½ cup sugar

Split open the baobab fruit and scoop the pulp into a large bowl. Add the water and set aside to soak overnight. Remove and discard the seeds and return the pulp to the water. Stir until well combined and thick. Strain the baobab mixture through a cheesecloth-lined sieve into an airtight container and discard the solids. Add the sugar and stir until dissolved. Cover and store in the refrigerator for up to 1 week.

NOTE: If baobab fruit is unavailable, simply add 1 cup baobab powder to the water and sugar and stir until well combined.

ZIMBABWE

Home to five UNESCO World Heritage Sites, including the 13,000-year-old Matobo Hills rock art complex and thunderous Victoria Falls, Zimbabwe doesn't lack for ancient and natural wonders, and its current human state of affairs is just as fascinating. The landlocked country holds the Guinness World Record for having the most official languages with sixteen, and is one of the few multicurrency states, where the Zimbabwean dollar, United States dollar, and South African rand are all considered legal tender. Whatever their desired method of payment, Zimbabweans prefer to spend their drinking money on beer, such as maize-based Zambezi, the national lager that's enjoyed throughout Africa for its full body and smooth finish.

That's not to say that Zimbabwe, the successor state to the British colony of Southern Rhodesia, is bereft of cocktail history. In fact, it's the birthplace of one of the most unique spins on the classic Negroni. While its exact origins are unknown, most recipes for the Zimbabwean version up the amount of London dry gin (still one of the country's most popular imported spirits) and add orange juice and a sugar rim, creating a funky, citrusy, and bittersweet refresher that retains much of the bold character of the Campari and sweet vermouth–backed original.

Zimbabwe-Style Negroni
Makes 1 drink

Superfine sugar, for rimming the glass
1 lime wedge, for rimming the glass
1½ ounces gin
1 ounce fresh orange juice
½ ounce Campari
½ ounce sweet vermouth

Spread some sugar over a small plate. Run the lime wedge around the rim of a double rocks glass, then dip the rim in the sugar to coat. Fill the glass with ice and set aside. Combine the gin, orange juice, Campari, and sweet vermouth in an ice-filled shaker. Shake vigorously and then strain into the prepared glass.

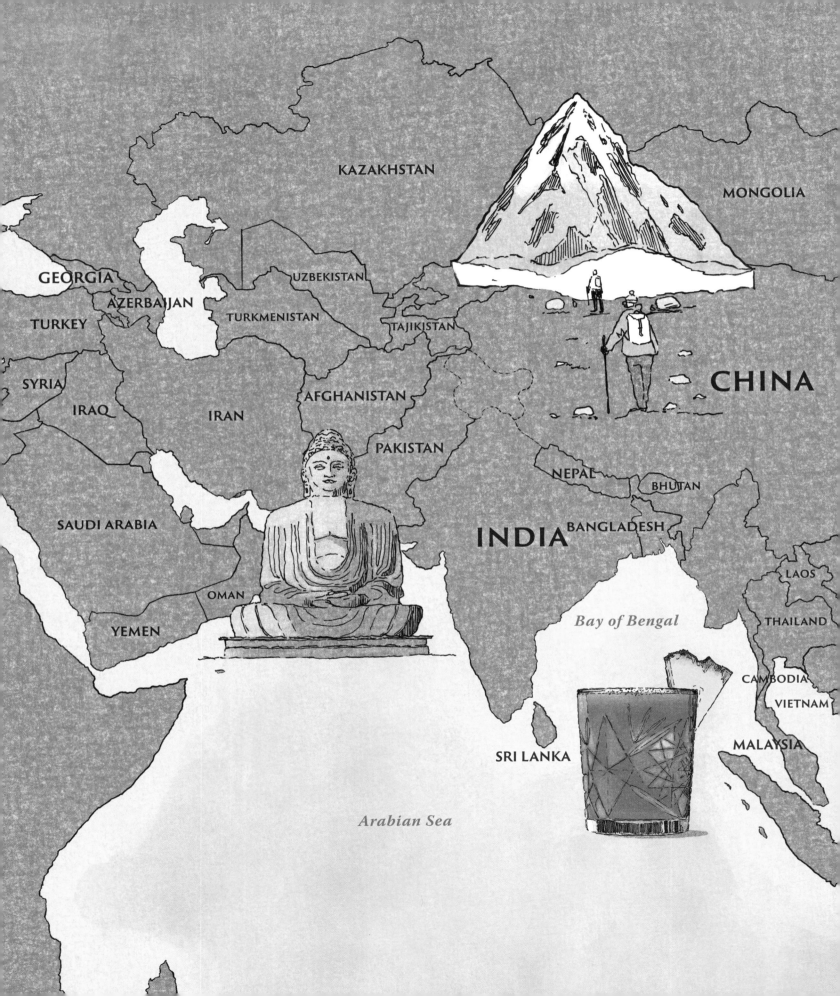

KAZAKHSTAN

MONGOLIA

GEORGIA

AZERBAIJAN

UZBEKISTAN

TURKEY

TURKMENISTAN

TAJIKISTAN

CHINA

SYRIA

IRAQ

IRAN

AFGHANISTAN

PAKISTAN

NEPAL

BHUTAN

SAUDI ARABIA

INDIA

BANGLADESH

LAOS

OMAN

THAILAND

YEMEN

Bay of Bengal

CAMBODIA

VIETNAM

MALAYSIA

SRI LANKA

Arabian Sea

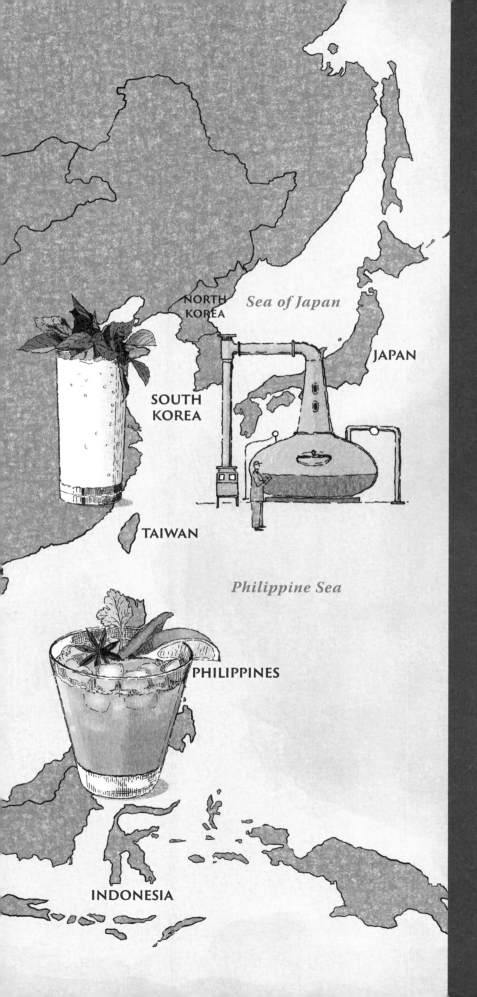

NORTH
KOREA

Sea of Japan

JAPAN

SOUTH
KOREA

TAIWAN

Philippine Sea

PHILIPPINES

INDONESIA

ASIA

AFGHANISTAN

To an entire generation, Afghanistan has been the poster child for conflict and Western ineptitude in the Middle East. But the land referred to as "the Heart of Asia" is much more than its cursory portrayal as a hopeless battlefield. The birthplace of oil painting, this landlocked country has been a Silk Road–influenced melting pot of religions, cuisines, and languages for centuries, many of which have contributed to today's agrarian, rug-making culture that exists alongside an array of untouched landscapes and archaeological wonders like the Gardens of Babur. But don't expect to find any alcohol here, as unlike other more laid-back Islamic countries, it's expressly forbidden, even for the rare non-Muslim tourist, with extreme penalties if you're caught sneaking a nip.

With one of the largest annual poppy yields, Afghanistan is also unfortunately linked to the flower's notorious by-product, opium, producing more of the drug than anywhere else. But the country's exceptionally fertile soil also nourishes dozens of benign crops like cotton, grapes, almonds, saffron, and cherries, which are made into a sour syrup that adds a nice tangy depth to fizzy drinks like the Bubbly Afghan Cherry. First described on the *Afghan Culture Unveiled* blog, this festive and fruity number mixes that traditional modifier with vodka—the mother spirit of Russia, Afghanistan's neighbor to the north—as well as Champagne and a hint of sweetness. It's an elegant party favor bursting with cherry goodness, with enough juice to spruce up any occasion or give you the courage to check out one of the world's least-visited locales.

Bubbly Afghan Cherry

Makes 1 drink

Superfine sugar, for rimming the glass
1 lime wedge, for rimming the glass
1 ounce vodka
¼ ounce sour cherry syrup
Champagne, to top
1 orange twist, for garnish

Spread some sugar over a small plate. Run the lime wedge around the rim of a Champagne flute or coupe, then dip the rim in the sugar to coat; set aside. Combine the vodka and sour cherry syrup in an ice-filled mixing glass. Stir with a long-handled spoon until well chilled and then strain into the prepared flute or coupe. Top with Champagne. Place the orange twist in the glass.

ARMENIA

One of the most ancient countries to have remained culturally and (relatively) geographically intact, Armenia boasts plenty of historical firsts. It was the earliest state to adopt Christianity as its official religion and is home to some of that faith's oldest surviving monuments and communities, whose wine-based rituals have never lacked for supplies in the grape-loving Caucasus republic. In fact, Armenians have been making wine for nearly as long as their Georgian neighbors, with archaeologists recently discovering what is thought to be—at 6,100 years old—the oldest winery in the world, found in a cave near the village of Areni.

While Armenia continues to produce excellent wines, including some truly delightful pomegranate and apricot varieties, the country's most sought-after boozy export is now brandy. The biggest brand, by far, is Ararat—named after the mountain that looms just across the border with Turkey and is the alleged resting place of Noah's Ark—which has been produced using white grapes by the Yerevan Brandy Company since 1887. Usually aged between three and thirty years (and in some cases up to seventy years) before bottling, the spirit is revered throughout the Caucasus region for its fruity nose and rich, oaky finish. Both of those exceptional qualities make it a lovely starting point for the Ararat Sweet & Sour, a funkier but not too sweet sidecar riff inspired by centuries of Armenian agriculture and booze-making. So exquisitely fresh and summery, you'd want to keep drinking them even if your lifespan was as long as their incredibly ancient place of origin.

WINSTON CHURCHILL apparently fell in love with Armenian brandy after a case of twenty-five-year-old Ararat Dvin was gifted to him by Josef Stalin during World War II. From then on, he allegedly had 400 bottles of the stuff shipped to his home each year.

Ararat Sweet & Sour

Makes 1 drink

1½ ounces Armenian brandy, such as Ararat 5-Star

¾ ounce fresh lemon juice

½ ounce peach liqueur

1 heaping spoonful white peach puree

1 strawberry, for garnish

Combine the brandy, lemon juice, peach liqueur, and peach puree in an ice-filled shaker. Shake vigorously and then strain into a coupe or wineglass. Skewer the strawberry with toothpicks and perch it on the rim of the glass.

AZERBAIJAN

Calling something "geologically flatulent" seems like a somewhat aggressive insult, but it's the best way to describe mud volcanoes, which appear much more frequently in Azerbaijan than anywhere else. And these cone-shaped structures that belch out methane and a muddy mix of water and occasionally erupt with thick gray mud aren't the country's only subjects of nature-related disses. The name of the capital Baku comes from a Persian phrase that means "wind-pounded city," referring to its frequently terrible weather. Azerbaijanis do little in the way of boozing to soothe their nerves in the face of so many landscape-related affronts; only 1 percent of the population partakes of the former Soviet republic's most popular spirit, vodka. And the average citizen downs about 7 liters of beer a year, which sounds like a normal week for many Western brew heads.

As with much of Western Asia, Muslim-majority Azerbaijanis are crazy about sharbat, a syrupy and satisfying tonic that was first described by Persian physician Ismail Gorgani nearly 800 years ago. Every country has its preferred ingredients, and in Azerbaijan those typically include lemon, apricot, orange, cherry, rose petals, basil, mint, saffron, and cardamom, many of which also factor in the Caspian Sea Sharbat. Named for the vast inland sea that forms the country's eastern border, this slightly sweet, fruity, grassy, floral, and herbal hodgepodge has enough vodka to quickly make you forget about the weather or any potentially devastating geographical anomalies, or just about anything else that happens to be bothering you.

Caspian Sea Sharbat

Makes 1 drink

1½ ounces vodka

¾ ounce apricot liqueur

¾ ounce fresh lemon juice

¼ ounce pomegranate syrup (page 5)

5 or 6 mint leaves, plus 1 sprig for garnish

2 drops rose water

Combine the vodka, apricot liqueur, lemon juice, pomegranate syrup, mint leaves, and rose water in an ice-filled shaker. Shake vigorously and then strain into a double rocks glass over ice. Garnish with the mint sprig.

BOTH THE PERSIAN word *sharbat* and the Turkish word *sherbet* derive from the Arabic *sharba*, meaning "a drink," and *shariba*, "to drink." *Sherbet* entered the English language as *sorbet*, which now refers to an iced dessert or palate cleanser rather than a drink, whereas the word in the Azerbaijani language has retained its original meaning.

BAHRAIN

In the Arab world, Bahrain is unique in many ways. At 295 square miles, it's the smallest country in the Persian Gulf region (as well as the third smallest in Asia) and the only one that's comprised entirely of islands. It's also home to Dive Bahrain, the world's largest underwater theme park—featuring a sunken Boeing 747 jet—and the first Formula 1 Grand Prix race in the Middle East, while boasting a diversified economy that's increasingly reliant on banking, retail, and tourism rather than oil. However, many aspects of this microstate are in line with its largest neighbors, including its powerful monarchy, devotion to Islam (which has been practiced here since the seventh century), and a love of coffee—or qahwah—which is the national drink.

When they want to cool down in the arid climate, Bahrainis infuse icy drinks with sharbat syrup, a rose-flavored sweetener that originated on the Indian subcontinent and is found throughout Asia. Its summery floral bouquet is also the inspiration for the Desert Rose Fizz, a creamy riff on the many Tom Collinses that were undoubtedly quaffed by gin-loving British diplomats when Bahrain was a protectorate of the United Kingdom from 1892 to 1971. Bright, supple, and citrusy, with a pleasantly fruity burst of raspberry, it's just the thing for transporting your taste buds to an extraordinary island oasis.

Desert Rose Fizz

Makes 1 drink

1½ ounces London dry gin

¾ ounce rose syrup, such as Monin

¾ ounce fresh lemon juice

¾ ounce heavy cream

3 or 4 raspberries

Club soda, to top

Rose water, in an atomizer

Combine the gin, rose syrup, lemon juice, cream, and raspberries in an ice-filled shaker. Shake vigorously and then strain into a fizz glass. Top with club soda. Spritz with rose water.

BANGLADESH

There's no question that British colonialism created more than its share of geographical anomalies. The fact that Bangladesh and Pakistan—despite being separated by almost a thousand miles of Indian territory—shared the same government for more than thirty years has got to be one of the weirdest. Since its 1971 victory in a civil war backed by India, Bangladesh has established an independent identity as an Islamic republic with economic and political power concentrated in its capital, Dhaka, the most densely populated city in the world. However, Bangladesh does share many similarities with its neighbors on the Indian subcontinent, including a propensity for cricket, massive amounts of textile exports, and an unwavering love for a glass of lassi on hot summer days.

Lassi, a smoothie-like blend of yogurt and water, originated in India centuries ago and can be spruced up with everything from mangoes, strawberries, and rose water to ginger, green chiles, and pistachios. There's even a version called bhang lassi that features liquid cannabis extract and is especially popular in areas where boozing isn't. Those who do condone (alcoholically) intoxicating beverages would be wise to try the Flutterby Lassi. Based on a recipe from London's Gymkhana restaurant that was adapted in André Darlington and Tenaya Darlington's *The New Cocktail Hour* (2016), this funky, digestion-aiding lineup of cucumber, dill, yogurt, and absinthe is a tongue-tingling tonic for when it's hotter outside than a Bangladeshi mangrove forest.

Flutterby Lassi

Makes 1 drink

3 small dill sprigs

2 slices peeled English (seedless) cucumber

Scant ¼ cup plain whole-milk yogurt

1 ounce absinthe

½ ounce fresh lime juice

½ ounce simple syrup (page 5)

1 long strip of cucumber peel, for garnish

Muddle 2 dill sprigs and the cucumber slices in a shaker. Fill the shaker halfway with ice, then add the yogurt, absinthe, lime juice, and simple syrup. Shake vigorously and then double-strain into a large coupe or tumbler. Garnish with the remaining dill sprig and the cucumber peel.

MUSLIMS IN BANGLADESH need a doctor's prescription in order to purchase alcohol. But even with this golden ticket, the booze options are slim. Until 2003, the only distiller in the country was the state-owned Carew & Co, which produces brandy, gin, rum, whisky, and vodka in limited quantities. Today, Carew's only competition is the private Jamuna Distillery, which specializes in a similar range of spirits.

BHUTAN

Most governments would agree that having happy citizens is one indicator of a nation's success. Bhutan's former king Jigme Singye Wangchuck took that idea to extremes when he introduced the concept of "Gross National Happiness" to determine a country's well-being instead of its gross domestic product. According to that system—which accounts for factors like environmental conservation and cultural preservation—tiny and isolated Bhutan is far happier than its wealthier and more developed neighbors like India. Given the Himalayan kingdom's transcendent mountain scenery, emphasis on family, and adherence to peaceful Buddhist teachings, that shouldn't come as too much of a surprise. It also helps that Bhutan has a top-notch booze culture, where serving a loved one or guest alcohol is a sign of great honor and respect.

Ara, the most popular drink, is a fermented, grain-based beverage that's enjoyed liberally at Bhutan's famous archery tournaments (by both spectators and competitors), but there are plenty of locally made beers, whiskeys, and even wines from which to choose. For those trekking to high-altitude points of interest like the cliffhanging Tiger's Nest Monastery, a piping-hot, throat-and-belly-soothing libation like the Dragon Warmer is essential. The favorite drink of Bhutanese hikers, it's also a respectful shoutout to the symbol of the nation—Bhutan has long been called "the Land of the Dragon" because of its jagged topography and frequently stormy weather. However, there's nothing mythological about the effects of infusing dark rum with steamy apple juice, honey, and cinnamon. Meaning, your Gross Personal Happiness will surely increase after a few sips.

THE PRODUCTION OF ARA, while extremely popular, is largely unregulated and thus discouraged by the government. In lieu of jail time, those who are caught selling large amounts of the fermented beverage are sentenced to prolonged periods of meditation at one of the country's many Buddhist monasteries.

Dragon Warmer
Makes 1 drink

4 ounces apple juice

¼ cinnamon stick

1 barspoon honey

1½ ounces dark rum

1 lemon wheel, for garnish

1 cinnamon stick, for garnish

Combine the apple juice and cinnamon stick in a small saucepan and bring to a boil over medium heat. Reduce the heat to low and simmer for 5 minutes. Remove from the heat and let cool for 2 to 3 minutes. Add the honey and stir until dissolved. Pour into a mug or heat-safe glass and add the rum. Stir well. Place the lemon wheel and cinnamon stick in the mug or glass.

BRUNEI

Brunei's formal name, Brunei Darussalam, means "Abode of Peace" in the Malay language, and that's a fairly accurate description of the small, oil-rich semi-enclave. Nestled between the Malaysian state of Sarawak and the coastline on the island of Borneo and ruled by absolute monarch Sultan Hassanal Bolkiah since 1967, the country ranks high on the Human Development Index, boasts a relatively low crime rate, and provides free medical care and education to its citizens, who have one of the longest life expectancies in Southeast Asia. Some of that peace is also probably due to the state religion, a form of Islam that encourages strict punishments for most legal transgressions.

It goes without saying that partaking of your favorite boozy beverage could be a potentially catastrophic faux pas in the conservative nation. Many observant Bruneians prefer their (nonalcoholic) refreshment in the form of chilled coconut milk, which is also a favorite ingredient in the local cuisine. The flavors and textures of this silky indulgence are succulently re-created in the Sherry Colada, a lush and nutty tropical sipper from bartender Adam Minegar at New York's Raines Law Room. Its sherry base is a longtime favorite of the British, who occupied Brunei until 1984, and whose legal system is still partially used by the country's current government. If there was a Cocktail Development Index, this deliciously low-proof take on a warm-weather classic would have a ranking that's off the charts.

Sherry Colada

Makes 1 drink

2 ounces amontillado sherry

2 ounces pineapple juice

¾ ounce coconut syrup, such as Wildly Organic Coconut Syrup

Splash of heavy cream

1 lime wedge

Pinch of freshly grated nutmeg, for garnish

Combine the sherry, pineapple juice, coconut syrup, cream, and lime wedge in an ice-filled shaker. Shake vigorously and then strain into a double rocks glass over ice. Sprinkle with the nutmeg.

CAMBODIA

The Kingdom of Cambodia is the only country to feature a building on its flag, which, if you've ever visited the Angkor Wat temple complex, makes quite a bit of sense. Hidden deep in the jungle near the city of Siem Reap, it's the largest religious monument on Earth, featuring exquisitely detailed bas-reliefs, statues, moats, and towers built nearly 900 years ago. For Cambodians, many of whom adhere to both Buddhist beliefs and the animist traditions of the Khmer people, Angkor Wat is still considered the soul of the country, even as many aspects of society have raced toward modernity.

Like the local Cambodian alcohol industry, which is dominated by Sombai, a liqueur manufacturer in Siem Reap whose infused rice wines (*som bai* means "some rice, please" in the Khmer language) have become a new source of national pride since first being produced in 2012. Consumed neat, on the rocks, or in cocktails like the Sombai Fizz—an easy-to-fix mix of Sombai, lemon juice, and lemon soda—the eight uniquely flavored liqueurs contain a plethora of widely grown spices, herbs, roots, and fruit, such as lemongrass, lime, tamarind, ginger, galangal, and chile.

There's also a budding mixology scene centered in the capital city of Phnom Penh, where drink-slingers like Annemarie Sagoi fuse Western ingredients and authentic Cambodian flavors to create drinks that feel both timeless and exhilarating—like the Cambodian Coley, which Sagoi first served at the now-defunct Le Boutier bar in 2016. A spirit-forward homage to sweet yet herbaceous martini variations like the Hanky-Panky, its far-flung blend of gin, sherry, cherry brandy, sweet vermouth, and Fernet-Branca is spiced up with a misting of locally produced Kampot pepper tincture for a fascinating, soulful cocktail with a global appeal.

Cambodian Coley

Makes 1 drink

1¼ ounces dry gin

¾ ounce fino sherry

½ ounce Cherry Heering

¼ ounce sweet vermouth

1 barspoon Fernet-Branca

3 dashes Angostura bitters

Kampot pepper tincture, such as Tomoka Cocktail Company, in an atomizer

1 lemon twist, for garnish

Combine the gin, sherry, Cherry Heering, vermouth, fernet, and bitters in a double rocks glass. Add ice and stir with a long-handled spoon for 5 or 6 seconds. Spritz with the Kampot pepper tincture. Place the lemon twist in the glass beside the ice.

WHEN DRINKING with friends in Cambodia, it's considered proper etiquette to say *choul muoy* ("cheers" in Khmer) with every sip of alcohol you take. Meaning that when you take a sip, all your drinking companions must follow suit. Not only that, but everyone's glasses or bottles must touch for the toast to be considered proper.

CHINA

There's a famous Chinese proverb that translates to "With a close friend, a thousand cups of wine are too little." It's a beautiful summary of China's ancient and highly social drinking culture, where friends and family members are expected to constantly raise glasses together at everything from festivals, weddings, and birthday parties to casual meals at home. Building relationships through booze also extends to the Chinese corporate workplace, with many clearheaded executives designating junior employees as proxy drinkers for the seemingly endless celebratory shots at business functions.

The most popular spirit to consume after saying *ganbai* (a word that conveys cheers and literally means "empty cup") is baijiu. It's a funky, colorless liquor that's usually distilled from fermented sorghum, rice, or other grains, is created using qu, a type of Asian yeast starter, and has a similar flavor to Korean soju but with a significantly higher alcohol content. One of the world's oldest distilled beverages, its exact origins are unclear, though poets were praising a prototypical version of the stuff that was being produced during the Tang dynasty (618 to 907 CE). Throughout most of the drink's history it was taken straight alongside food, in wildly varying quantities depending on one's tolerance. Though lately its unique aromatics have been worked into some very delightful cocktails.

Bartenders who have dabbled with China's national hooch claim that the key to crafting a successful baijiu-based libation is to pair the liquor's intensity with other equally bold flavors, a feat that can be accomplished in a myriad of styles. Boston's Nick Lappen takes a smoky, old-fashioned-esque approach with his Golden Years, which combines baijiu, Scotch, maple syrup, fish sauce, and a hint of five-spice, whose flavors (sweet, bitter, sour, salty, savory) represent the five traditional elements of Chinese cooking. While it also includes some of the same flavors, Chockie Tom's Dan Dan Tai goes on an entirely different path, using bright tiki influences and funky Jamaican rum to create a drink that feels both authentically Chinese and highly accessible to anyone who enjoys a complex and spicy sipper.

Golden Years

Makes 1 drink

1½ ounces rice-aroma baijiu

½ ounce Scotch, preferably Compass Box Artist Blend

¼ ounce pure maple syrup

6 dashes Bittermens Xocolatl Mole bitters

3 drops Red Boat fish sauce

1 dash Bitter Queens Shanghai Shirley Five-Spice bitters

Combine all the ingredients in a double rocks glass. Add ice and stir with a long-handled spoon for 5 or 6 seconds.

Dan Dan Tai

Makes 1 drink

1 thin orange slice, for garnish

Chili powder, for dusting

Sugar, for dusting

1 ounce Jamaican rum, preferably Hamilton Jamaican Pot Still Black Rum

½ ounce strong-aroma baijiu, preferably Ming River

½ ounce rhum agricole, preferably Clément VSOP Rhum Agricole Vieux

½ ounce curaçao

½ ounce Five-Spice Peanut Orgeat (recipe follows)

½ ounce fresh lemon juice

Crushed ice

1 pineapple leaf, for garnish

1 basil sprig, for garnish

Dust the orange slice with chili powder and sugar; set aside for garnish. Combine the rum, baijiu, rhum agricole, curaçao, orgeat, and lemon juice in a shaker. Pour into a tall glass filled two-thirds of the way with crushed ice. Add a straw and top with more crushed ice. Garnish with the pineapple leaf, chili-sugar-dusted orange slice, and basil sprig.

Five-Spice Peanut Orgeat
Makes about 2 cups
2 cups raw unsalted peanuts
2 cups hot water
2 cups sugar, or as needed
4 teaspoons Chinese five-spice powder, or as needed
Pinch of MSG

Place the peanuts in a large bowl. Pour the hot water over the peanuts, cover with plastic wrap, and let stand at room temperature for 12 hours. Strain the soaking water through a fine-mesh sieve into a measuring cup (discard the peanuts). Note the amount of water, then pour it into a saucepan over low heat and add an equal amount of sugar. Add 1 teaspoon of five-spice powder for every cup of water and sugar. Heat gently over low heat, stirring, until the sugar has dissolved; don't let the mixture boil. Add the MSG and stir to combine. Remove from the heat and let cool. Store in an airtight container in the refrigerator for up to 1 month.

CHINA CAN LAY CLAIM to having some of the strangest boozy beverages—including a rice wine that's fortified with fetal mice and another infused with snake venom—but Tezhi Sanbian Jiu or "Three-Penis Liquor" might be the wildest of these. True to its name, this murky spirit is infused with deer penis, seal penis, and Cantonese dog penis and purportedly has a vinegary, slightly sweet flavor that tastes a little like spoiled port. According to traditional Chinese medicine practitioners, consuming animal genitalia is excellent for stimulating the male libido.

GEORGIA

Though Georgia in its current incarnation is a relatively recent political entity, there's much that's ancient about the former Soviet republic. Boasting three UNESCO World Heritage Sites, one of the oldest continuously inhabited cities in the world (Kutaisi), and a nearly 2,000-year-old official language, it's also considered the birthplace of wine. Georgians were fermenting grape juice in clay pots as early as 6000 BCE, and their reverence for the fruit continues to this day in the form of chacha, the country's national spirit. Made with pomace, the pulp remaining from pressed-off wine grapes, this clear, heady brandy is a ubiquitous presence in old-school Georgian celebrations and long-standing culinary traditions.

Chacha might be hard to come by outside of Western Asia or Eastern Europe, but a new generation of Georgian bartenders working in the capital city of Tbilisi are making sure visitors get introduced to the spirit in exciting and unexpected ways. Like the Rustaveli, one of the signature drinks at cocktail den 41 Gradus. This powerfully aromatic Manhattan variation, named after locally beloved Georgian poet Shota Rustaveli, is an unapologetic ode to chacha's bold and complex notes, adorned with sweet vermouth and absinthe for an herbaceous, full-bodied finish. A must-drink if you find yourself in the Caucasus region or are lucky enough to nab a bottle of the area's tastiest liquid treasure when it's available from online retailers like Cask Cartel.

Rustaveli

Makes 1 drink

1 ounce chacha

1 ounce sweet vermouth

1 teaspoon Cynar

5 drops absinthe

1 brandied cherry, for garnish

Combine the chacha, vermouth, Cynar, and absinthe in an ice-filled mixing glass. Stir with a long-handled spoon for 20 to 30 seconds and then strain into a coupe. Drop the brandied cherry into the glass.

LIKE MANY COUNTRIES, Georgia's drinking culture involves copious amounts of toasting. What's unique here is appointment of a *tamada*, or toastmaster, before any serious round of drinking. Throughout the evening, the tamada is expected to randomly propose twenty-five to thirty toasts and deliver an eloquent speech during each of them. Each toast must be performed with wine or chacha. To toast with anything else is considered an "anti-toast," which is a major insult to the toastee.

INDIA

The most populous country on Earth, India is a vast land of varying landscapes, languages, and cuisines, the birthplace of several major religions and home to more than 1.4 billion citizens who form an immense and intricate cultural mosaic, representing what many believe to be the planet's oldest continuous civilization. Alcohol has a similarly long and complex history on the Indian subcontinent, dating to at least 3000 BCE, when the act of drinking fermented beverages was first mentioned in writings referencing the ancient Harappan civilization. The production of traditional hooch is still abundant just about everywhere, from the rice and palm wines brewed by indigenous tribes in the northern provinces to tropical flower and saffron-infused liqueurs found in the south to Feni, a double-distilled liquor made with cashew apples that's only produced in the coastal state of Goa.

While you may find these and other local beverages on Indian bar menus, the cocktail list is more likely to be highlighted by drinks featuring globally popular spirits like rum and whiskey (both of which are now also produced domestically) embellished by homegrown flavors. Like mango lassi, a ubiquitous fruit and yogurt smoothie that reaches its full potential in Kristina Preka's Boozy Mango and Makrut Lime Lassi, thanks to a little citrus and a lot of tropically inclined rum that vibes deliciously with the milky texture. If sour and spicy is more your thing, try the Tamarind Ginger Margarita (page 93), adapted from a recipe on the *Zesty South Indian Kitchen* blog. This bright and peppery fusion of Asian and Western ingredients is dominated by its titular fruit, which is widely cultivated throughout Southern India. And if you're feeling colder than a mountaineer trapped on Kangchenjunga, India's highest peak in the Himalayas, the cardamom and star anise–infused Indian Hot Toddy (page 93) from Puja Thomas-Patel is your ticket to instant belly-warming bliss.

Boozy Mango and Makrut Lime Lassi
Makes 1 drink

4 ounces ripe mango, coarsely chopped

4 ounces plain yogurt, preferably full-fat

1 ounce buttermilk

1 ounce aged rum

1 ounce Makrut Lime Syrup (recipe follows)

¼ ounce fresh lime juice

Pinch of kosher salt

Coarsely chopped toasted pistachios, for garnish

Green cardamom powder, for garnish

Puree the mango chunks in a blender. Add the yogurt, buttermilk, rum, makrut lime syrup, lime juice, salt, and a bit of ice and puree until smooth. Pour into a chilled Collins glass. Sprinkle with the pistachios and cardamom.

Makrut Lime Syrup
Makes ½ cup

½ cup water

½ cup sugar

16 makrut lime leaves

Combine all the ingredients in a small saucepan and bring to a boil over high heat. Remove from the heat and let cool to room temperature. Strain the syrup through a fine-mesh sieve into a glass bottle with a lid. Use immediately or refrigerate for up to 1 week.

Tamarind Ginger Margarita

Makes 1 drink

Tajín seasoning, for rimming the glass

1 lemon wedge, for rimming the glass

2 ounces Tamarind Concentrate (recipe follows)

1½ ounces tequila

¾ ounce ginger syrup (page 5)

½ ounce Cointreau

½ ounce fresh lemon juice

1 lemon wedge, for garnish

Spread some Tajín over a small plate. Run the lemon wedge around the rim of a double rocks glass, then dip the rim into the Tajín to coat; add ice and set aside. Combine the tamarind concentrate, tequila, ginger syrup, Cointreau, and lemon juice in an ice-filled shaker. Shake vigorously and then strain into the prepared glass. Perch the lemon wedge on the rim of the glass.

Tamarind Concentrate

Makes about ½ cup

¼ cup tamarind paste

⅓ cup water

Combine the tamarind paste and water in a small jar and stir until the paste has dissolved completely. Cover and store in the refrigerator for up to 10 days.

Indian Hot Toddy

Makes 1 drink

1 cup water

1 slice fresh ginger, about ¼ inch thick

½ ounce fresh lemon juice

1 tablespoon brown sugar

2 green or brown cardamom pods

½ cinnamon stick

1 star anise pod

2 ounces Indian whisky or bourbon

1½ ounces bourbon

1 lemon wedge, for garnish

Combine the water and ginger in a small saucepan and bring to a boil over medium heat. Meanwhile, combine the lemon juice, brown sugar, cardamom pods, cinnamon stick, and star anise in a mug. Pour the boiling water into the mug. Add the whisky and bourbon and stir until well blended, then remove the ginger and spices, except for the star anise pods. Perch the lemon wedge on the rim of the mug.

NO MATTER how thirsty you get while boozing in an Indian home, never refill your own glass before offering to top off your host's. Filling your fellow drinkers' glasses is a sign of great friendship, and failure to do so is a sign that the friendship isn't destined to last. On the other hand, don't stress if you accidentally break a bottle. In India, it's actually considered good luck.

Boozy Mango and Makrut Lime Lassi (page 91)

INDONESIA

The largest country in the world comprised solely of islands, Indonesia is a megadiverse archipelago filled with plant and animal species—like the Komodo dragon and Javan rhinoceros—that are found nowhere else on Earth. It's also mega-populated, with more than 255 million inhabitants who speak around 700 different languages and whose various indigenous cultures are often combined with Chinese, European, Indian, Middle Eastern, and South Pacific influences. If there's one unifying element, it's red rice, which is the foundation of all Indonesian cuisine and a major ingredient in the country's most historically significant spirit, Batavia arrack.

The funky, vegetal, and slightly smoky sugarcane distillate dates to the 1600s, when the pot still was introduced to Indonesia by Dutch traders, who shortly thereafter began exporting it to Europe. Often described as a precursor to rum, Batavia arrack enjoyed its greatest popularity in the eighteenth and nineteenth centuries, when European and American drink-makers highlighted it alongside other "exotic" ingredients in the earliest punches. And though it fell out of favor in the cocktail world by the early twentieth century, it's made a significant comeback in recent years as a niche ingredient for arrack enthusiasts who embrace its unique ambiance.

That's not to say that the somewhat divisive liquor should always be the star of the show. Instead, as Chicago-based beverage director Guillermo Bravo explains in a 2022 interview with *Punch*, Batavia arrack should be used "like a spice," providing an interestingly warm and fortifying counterpoint to the drink's foundational elements. That's certainly the vibe of Bravo's Jakartian Peardition, a fruity and aromatic homage to the punches of earlier centuries that also manages to feel fresh and palate-piquing.

Batavia arrack isn't the only rice-derived spirit native to Indonesia. On Bali—part of the country's only Hindu-majority province—residents have been using brem, a fermented glutinous rice liqueur with a sweet yet slightly acidic flavor profile, in offering ceremonies for more than 1,000 years. Much more recently, brem has found its way into cocktails like the wonderfully bittersweet and herbal Kadek Manhattan, which is served at Room 4 Dessert in Ubud, Bali, a necessary pit-stop on any trip to this lush and mystical island.

Jakartian Peardition

Makes 1 drink

1 ounce Batavia arrack

¾ ounce oloroso sherry, preferably Lustau

¾ ounce fresh lime juice

½ ounce pear brandy, such as Clear Creek Williams

½ ounce fresh grapefruit juice

½ ounce orgeat

¼ ounce cinnamon syrup (page 4)

Combine all the ingredients in an ice-filled shaker. Shake vigorously and then strain into a coupe.

Kadek Manhattan

Makes 1 drink

1 ounce bourbon

1 ounce brem

½ ounce tawny port

1 makrut lime leaf, for garnish

Combine the bourbon, brem, and port in a rocks glass. Add ice and stir with a long-handled spoon for 5 or 6 seconds. Garnish with the makrut lime leaf.

IRAN

What do Persian cats, Zoroastrianism, and kebabs have in common? They all originated in Iran, one of the Middle East's oldest and most multifaceted countries. The birthplace of the highly influential Persian Empire, it was a center for art, religion, and literature long before merchants and traders from the Arabian Peninsula arrived and ushered in the Islamic era. Those same Arabs brought the earliest pot stills and a knowledge of spirits-making that became an underground industry in 1979 when alcohol was made illegal under the current political regime. That surreptitious tradition continues in the form of aragh sagi, an aromatic moonshine produced from fermented raisins. It's famous for its impressive alcohol content (up to 80% ABV) and being pretty much the only way parched Iranians can sneak a buzz.

Due to its clearness and potency, aragh sagi is often referred to as Persian vodka, though flavor-wise, it's apparently much closer to Italian grappa, a fiery pomace brandy. But unless you've spent time in Iran or are willing to illegally smuggle a bottle out of the country, you may never know for sure. There are, however, easy-to-obtain Iranian ingredients that are very cocktail-friendly. Like sekanjabin syrup, a mixture of honey, vinegar, and mint that's prized as an immune system strengthener and a cure-all for just about any imaginable ailment. Medical efficacy aside, it also works as a delightful modifier in the Persian Maid, a fresh, floral, cucumber-infused potation that also includes rose water, another staple in Iranian kitchens.

Persian Maid

Makes 1 drink

2 ounces vodka

1 ounce Sekanjabin Syrup (recipe follows)

¾ ounce fresh lime juice

2 drops rose water

3 thin cucumber slices

1 mint sprig, for garnish

Combine the vodka, sekanjabin syrup, lime juice, rose water, and 2 cucumber slices in an ice-filled shaker. Shake vigorously and then strain into a double rocks glass over ice. Skewer the remaining cucumber slice with the mint sprig and perch them on the rim of the glass.

Sekanjabin Syrup

Makes about 3 cups

2 cups orange blossom honey

1¼ cups water

½ cup white wine vinegar

8 to 10 mint leaves

Combine the honey and water in a medium saucepan. Bring to a boil, stirring to dissolve the honey. Add the vinegar, reduce the heat to low, and simmer until the flavors combine, 5 to 7 minutes. Remove from the heat. Add the mint leaves and let cool to room temperature, then remove and discard the mint leaves. Store in an airtight container in the refrigerator for up to 1 month.

IRAQ

There's old, and then there's Mesopotamia old. Thousands of years before ancient wonders like the Great Pyramid of Giza and Stonehenge were constructed, the area encompassing much of modern-day Iraq was filled with bustling urban centers, large-scale agricultural activity, and beer. Lots and lots of beer. For cultures like the Sumerians, Akkadians, and Babylonians, sudsy draughts were the daily beverages of choice and a vital component of just about every social (and intimate) interaction, celebrated—and occasionally lamented—in poetry, song, and art. People from all walks of life were constantly buzzed at home, on the job, at feasts and festivals, in the temple, and at the neighborhood tavern, where they would sip their favorite brews through long reedy straws from communal ceramic pots that were not unlike today's Scorpion Bowls.

Though several booze-loving archaeologists have attempted experiments to re-create Mesopotamian beer (which most likely had a malted barley base and may have included date syrup, and a variety of roasted and toasted grains), the exact flavor and alcohol content of the 4,000-year-old (or older) drink is still unknown. That's not the case with Iraq's traditional spirit, arak, which is still produced using time-honored methods in the northern region of Nineveh by members of the country's dwindling Yazidi and Christian communities. The date-based, anise-flavored liquor also forms the most prominent part of the Mesopotamian Sour, a frothy, herbaceous sipper that also includes honey, mint, and rose water, all important components of both ancient and modern Iraqi cooking. Skip the straws and communal vessel, as you'll probably want to keep this smooth slice of liquid history all to yourself.

Mesopotamian Sour

Makes 1 drink

1½ ounces arak

¾ ounce fresh lemon juice

¾ ounce honey syrup (page 5)

5 or 6 mint leaves

2 drops rose water

1 egg white

Combine all the ingredients in a shaker. Shake without ice for 5 or 6 seconds to emulsify the egg white, then add ice and shake vigorously. Strain into a coupe.

THE FIRST WRITTEN regulation on the sale of alcohol appeared in Mesopotamia around 1772 BCE in the Code of Hammurabi, specifically stating that beer could only be bartered for barley: "If a beer seller do not receive barley as the price for beer, but if she receive money or make the beer a measure smaller than the barley measure received, they shall throw her into the water."

ISRAEL

Israel as a modern political entity has only existed since 1948. Yet this New Jersey–size sliver of the Middle East—particularly its capital, Jerusalem—has been revered for ages by practitioners of Judaism, Christianity, and Islam as the epicenter of the Holy Land and an integral place in their spiritual lives. That's not to say there isn't any secular fun to be had. Tel Aviv, the country's second-largest city, is the region's premier nightlife destination, is renowned for its party and restaurant scenes, inclusivity, and twenty-four-hour culture. Interestingly, it's also considered the most vegan-friendly town in the world.

Whatever their dietary preferences, traditional-minded Israelis in the mood to let loose (or recover from a hearty plate of hummus or falafel) like to reach for a chilled bottle of arak, the national spirit, whose strong aniseed properties make it an excellent choice before, during, and after meals, or as a relatively stomach-friendly late-night reviver. Widely produced in many Arab countries since the invention of alembic distillation in the twelfth century, the herbally infused grape brandy is enjoyed far more openly in Israel than in predominantly Muslim locales like Jordan and Syria, at nearly every street-corner café and beverage stand. It also constitutes the base of the Blushed Arak, the most popular Israeli street cocktail, which loosely refers to any drink featuring arak, citrus, and herbs. The following recipe, an adaptation of one by New York–based Israeli chef Shlomo Schwartz, combines the aniseed vibes with fresh grapefruit, lemon, and earthy sage for an authentically Middle Eastern libation that's bright and light but with a pleasantly peppery finish.

Blushed Arak

Makes 1 drink

1½ ounces arak
1½ ounces fresh grapefruit juice
1 ounce fresh lemon juice
¾ ounce Sage Syrup (recipe follows)
2 small grapefruit segments
1 sage leaf, for garnish

Combine the arak, grapefruit juice, lemon juice, sage syrup, and grapefruit segments in an ice-filled shaker. Shake vigorously and then strain into a double rocks glass over ice. Garnish with the sage leaf.

Sage Syrup

Makes 1 cup

1 cup superfine sugar
1 cup water
6 sage leaves

Combine the sugar, water, and sage leaves in a small saucepan. Bring to a boil and cook for 2 minutes. Remove from the heat, discard the sage leaves, and let cool to room temperature. Store in an airtight container in the refrigerator for up to 1 week.

THE EARLIEST EVIDENCE of intentional human alcohol production was discovered at a prehistoric burial site near the modern-day city of Haifa in 2021. Archaeologists found traces of 13,000-year-old beer that they believe may have been used for feasts honoring the dead.

JAPAN

Attention to detail is paramount to Japanese culture. This philosophy—known as *kodawari*, or "the uncompromising and relentless pursuit of perfection"—is plainly evident in the work of the country's best artisans, architects, sushi chefs, and cocktail bartenders. And its whisky makers. Lately one of the planet's most sought-after spirits, Japanese whisky was first privately produced in the late 1800s as an attempt to re-create the flavors of Scotch. And while the first industrial distillery—Yamazaki—opened in 1923, it wouldn't be until the early 2000s that the international spirits community would recognize the malted, grain-based liquor's exceptional quality. Since then, blended and single-malt whiskies from Japan's two largest companies, Suntory and Nikka, have won dozens of awards and are at the center of a thriving global market, with some rare bottles fetching prices in the hundreds of thousands of dollars.

You might have to shell out a bit more cash in order to appreciate Japanese whisky's characteristic dry smoothness and floral, peaty, citrusy, and oaky notes. But it's well worth it, whether you take your tipples neat, as a haibōru (a locally popular combination of whisky and soda water in a highball glass) or integrated into a spirit-forward sipper such as Sam Ross's Improved Yokohama Cocktail. A mash-up of classics like the Monte Carlo and Improved Whiskey Cocktail and named for the major Japanese port in Tokyo Bay, it works just as well with either blended or single-malt varieties thanks to the balanced versatility of Bénédictine and a hint of absinthe.

A thousand years before the Japanese were making whisky, they were brewing sake, a rice wine that's considered godfather of the country's spirits culture. Best known as a companion to omakase adventurers or dropped in beer and chugged in sake bomb form, it's made with rice that's been polished to expose its starchy interior, yeast, and koji, a kind of fermentation-inducing mold. And while most sake enthusiasts prefer theirs neat at room temperature or slightly chilled, it's found its way into an impressively vast array of cocktails that highlight its distinctive undertones of fruit, nuts, and umami. Like the Tamagozake, a steamy soother that's sort of a cross between a toddy and eggnog and has been used traditionally as a home remedy for the common cold. Or the Kyoto Sour (page 101) from drinks consultant Paul Tanguay, a surprising and versatile sipper that enhances sake's fruity notes with lots of citrus, spice, and a hint of agave-based sweetness.

Japan's other famous rice-based booze is shōchū, a stronger spirit that's also usually made with barley, sweet potatoes, buckwheat, or brown sugar. Somewhat similar to Korean soju and distilled at up to 43% ABV, it's a favorite of bartenders like Kenta Goto, the creative force behind New York's Bar Goto, who uses it as a savory, earthy base in his Koji-San (page 101), a vegetal, margarita-esque potation with beautiful hints of smoke and heat.

Improved Yokohama Cocktail

Makes 1 drink

2 ounces Japanese whisky

½ ounce Bénédictine

4 or 5 dashes Angostura bitters

1 dash absinthe

1 lemon twist, for garnish

Combine the whisky, Bénédictine, bitters, and absinthe in a rocks glass. Add ice and stir with a long-handled spoon for 5 or 6 seconds. Place the lemon twist in the glass beside the ice.

Tamagozake

Makes 1 drink

6 ounces sake

½ ounce honey

1 egg

Combine all the ingredients in a medium saucepan. Heat over low heat, whisking continuously, until the mixture has thinned out and turned a semi-opaque yellow color like a really well-mixed egg for scrambled eggs, about 5 minutes; be careful not to fully cook the egg. Pour into a tall heat-safe glass or mug.

Kyoto Sour

Makes 1 drink

3 grapefruit slices

2 dashes green Tabasco sauce

3 ounces sake, such as Gekkeikan Haiku

¾ ounce agave nectar

½ ounce fresh lemon juice

1 mint sprig, for garnish

In a shaker, muddle 2 grapefruit slices and the Tabasco. Add the sake, agave nectar, and lemon juice, then add ice and shake vigorously. Strain into a double rocks glass over ice. Garnish with the mint sprig and the remaining grapefruit slice.

Koji-San

Makes 1 drink

1 ounce plus 5 teaspoons shōchū, preferably Iichiko Saiten

⅘ ounce cane syrup

¾ ounce fresh lime juice

1 teaspoon mezcal

¼ ounce celery juice

Combine the shōchū, cane syrup, lime juice, and mezcal in an ice-filled shaker. Shake vigorously and then strain into a double rocks glass over ice. Float the celery juice on top by pouring it over the back of a spoon into the glass.

THE WORD *sake* simply means "alcohol" in Japan, whereas the rice-based drink that the rest of the world knows as sake is in fact called *nihonshu* in Japanese.

Japan / Improved Yokohama Cocktail (page 99)

JORDAN

Jordan is one of the most fascinating countries to visit in the Levant, a deeply historical region that functions as a land bridge between Africa and Eurasia. Famous for archaeological sites like the ancient Petra complex with its rock-cut architecture, a vibrant arts culture, and delightfully seasoned cuisine, it's also home to some of the world's oldest cities and an overabundance of natural wonders. The most well-known of these is the Dead Sea, a saline lake that's nearly ten times saltier than any ocean. It's such an unearthly place that no animals and plants can survive there, but humans have been taking advantage of the unique water's therapeutic properties for at least several thousand years.

It's also the inspiration for the Dead Sea Rickey, a variation of the classic Mexican Firing Squad with some Jordanian touches, including, of course, a pinch of salt. The drink also features pomegranate syrup, which derives from one of the Levant's most significant crops, as well as arak, the grape-based, anise-flavored liquor that's the traditional spirit of the now mostly Muslim region. The smokiness of mezcal conjures the sensation of roasting lamb meat, a ubiquitous ingredient in Jordan's culinary creations, while the bright citrus and fizzy soda creates an effervescence that's not dissimilar to peacefully floating along on the cocktail's namesake body of water. And though it's nearly impossible to drown in the absurdly buoyant Dead Sea, we still recommend waiting a bit to swim after downing a few of these effervescent beauties.

Dead Sea Rickey

Makes 1 drink

2 ounces mezcal

¾ ounce pomegranate syrup (page 5)

¾ ounce fresh lime juice

1 barspoon arak

Pinch of sea salt

Club soda, to top

1 lime wedge, for garnish

Combine the mezcal, pomegranate syrup, lime juice, arak, and salt in a shaker. Add 1 or 2 ice pebbles, shake briefly, and pour into a tall glass filled with ice. Top with club soda. Perch the lime wedge on the rim of the glass.

KAZAKHSTAN

You'd think that Kazakhstan, as the largest predominantly Muslim country in the world by land area, wouldn't have much of a drinking culture, if any. But many citizens of Central Asia's economic and political leader enjoy their tipples eagerly and often. Maybe it's due to decades of Russian influence or living along centuries-old transcontinental trade routes. Or maybe it's loneliness: This barren landscape of low-lying plains, impenetrable mountain ranges, vast deserts, and plateaus is one of the most sparsely populated places in the world, averaging a mere 15 people per square mile.

While beer, wine, and koumiss and shubat—fermented mare's milk and camel's milk, respectively—are widely available in even the most remote regions, the country's most popular alcoholic drink is a throwback to its years as a Soviet republic: vodka, cold and straight, no sipping allowed. Knocking back shots until the bottle's empty (the traditional factor for determining an evening's end) is a primarily masculine pastime, however, as many female imbibers prefer brandy taken at a more leisurely pace.

Featuring both spirits of choice, the Stay Up Later is also an homage to Kazakhstan's most famous native fruit, the apple, which still grows wild in the Tian Shan mountains. This tall, tangy, slightly sour and creamy cocktail is a mashup of two 1940s classics, the Stay Up Late and the Apple Blow Fizz, and is a can't-miss refresher for when it's as hot as the Kazakh Steppe. Feel free to substitute mare's or camel's milk for the heavy cream, but good luck finding those at your local farmers' market.

Stay Up Later
Makes 1 drink

1½ ounces vodka

¾ ounce fresh lemon juice

½ ounce apple brandy

½ ounce simple syrup (page 5)

½ ounce heavy cream

1 egg white

Club soda, to top

1 thin apple slice, for garnish

Combine the vodka, lemon juice, apple brandy, simple syrup, cream, and egg white in a shaker. Shake without ice for 5 or 6 seconds to emulsify the egg white, then add ice and shake vigorously. Strain into a tall glass filled with ice. Top with club soda. Perch the apple slice on the rim of the glass.

EVEN IF YOU'RE not a fan of koumiss, it's best to finish your glass when presented with one by a Kazakhstani host. Any leftovers will be poured back into a jug to continue to ferment until you're offered a second glass, which you'll be expected to finish.

Kazakhstan / Stay Up Later (page 103)

KUWAIT

Sandwiched between Iraq and Saudi Arabia, tiny Kuwait, on the surface, resembles much of the surrounding region, with sweltering deserts that average more than 110 degrees Fahrenheit during the summer and a balmy Persian Gulf coastline where most of the population resides. What makes this constitutional monarchy of particular interest to the global community is what lies beneath its sands; namely, the world's sixth-largest oil reserve, which accounts for roughly 9 percent of all reserves on the planet. All that black gold has made Kuwait one of the richest countries and made a minority of ethnic Kuwaitis in their own land, due to the influx of foreign petroleum industry workers.

During long workdays in the oil fields or in the ultramodern capital and economic powerhouse Kuwait City, both natives and expats keep a pep in their step with the country's national drink, kahwah, or Arabic coffee, a favorite in every Gulf state. For a much lighter and smoother buzz, they also love their loomi, an iced tea made from dried black limes that are renowned in many Middle Eastern cuisines for their tangy and intense flavor. The Loomi Cocktail, based on a recipe that originally appeared in the *New York Times*, allows the aromatic tea's tart and slightly bitter vibes to shine through, while keeping things balanced with the addition of mint, honey, and aged rum. The result is a pleasantly puckering, julep-like concoction that's as easy to whip up as it is to wash down.

Loomi Cocktail

Makes 1 drink

6 mint leaves, plus 1 sprig for garnish
5 ounces chilled Dried Lime Tea (recipe follows)
1½ ounces rum
1 teaspoon honey
1 dash Angostura bitters
Crushed ice

Combine the mint leaves and a splash of the tea in a shaker. Muddle, then add the rest of the tea, the rum, honey, and bitters. Add ice and shake vigorously. Strain into a tall glass filled two-thirds of the way with crushed ice. Add a straw, top with more crushed ice, and garnish with the mint sprig.

Dried Lime Tea

Makes 4 cups

2 loomi omani (dried limes)
4 cups water
¼ cup sugar, or to taste

Break the dried limes into several pieces and place in a small saucepan. Add the water and bring to a boil over high heat, then reduce the heat to medium-low and simmer for 4 minutes. Remove from the heat and strain through cheesecloth or a coffee filter; discard the solids. Add the sugar and stir until dissolved, then let cool to room temperature. Store in an airtight container in the refrigerator for up to 1 week.

KYRGYZSTAN

Don't let Kyrgyzstan's unspoiled mountain ranges, placid lakes, and meditative glaciers lull you into false sense of serenity. When it's time to drink with this Central Asian nation's rowdy residents, it's best to prepare your liver for an epic onslaught. Though the Kyrgyz have their pick of traditional fermented beverages like koumiss or shubat (see page 103), the day's bracer usually consists of vodka shots, which are slugged liberally at just about every festivity, meeting, and family meal. Guests are expected to join in the seemingly endless toasts until all the nearby bottles are kicked unless they claim abstinence on religious grounds. Which, even in this Muslim country, might not prevent you from getting coaxed into a night of fantastically aggressive drinking.

Thankfully, Kyrgyz cuisine is robust enough to mitigate some of the effects of all that vodka. Like paloo, a popular meat and rice–based stew with spicy and peppery notes that's also the inspiration for the Red Eye to Bishkek. Named after Kyrgyzstan's capital, this variation on the Bull Shot—a 1960s American classic pairing vodka and Worcestershire sauce with beef consommé—adds chile pepper flavor alongside hot sauce, onion, and garlic, with a celery salt rim befitting its ultra-savory Bloody Mary–esque vibes. You'll want to sip this one slowly to take in its many layers of flavor, even if you find yourself smack dab in the middle of a Kyrgyzstan shot fest.

Red Eye to Bishkek

Makes 1 drink

Celery salt, for rimming the glass

1 lemon wedge, for rimming the glass

3 ounces beef consommé (or canned beef stock, such as Campbell's)

2 ounces vodka

½ ounce fresh lemon juice

3 dashes Worcestershire sauce

3 dashes hot sauce, such as Cholula

Pinch of chili powder

Pinch of onion powder

Pinch of garlic powder

Spread some celery salt over a small plate. Run the lemon wedge around the rim of a tall glass, then dip the rim into the salt mix to coat. Fill the glass with cracked ice and set aside. Combine the beef consommé, vodka, lemon juice, Worcestershire, hot sauce, chili powder, onion powder, and garlic powder in a shaker. Add 1 or 2 ice pebbles, shake briefly, and pour into the prepared glass.

THERE ARE NO AGE restrictions on the purchase and use of alcoholic beverages in Kyrgyzstan. And while there are some regulations or prohibitions about bringing booze to schools and universities, it's not uncommon to see teenagers buying vodka and beer for themselves at most neighborhood shops.

LAOS

Though the Lao people have called the mountainous and densely forested interior of the Indochinese Peninsula home for nearly a millennium, the political landscape in which they've lived has been in a constant state of flux. Originally the regionally powerful kingdom of Lan Xang, it was ransacked by Chinese bandits in the nineteenth century, then became part of French Indochina, was occupied by Thailand, Imperial Japan, and France again, before achieving independence as the one-party socialist state that's existed since 1975.

Despite their turbulent history, Laotians are known throughout Asia as extremely laid-back and welcoming, perhaps due to the ubiquity of Lao-Lao, a rice whiskey that's the country's national spirit. Traditionally served as a pair of tall shots at festivities—where imbibers are expected to finish each in a single gulp—it's often infused with everything from honey to scorpions.

Thankfully, you don't have to pound shots of insect-laden booze to appreciate Laotian culture, as some of the country's other gastronomic staples have inspired highly palatable potations like the Lost in Laos, which first appeared in Los Angeles bartender Matthew Biancaniello's *Eat Your Drink* (2016). Highlighting flavors from across the Indochina Peninsula like coconut, turmeric, and makrut lime, as well as green Chartreuse (a nod to the French language that's still understood and spoken by many Laotians), it's spicy, herbaceous, citrusy, creamy, and, like the best cocktails, a feast for both the eyes and taste buds.

THE LAOTIAN PROCLIVITY for infusing liquor with dead animals not only makes for some great travel stories, it's also been responsible for at least one surprising scientific discovery. In 1999, a Lao biologist attending a wedding in the rural northern region of the country noticed an unusual salamander that had been infused in a bottle of the local alcohol. He soon realized that the amphibian belonged to a previously unknown species, much to the amusement of the villagers, who had been catching the intoxication-inducing critters for years.

Lost in Laos

Makes 1 drink

¾ ounce fresh lime juice

½ ounce green Chartreuse

½ ounce agave syrup

¼ ounce freshly ground turmeric

6 makrut lime leaves

2 ounces gin

2 ounces unsweetened full-fat coconut milk

1 Thai basil sprig, for garnish

Combine the lime juice, Chartreuse, agave syrup, turmeric, and 3 makrut lime leaves in a shaker, then add the gin, coconut milk, and ice. Shake vigorously, then strain into a Collins glass filled with ice. Garnish with the remaining 3 makrut lime leaves and the Thai basil sprig.

LEBANON

The second-smallest country in the Middle East (and continental Asia), Lebanon is nevertheless a melting pot of epic proportions. Located at the crossroads of the Mediterranean Basin and the Arabian hinterland, it's a truly unique place where East meets West, modernity collides with tradition, and Christianity and Islam exist side by side in relative peace. Visitors to this incredibly ancient land can expect to find Roman ruins and villages with more than 7,000 years of history just down the road from glamorous beach resorts and raucous cities where you're likely to see secular partiers downing chilled glasses of arak, the country's traditional spirit, while nearby worshippers head to a mosque or church for evening prayers.

With all that cultural intermingling, you'd expect to find some surprising and delectable culinary creations. One of these, za'atar, is a blend of its namesake herb with far-flung elements like marjoram, thyme, sumac, toasted sesame seeds, and, occasionally, citrus zest. Popular throughout Southwest Asia and Northern Africa as both an ingredient in cooking and an infusion in dipping oils, it also forms the savory and sweet backbone of a cocktail syrup created by bartender Whitney Neal at Sitti, a Lebanese eatery in Raleigh, North Carolina. A prominent component of Neal's Za'tar Paloma, the syrup gives the fresh take on the Mexican classic a nice level of Middle Eastern depth and complexity, while maintaining the citrusy freshness of the original drink.

Za'atar Paloma

Makes 1 drink

1½ ounces silver tequila

1 ounce fresh grapefruit juice

1 ounce Za'atar simple syrup (recipe follows)

½ ounce fresh lime juice

Club soda, to top

1 lime wheel, for garnish

Combine the tequila, grapefruit juice, and za'atar simple syrup in a shaker. Shake without ice and then pour into a Collins glass filled with ice. Top with club soda. Perch the lime wheel on the rim of the glass.

Za'atar Simple Syrup

Makes 2 cups

2 cups sugar

2 cups water

¼ cup za'atar

Combine the sugar and water in a medium saucepan and heat over medium heat, stirring, until the sugar has dissolved. Remove from the heat and add the za'atar. Let stand for 3 hours. Strain through a fine-mesh sieve into an airtight container. Cover and store in the refrigerator for up to 1 month.

IN THE CITY of Zahlé, the epicenter of Lebanon's arak industry and home to most of its distilleries, the national hooch is an integral part of daily life, including most meals. A common Zahlé breakfast consists of a small glass of eye-opening "lion's milk"—arak diluted in cold water—accompanied by a hearty slab of liver with fresh mint and onions.

MALAYSIA

It's good to be the king. But if you're the reigning constitutional ruler of Malaysia, you'd better take advantage of the high life while you can. The Southeast Asian country occupying parts of the Malay Peninsula and the island of Borneo is the only nation in the world with a rotating monarchy system, in which the head of state is selected from one of nine Malay royal families—the remnants of an ancient, class-based feudal system—every five years. Incumbents are expected to gracefully hand over the crown at the end of their term, with no chance for reelection.

When Malaysians want to discuss their wacky politics over a drink, they usually choose beer, which accounts for more than 75 percent of the country's yearly alcohol consumption. Which means that Malaysia's signature classic cocktail, the Jungle Bird, has the rare distinction of being far more popular outside its place of origin. The inspiration for the names of several American watering holes, this luscious exemplar of 1970s tiki alchemy was the brainchild of Jeffrey Ong, when he was beverage director at Kuala Lumpur Hilton's Aviary Bar in the heart of Malaysia's capital. It first appeared in print in John J. Poister's *New American Bartender's Guide* (1989) and was tweaked again in the 2000s by Brooklyn's Giuseppe González, who substituted blackstrap rum instead of the original Jamaican or Puerto Rican rum base. That former spirit's richness pairs exceptionally well with Campari's herbal bitterness, alongside just enough pineapple-powered sweetness for a rum revelation whose influence has had a far longer shelf life than any Malaysian king.

Jungle Bird

Makes 1 drink

1½ ounces blackstrap rum

1½ ounces pineapple juice

¾ ounce Campari

½ ounce fresh lime juice

½ ounce simple syrup (page 5)

1 pineapple wedge, for garnish

Combine the rum, pineapple juice, Campari, lime juice, and simple syrup in an ice-filled shaker. Shake vigorously and then strain into a double rocks glass over ice. Perch the pineapple wedge on the rim of the glass.

MALDIVES

Possessing a territory—including water—that spans nearly 35,000 square miles of the Indian Ocean, the Maldives has the unique distinction of being one of the most geographically dispersed nations but also the smallest country in Asia by land area. It's also the lowest lying island country on the planet, having an average elevation just shy of five feet, with its tallest point, located on the eighth tee of the archipelago's only golf course, rising to a relatively gargantuan 17 feet. For centuries, this unparalleled proximity to the sea fueled a maritime lifestyle based primarily on fishing and oceanic trade. But a recent tourism boom has led to a massive economic shift, with large portions of the tranquil landscape—as well as several entire islands—being converted into high-end holiday destinations.

These stunningly curated slices of palm tree–dotted paradise are the only places to score a drink in the conservative Muslim country. Which is why vacationers tend to stay close to their resorts, where they're treated to bar menus as enticing as a South Asian sunset. Alongside the usual beachy suspects like the Tequila Sunrise and mojito can be found a few stimulating homegrown favorites like the Maldivian Lady. It's a tiki-fied take on the classic Perfect Lady that marries standard ingredients like rum and pineapple with apricot brandy, giving the drink a fruity depth and nuance that's uncommon among its tropical peers. Unfortunately, the Maldives might be mostly underwater in as little as a couple decades, but you'll always be able to whip up one of these in its honor.

Maldivian Lady

Makes 1 drink

1½ ounces white rum
¾ ounce apricot liqueur
½ ounce pineapple juice
½ ounce fresh orange juice
¼ ounce pomegranate syrup (page 5)
Crushed ice
1 pineapple wedge, for garnish
1 brandied cherry, for garnish

Combine the rum, apricot liqueur, pineapple juice, orange juice, and pomegranate syrup in a shaker. Pour into a tall glass filled two-thirds of the way with crushed ice. Add a straw and top with more crushed ice. Garnish with the pineapple wedge and brandied cherry.

THE MALDIVES' religious-minded authorities take the country's policy of only allowing drinking on resorts very seriously. Alcohol imports are completely banned, with all baggage x-rayed upon arrival.

MONGOLIA

If making lots of new friends is one of your travel goals, you might want to recalibrate your objectives before a trip to Mongolia. Outside of the capital city of Ulaanbaatar, the world's most sparsely populated sovereign state is a largely vacant, breathtakingly vast land of grassy steppes, cold deserts, and mountains that's home to stunning natural vistas and a few widely dispersed clans of nomadic herders. If you're lucky enough to encounter a group of these yurt-dwelling, horseback-riding traditionalists, you'll probably be welcomed with a chilled glass of airag, or fermented horse milk. This slightly sour and salty beverage has been brewed in Central Asia for thousands of years, clocks in at around 2% ABV, and is considered Mongolia's national drink.

In recent decades, however, urbanized Mongolians living in and around the country's few urban centers have shown a preference for stronger potations to combat the notoriously bone-chilling climate. Most notably vodka, the majority of which is imported from neighboring Russia. But there are several prominent beverage companies operating in Ulaanbaatar, including APU Company, which produces several vodkas made with locally grown wheat and artesian water from the Bogd Khan Uul, the world's oldest nature reserve. APU is also responsible for the Mongolian Lady, a sweet and bubbly Aperol Spritz variation that's guaranteed to get the party started and make you look as hospitable as one of Mongolia's famously friendly nomads. Because who doesn't like a boozier take on an all-time favorite summertime staple?

DURING TSAGAAN SAR, the Mongolian New Year, airag is offered to all guests as part of an elaborate welcoming ceremony. In the past, servants who were late to the festivities were forced to chug 5 to 10 liters of the horse-based brew as punishment.

Mongolian Lady

Makes 1 drink

1½ ounces Mongolian vodka, such as Eden

½ ounce Aperol

½ ounce fresh lemon juice

½ ounce honey syrup (page 5)

Sparkling wine, to top

1 lemon twist, for garnish

Combine the vodka, Aperol, lemon juice, and honey syrup in an ice-filled shaker. Shake vigorously and then strain into a large Champagne flute. Top with sparkling wine. Place the lemon twist in the glass.

MYANMAR

To most of the world, Myanmar—officially known as Burma until 1989—is a bit of a mystery. That's because for nearly more than seventy years, the largest country by area in Southeast Asia has been entangled in near-constant civil war and virtually closed to tourism. It's a shame, as this slice of the Indochinese Peninsula is brimming with gorgeous temples, rare wildlife, and plenty of rivers, jungles, and towering mountains just begging to be explored.

Strangely enough, this mostly dry (booze-wise), heavily Buddhist-influenced country is also the home of one of history's most enduring and highly regarded gin cocktails. A throwback to the days when Myanmar was occupied by the United Kingdom (1824–1948), the Pegu Club was the signature drink of the famous social institution of the same name, a boozy outpost where its members—mostly well-to-do British military officers and politicians—could kick back and commiserate after long days spent enforcing their colonialist dogma. The beautifully dry, tart, and airy concoction was first described in Harry MacElhone's 1927 tome *Barflies and Cocktails*, though its origins may reach as far back as the 1860s, the earliest days of the club. In the twenty-first century, this deceptively stiff serving of juniper and citrus has enjoyed a major renaissance, appearing on hundreds of menus and inspiring New York's influential craft cocktail den Pegu Club, which was fronted by legendary bartender Audrey Saunders until closing its doors in 2020.

Even if a trip to Myanmar isn't in the cards—or possible—the Pegu Club should still be on every cocktail fan's radar.

Pegu Club
Makes 1 drink

2 ounces London dry gin

¾ ounce curaçao

¾ ounce fresh lime juice

2 dashes Angostura bitters

1 dash orange bitters

Combine all the ingredients in an ice-filled shaker. Shake vigorously and strain into a coupe.

NEPAL

As the gateway to Mount Everest and several other of the world's mightiest peaks, Nepal is a nation of extremes. Mile-high metropolises like Kathmandu are considered valleys in the "roof of the world," where countless Buddhist and Hindu monuments, temples, and shrines loom around every city block and mountain trail and seem as old as the rocks themselves, and where even the simple act of breathing can be a challenge for those with little experience in high altitudes. Few things come easy here, unless you're in the mood for a drink. Beers from domestic brands like Nepal Ice, Gurkha, and Everest Lager can be had in every restaurant and corner shop for less than a dollar, while local distilleries churn out an impressive collection of spirits, from vodkas, gins, and single-malt whiskies to the iconic Khukri Spiced Rum.

In a place where elevation-related records are routine, it's no surprise that Nepal is home to the world's highest and most remote Irish pub. Located in the town of Namche Bazaar, a popular trekking destination in the Khumbu region, the straightforwardly named The Irish Pub warms its hike-weary customers' hearts with shots of Baileys, pints of Guinness, and its signature cocktail, the Himalayan Hot Toddy. In this hot and heavy sipper, a bountiful dose of Irish whiskey joins forces with mango juice—the most popular Nepalese nectar—as well as lime and cardamom for an explosively flavorful act of cultural collaboration that's just as delicious when sipped at sea level or on top of the planet's tallest peaks.

Himalayan Hot Toddy

Makes 1 drink

5 ounces mango juice

3 green cardamom pods

1½ ounces Irish whiskey

1 lime wedge, for garnish

Combine the mango juice and cardamom pods in a small saucepan and bring to a simmer over medium heat. Pour into a toddy glass and add the whiskey. Perch the lime wedge on the rim of the glass.

TO KEEP ITS GUINNESS taps flowing, The Irish Bar relies on one of the oldest forms of Himalayan transportation: donkeys. A special herd of "Guinness donkeys" routinely makes the trek to Namche Bazaar from a nearby valley, with each animal carrying two kegs.

Nepal / Himalayan Hot Toddy (page 113)

NORTH KOREA

It's rather difficult to discuss North Korea from a societal or historical perspective, given that the outside world knows so little about the one-party socialist republic. That's thanks to dictator Kim Jong-un's policy of *juche*, or "self-reliance," an ideology that's cut the country off completely from external media, trade, and immigration since Kim's grandfather Kim Il-sung rose to power in the 1940s. What can be understood, officially, about North Korea's spirits culture comes from a single 2019 press release in which the "supreme leader" declared soju to be the state's national liquor, embodying the "innocent and tender hearts" of its people. Although, given the stories about North Korea's pervasive human rights violations, frequent famines, and massive forced labor camps, it's unclear what reasons those people would have to raise a celebratory glass.

Whether or not North Korea's soju etiquette is as complex as neighboring South Korea's is also unknown. But it's easy to see (and taste), no matter where you're from, that this distilled rice wine makes an interestingly tangy, bittersweet addition to a wide array of cocktails. The 38th Parallel—named for the line of latitude that roughly demarcates North and South Korea—fits the bill perfectly. A far-flung, spirit-forward blend of maple soju, Punt e Mes, and Becherovka (from formerly socialist Czechia) that was first described on the *A Bar Above* blog by Julia Tunstall, it's got a sweet and earthy nose with a subtle herbal finish that begs to be repeated. Which is perfectly fine, due to its relatively low alcohol content. It might take some work to track down all the ingredients, but they're still infinitely more accessible than East Asia's Hermit Kingdom.

38th Parallel

Makes 1 drink

1½ ounces maple soju

½ ounce Punt e Mes

½ ounce Becherovka

1 lemon twist, for garnish

Combine the soju, Punt e Mes, and Becherovka in a rocks glass. Add ice and stir with a long-handled spoon for 5 or 6 seconds. Place the lemon twist in the glass beside the ice.

OMAN

Arabian Peninsula countries like Saudi Arabia, the United Arab Emirates, and Qatar get most of the region's media attention. And most Omanis are perfectly fine with that. For decades, they've been building an economically powerful oasis based on oil and tourism that's filled with Instagrammable beaches, ornate architecture, UNESCO World Heritage Sites, and one of the few remaining frankincense forests in Asia. The oldest continuously independent state in the Arab world, Oman is known for being the home of both the Persian Gulf's finest shipbuilders and its most aggressive caffeine enthusiasts. In between cups of spice-infused *kahwa* (coffee), Omanis absolutely feast on Mountain Dew, so much so that it has the highest rate of consumption of any drink in any Middle Eastern country.

While you're more than welcome to "do the Dew" in Oman, be careful if you decide to imbibe something stronger. Tourists need a special license just to drink at the handful of hotel bars that serve alcohol, and acting even a little tipsy in public means serious fines or a potential prison sentence. Which means, be safely out of the otherwise chill sultanate when fixing an Arabian-style version of the Café con Leche Flip, one of the lovelier coffee-forward potations to emerge from Sasha Petraske's legendary Manhattan cocktail den, Milk & Honey, in the early 2000s.

Black rum, coffee liqueur, cream, and egg yolk harmonize with allspice and an Omani-specific spice-salt rim to highlight the country's tastiest flavors with none of its booze-based restrictions.

Café con Leche, Arabian-Style

Makes 1 drink

Omani Spice-Salt Mix (recipe follows), for rimming the glass

1 lime wedge, for rimming the glass

1 ounce black rum, such as Gosling's Black Seal Rum

1 ounce coffee liqueur

¾ ounce heavy cream

½ ounce simple syrup (page 5)

¼ ounce allspice

1 egg yolk

Spread some Omani spice-salt mix over a small plate. Run the lime wedge around the rim of a sour glass, then dip the rim into the spice mix to coat; set aside. Combine the rum, coffee liqueur, cream, simple syrup, allspice, and egg yolk in a shaker. Shake without ice for 5 or 6 seconds to emulsify the egg yolk, then add ice and shake vigorously. Strain into the prepared glass.

Omani Spice-Salt Mix

Makes about 2½ tablespoons

1 tablespoon ground coriander

1 tablespoon ground cumin

½ teaspoon ground cinnamon

½ teaspoon freshly ground black pepper

½ teaspoon sea salt

2 or 3 whole cloves, ground (about ⅛ teaspoon)

Combine all the ingredients in a jar and mix thoroughly. Cover and store in a cool, dark place for up to 6 months.

PAKISTAN

Home to five of the thirteen tallest mountain peaks and the three highest mountain ranges in the world—the Hindu Kush, Karakoram, and Himalayas—northern Pakistan is no stranger to bone-numbingly frigid weather conditions. Yet the rest of the country, especially the low-lying plains in the South Asian country's southern interior, tends to be one of the hottest places on Earth. Summer temperatures here average around 100 degrees Fahrenheit and Jacobabad, the region's hottest city, has frequently experienced drought-inducing hot spells of up to 128 degrees in recent years, often followed by devastating monsoon rains.

Surviving such extreme temperatures requires some serious refreshment. To beat the heat, Pakistanis like to whip up a tall and citrusy Limca, a lemonade-like punch featuring the South Asian spice cumin, lime juice, and lemon-lime soda. A perfect beverage both for rehydrating purposes and experiencing a burst of some of Pakistan's most widely used culinary flavors, it's also been purported to flush toxins from the liver and improve digestion. My cocktail version of this popular cooler, the Limca Haram—or "Forbidden Limca," as the public consumption of alcohol in Pakistan is highly illegal and can result in hefty fines or even jail time—adds London dry gin as a base spirit, as both a nod to the country's colonial past and the English language, which, alongside Urdu, is one of Pakistan's official forms of communication. The gin's notes of juniper and citrus provide further balance to the spicy mélange, for a tipple that will rejuvenate the body (besides the liver, probably) in any climate.

Limca Haram

Makes 1 drink

2 ounces gin

½ ounce fresh lemon juice

½ ounce simple syrup (page 5)

3 lime wedges

Pinch of freshly ground cumin

Lemon-lime soda, to top

Combine the gin, lemon juice, simple syrup, 2 lime wedges, and the cumin in a shaker. Gently muddle, add cracked ice, and shake 8 to 10 times. Pour the contents of the shaker into a tall glass. Top with lemon-lime soda. Perch the remaining lime wedge on the rim of the glass.

BEFORE THE PASSAGE of a 1977 law banning the sale and use of alcohol, drinking was a popular Pakistani pastime. One of the country's deeply revered founders, Muhammad Ali Jinnah, was famous for his nightly dose of whiskey and soda. Even today, black market beer is relatively easy to come by; empty cans are a common sight in the gutters of Pakistan's cities and villages.

PHILIPPINES

Because two-dimensional world maps tend to exaggerate the size of countries near the poles, it's hard to get a feel for the Philippines' true size. Composed of 7,641 islands with a total area of 120,000 square miles, the Southeast Asian archipelago is nearly as long as the entire state of California. And with a population of more than 100 million, there's just as much cultural, linguistic, and environmental diversity as you'd expect, if not more. But no matter where you go or who you talk to regarding Filipino drinking customs, the conversation will most likely be about lambanog, a milky-white coconut palm liquor that's distilled using tubâ, a mildly alcoholic beverage derived from coconut sap that's aged for several days and was popular on the islands long before Spanish colonizers arrived in the 1500s.

The concept of social drinking—*tagayan* in the local Tagalog language—has always been held in high regard by Filipino imbibers, who often share a single large drinking container during quasi-ritualistic drinking sessions. Lambanog aficionados feeling the communal vibes like to make large batches of one of the country's most popular cocktails, the Lambanog Mule, which combines ginger, citrus, and juice from the carambola fruit, a star-shaped Southeast Asian delicacy that might be tough to find outside its native region, but can be replaced with pineapple juice in a pinch. Lambanog's notes of nuttiness and raisins (the liquor's traditional sweetening ingredient), as well as its crisp, clean finish, are much harder to replicate.

Lambanog Mule

Makes 1 drink

2 ounces lambanog

1 ounce carambola juice or pineapple juice (see headnote)

½ ounce fresh lemon juice

¾ ounce ginger syrup (page 5)

Club soda, to top

1 piece candied ginger, for garnish

Combine the lambanog, carambola juice, lemon juice, and ginger syrup in a shaker. Add 1 or 2 ice pebbles, shake briefly, and pour into an ice-filled Collins glass. Top with club soda. Skewer the piece of candied ginger with toothpicks and perch it on the rim of the glass.

MEZCAL AND TEQUILA as we know them today may never have existed without lambanog. Around 1569, a group of Filippino immigrants landed in Mexico and shortly thereafter established coconut plantations and began making their native liquor. Vino de coco, as lambanog was originally known, became so popular that Spanish colonial authorities, fearing that its sales would overtake those of imported liquors from Spain, banned its production indefinitely. But not before Mexicans were able to harness the Filipinos' distillation technologies and techniques, ultimately using them to create the first agave-based spirits.

QATAR

Hosting the 2022 World Cup put Qatar on the map for countless geographically challenged soccer fans. But the oil-rich, peninsular Arab country has been a highly influential economic and political force for decades, despite its mostly uninhabitable, scorching landscape and minute size. Ruled by the absurdly wealthy Al Thani family since the nineteenth century, Qataris have one of the highest per capita incomes in the world, a stunningly modern metropolis in the capital city of Doha, and taste for luxury cars and insanely valuable works of art. What they aren't into—as visiting World Cup attendees quickly discovered—is boozing it up. Libations are only sold to non-Muslim tourists at a handful of licensed hotel restaurants and bars, and expatriates living in Qatar can only obtain alcohol on a strict permit system.

Instead, Qataris like to get (mildly) lit with a cup of karak chai, a strong, milky, and moderately spiced tea that's sipped on nearly every street corner of Doha and in every outlying desert settlement. If you're in a country with friendlier drinking laws (which is to be assumed if you're reading this book), it's also an excellent starter in recipes for tea-inspired tipples, like the Dune Basher, named for the popular Qatari pastime of ripping through the desert at high speeds in luxury SUVs. Neutral vodka allows the flavors of homemade karak chai—adapted from a recipe that originally appeared in *Bon Appétit*—to fully express themselves, with ginger and honey supplying richness and depth. And, as the average well-heeled Qatari citizen can attest, flavorful opulence is about as on-brand as it gets in this cozy slice of Arabia.

Dune Basher

Makes 1 drink

2 ounces vodka

2 ounces Karak Chai (recipe follows)

½ ounce ginger syrup (page 5)

½ ounce honey syrup (page 5)

1 piece candied ginger, for garnish

1 cinnamon stick, for garnish

Combine the vodka, karak chai, ginger syrup, and honey syrup in an ice-filled shaker. Shake vigorously and then strain into a double rocks glass over ice. Skewer the piece of candied ginger with toothpicks and perch it on the rim of the glass. Place the cinnamon stick in the glass beside the ice.

Karak Chai

Makes about 6 cups

6 cups water

4 bags black tea

13 green cardamom pods, cracked

½ cinnamon stick

3 tablespoons sugar

1 teaspoon pure vanilla extract

1 cup evaporated milk

Bring the water to a boil in a medium pot over medium heat. Add the tea bags, cardamom pods, cinnamon, sugar, and vanilla and return to a boil. Stir in the evaporated milk and return to a boil again, making sure it doesn't boil over. Reduce the heat to medium-low and simmer until thick, creamy, and caramel in color, about 30 minutes. Pour the mixture through a fine-mesh strainer into an airtight container and let cool. Cover and store in the refrigerator for up to 1 week.

SAUDI ARABIA

When you control four-fifths of the preposterously oil-rich Arabian Peninsula, it means you're basically swimming in black gold. In fact, Saudi Arabia has access to more petroleum than any country in the world, with one of its oil fields—Ghawar—containing enough reserves to fill nearly five million Olympic-size swimming pools. The Royal House of Saud, estimated at around 15,000 members, has no qualms about flexing its incalculable wealth, buying up the most expensive art and luxury vehicles, funding professional soccer teams and golf leagues, and making its presence felt at every level of international politics. One thing that's not associated with the autocratic family—at least publicly—is upscale hooch (or spirits of any quality, for that matter), as Saudi Arabia enforces one of the strictest alcohol bans of any nation on the planet.

When well-heeled Saudis want to simulate the experience of popping a bottle of the good stuff, they reach for a glass of Saudi Champagne. Said to be a favorite of the royal family, the universally refreshing blend of apple juice, lemon, orange, mint, and sparkling water is super easy to make, and you won't have to dip into an oil-money trust fund to pay for its ingredients. If you want to get a bit fancier—and aren't subject to Sharia law—substitute the sparkling water with your favorite bubbly booze for a spritzy twist, creating a fruit-forward, low-ABV crowd pleaser that will have your taste buds living in the lap of luxury, at least temporarily.

Saudi Champagne

Makes 1 drink

1½ ounces unfiltered apple juice

¾ ounce fresh lemon juice

¾ ounce simple syrup (page 5)

5 or 6 mint leaves, plus 1 sprig for garnish

3 thin orange slices

2 dashes Angostura bitters

Champagne, to top

Combine the apple juice, lemon juice, simple syrup, mint leaves, 2 orange slices, and the bitters in an ice-filled shaker. Shake vigorously and then strain into an ice-filled Collins glass. Top with Champagne. Perch the remaining orange slice and the mint sprig on the rim of the glass.

SINGAPORE

In a part of Southeast Asia that's plentiful with magnificently shifting landscapes, impressive biodiversity, and exceptional cultural crossover, Singapore still manages to stand out. Spread across sixty-four islands at the southern tip of the Malay Peninsula, the wealthy, impeccably clean nation resembles a futuristic paradise where lush nature effortlessly coexists with eco-friendly skyscrapers, human-constructed waterfalls, the biggest retractable dome in the world, and the only zoo dedicated entirely to nocturnal animals. Only having gained full independence in 1959, the tiny country has become one of Asia's economic leaders, thanks to an emphasis on international trade, multiculturalism, and high quality of life standards.

Singapore's signature contribution to cocktail history, the Singapore Sling, was born long before the city-state became a shining example of prosperity and ambition. Created in 1915 by bartender Ngiam Tong Boon, it was first served at the legendary Long Bar at the still-extant Raffles Hotel. As with many other classic potations, the drink's recipe has changed over time. But even in its earliest heyday, the Singapore Sling seems to have been prone to variation, with author David A. Embury, who included it in his *The Fine Art of Mixing Drinks* (1948), commenting that "I have never seen any two [recipes] that were alike." Today, the Raffles Hotel serves two versions: one with a premixed batch that tastes like fruit punch and another with fresh juices that's shaken by hand. The following recipe sticks to the latter formula, a souped-up Collins-style refresher where gin, citrus, and herbal liqueur collide with notes of pineapple, orange, and cherry for a uniquely rich and complex finish that totally befits its namesake.

Singapore Sling

Makes 1 drink

1½ ounces gin

1 ounce Cointreau

1 ounce pineapple juice

¾ ounce fresh lemon juice

¼ ounce Bénédictine

Club soda, to top

Cherry Heering, for drizzling

1 orange slice, for garnish

Combine the gin, Cointreau, pineapple juice, lemon juice, and Bénédictine in a shaker. Add 1 or 2 ice pebbles, shake briefly, and pour into a tall glass filled with ice. Top with club soda and drizzle with a small amount of Cherry Heering. Perch the orange slice on the rim of the glass.

IN THE 1800s, the term "sling" was used to refer to any colorful drink that combined spirits, water, sweeteners, and other flavoring elements. According to Ngiam Tong Boon, the Singapore Sling's pink hue was meant to attract female customers.

Singapore / Singapore Sling (page 121)

SOUTH KOREA

Westerners tend to imagine South Korea, and especially its capital Seoul, as a futuristic metropolis, a trendy, high-tech playground where brightly lit billboards promote surgically enhanced fashionistas, the latest cars and phones, and the world's hottest boy bands. But many traditional aspects of Korean culture still permeate the modern milieu, such as the societal custom of deferring to one's elders; age-old dumpling, noodle, fish, and vegetable-based dishes that are still widely enjoyed; and a deep love for soju, the country's national spirit.

Dating to the thirteenth century, when Mongol invaders introduced Levantine pot stills to the Korean Peninsula, soju—which translates to "burned liquor"—was originally produced by distilling fermented rice wine. That is, until 1965, when the South Korean government forbade the use of rice in liquor due to grain shortages. Despite the lifting of rice prohibition in 1999, most modern soju is made by combining starch-based, high-proof ethanol with water and artificial sweeteners like saccharin, though it's preferable to crack open a traditionally made, grain-based bottle to experience this "neutral" spirit's buttery, malty, and faintly sweet notes.

Primarily consumed in shot form, soju drinking comes with a host of rules that have been an integral part of Korean society for centuries. Today, the spirit's subtle flavors are also employed as a base for cocktails like the Strawberry Soju Smash, which incorporates essential elements of South Korean cooking like lemon, ginger, and perilla (a plant with leaves that taste like a combination of basil and mint). As soju's alcohol content ranges from 13 to 53% ABV, this floral and festive tipple can work as both a low-ABV refresher or a stiff, fruit-forward nightcap.

ONE OF THE WILDEST ways to experience soju is in South Korea's infamous Tuna Tears Shot or *chamchi nunmulju*, as it's known in Korean. Traditionally served at Japanese-style seafood restaurants, the shooter is a combination of soju and the fluid from the eye of a tuna fish that's poured from a ceremonial tea kettle, with a thick, jellylike consistency that often requires servers to cut shot-sized portions from the kettle with scissors.

Strawberry Soju Smash
Makes 1 drink

2 ounces soju

¾ ounce ginger syrup (page 5)

4 lemon wedges

3 or 4 strawberries, halved

Small handful of perilla leaves (see Note)

Combine the soju, ginger syrup, lemon wedges, 2 or 3 strawberries, and perilla leaves in a shaker. Muddle, then fill the shaker with cracked ice and shake vigorously 3 or 4 times. Pour the contents of the shaker into a double rocks glass. Skewer the remaining halved strawberry with toothpicks and perch it on the rim of the glass.

NOTE: If perilla is unavailable, basil and/or mint leaves are an excellent substitute.

SRI LANKA

Sri Lanka is much more than a tear-shaped afterthought off the coast of the Indian subcontinent, with an ancient and diverse civilization that's worth more than a brief glance (and a few sips). Buzz-giving beverages have always been a part of the culture, courtesy of sap from the coconut palm, which has been tapped here since the earliest days of antiquity to make coconut wine, or toddy. That mild brew got a powerful level-up in the fifth century CE, when Arab traders introduced distilling techniques and created arrack (not to be confused with arak, the anise-flavored Middle Eastern spirit—see page 96), a rum-like liquor that's still a pervasive—and profitable—component of Sri Lanka's national identity.

The buttery, woodsy, and slightly sweet spirit is consumed neat, on the rocks, with coconut water or soda, but it's most popularly combined with ginger beer. That spicy, succulent blend has its fingerprints all over the Fruity Sri Lankan, a cocktail whose derivatives can be found at virtually all the country's Indian Ocean resorts, serene mountain hideaways, and urban toddy shops. Extracting the sap from coconut palms is still backbreaking, occasionally terrifying work, as toddy tappers must climb 50 feet or more up massive trunks armed with knives and gourds, balancing on precarious tightropes while painstakingly collecting the valuable nectar. That incredible effort, coupled with the Fruity Sri Lankan's notes of fresh pineapple, mint, and lime will have you appreciating this almost too easily chuggable South Asian delicacy even more.

Fruity Sri Lankan
Makes 1 drink

2 ounces coconut arrack (or an añejo coconut rum such as Coconut Cartel)
¾ ounce ginger syrup (page 5)
½ ounce fresh lime juice
½ ounce pineapple juice
6 mint leaves, plus 1 sprig for garnish
Club soda, to top
1 piece candied ginger, for garnish

Combine the coconut arrack, ginger syrup, lime juice, pineapple juice, and mint leaves in an ice-filled shaker. Shake vigorously and then strain into an ice-filled Collins glass. Top with club soda. Skewer the piece of candied ginger with toothpicks and perch it on the rim of the glass. Place the mint sprig in the glass beside the ice.

IT'S PERFECTLY legal for Sri Lanka's female citizens to enjoy a drink. But since 1955, women have been banned from buying alcohol in the country, a law that has faced an increasing amount of scrutiny in recent years.

SYRIA

Like most of the Middle East, Syria has an incredibly ancient history and more than enough still-extant archaeological attractions to prove it. And, as it is in far too much of the region, it's been afflicted by political turmoil for decades. Tourism has never been big here, and it's basically been nonexistent since the 2011 Arab Spring uprisings, which means that antiquity-minded travelers will have to wait to see wonders like Damascus's Umayyad Mosque, Sumerian clay tablets from the world's oldest library in the city of Elba, and other UNESCO World Heritage Sites like Aleppo, which was a major stop on the Silk Road.

But even if the political climate becomes stable enough to visit, don't expect to find any boozy refreshment after a tour. According to the World Bank, Syria is the ninth lightest drinking country in the world, with the average Syrian consuming around 0.3 liters of alcohol per year. And while anise-flavored arak is ostensibly the country's traditional spirit—just as it is in nearby Israel, Lebanon, and Jordan—it's nearly impossible to find. Instead, virtually every café serves limonana, or Arabic mint lemonade. In terms of summertime flavors, it's hard to beat the always-fresh combination of lemon juice, mint, and sugar, with a couple dashes of orange blossom water for an authentically Middle Eastern touch. Assuming you're in a place where arak is more readily available, turn that childhood favorite into an equally quenching adult beverage. If arak's potentially divisive flavor profile isn't your thing, feel free to substitute it with your favorite clear spirit. We won't tell anyone.

Spiked Limonana

Makes 1 drink

2 ounces arak

¾ ounce fresh lemon juice

¾ ounce simple syrup (page 5)

6 mint leaves, plus 1 sprig for garnish

2 drops orange blossom water

Club soda, to top

1 lemon wedge, for garnish

Combine the arak, lemon juice, simple syrup, mint leaves, and orange blossom water in an ice-filled shaker. Shake vigorously and then strain into an ice-filled Collins glass. Top with club soda. Perch the lemon wedge and mint sprig on the rim of the glass.

TAIWAN

Also known as Chinese Taipai, Taiwan is a large, densely populated island in the South China Sea that, though claimed by China, operates independently of the mainland superpower and is recognized as a sovereign nation by thirteen United Nations member states. Notwithstanding its complicated geopolitical status, Taiwan has become a highly developed, uniquely vibrant locale where traditional Chinese practices fuse with Western and greater South Asian influences, a flavorful milieu that's evident in its many cocktail dens, a handful of which routinely feature on lists of Asia's top fifty bars. As the majority of the population is ethnically Chinese, baijiu is the classic spirit of choice. Though, due to lucrative trade relationships with countries like the United States, you'll be able to find just about any spirit while visiting, especially in the larger cities like Taipei and Kaohsiung.

Taiwanese cocktail culture also extends to places like New York City, a major settling point for Taiwanese expats since the final schism with mainland China in 1949. In Manhattan, bartender and beverage director Shawn Chen serves group-friendly batches of the Chit-Cha Toddy, which uses osmanthus oolong tea from Taiwan, along with citrus, ginger, and popular Western ingredients like rye whiskey and Bénédictine. The result is nutty, delicate, and slightly spicy, a fragrant nod to the tea ceremonies that are an integral part of Chinese and Taiwanese social life. For even greater authenticity, Chen suggests serving the drink in a hollowed-out mini pumpkin with its top intact, or in a small, lidded cup called a gaiwan that mimics that gourd's shape.

Chit-Cha Toddy

Serves 12

4 cups water

2 tablespoons plus 2 teaspoons loose osmanthus oolong tea leaves

9 ounces rye whiskey

3 ounces Bénédictine

6 ounces fresh lemon juice

6 ounces ginger syrup (page 5)

3 ounces honey

Hollowed-out mini pumpkin, for serving (optional)

24 whole cloves, for garnish

12 lemon half-wheels, for garnish

12 mint leaves, for garnish

Cinnamon sugar, for garnish

Bring the water to a simmer in a medium saucepan. Remove from the heat, add the tea, and steep for 3 to 5 minutes. Strain the tea through a fine-mesh sieve into a punch bowl and add the rye, Bénédictine, lemon juice, ginger syrup, and honey. Stir with a wooden spoon until combined. Ladle into mugs, punch cups, or, if you're feeling ambitious, a hollowed-out mini pumpkin. Insert the spiky ends of 2 whole cloves into the flesh of each lemon half-wheel, leaving the bulbous ends of the cloves visible. Garnish each drink with a studded lemon half-wheel, mint leaf, and a small pinch of cinnamon sugar.

TAJIKISTAN

A major player in Silk Road commerce from the fifth to twelfth centuries, Tajikistan is also home to many of the highest mountain ranges found along the legendary trade route. Nearly 50 percent of the former Soviet republic has an elevation of around 10,000 feet above sea level and is now dotted by modern thoroughfares like the Pamir Highway, the world's second-highest road and a must-see destination for drivers and hikers looking to take in some of the most staggering scenery on Earth. The new infrastructure is also a boon to on-the-go nomadic tribes like the Kyrgyz, who still live in yurts, tend yak herds, and warm up from the often-frigid mountain climate with a steamy cup of green tea, the country's national drink.

Tearooms have long played a central role in Tajik culture as places of relaxation, hangouts for social lubrication, and important forums for discussing politics and other important issues of the day. Tajikistan's people may be big on talking, but they aren't especially fond of booze, consuming far less alcohol on average than their Central Asian neighbors like Kazakhstan, so don't expect to be offered any spiked green tea if you decide to visit. Instead, fix yourself a Green Goblin, a tea-based concoction that also includes vodka, a holdover from the Soviet era that's still a favorite of Tajiks who do like to indulge from time to time. Featuring cucumber, mint, and honey, it's vegetal, slightly sweet, herbaceous, (relatively) nutritious, and, most importantly, won't fail to get the conversation flowing.

Green Goblin

Makes 1 drink

2 ounces vodka

1 ounce brewed green tea, chilled

¾ ounce fresh lemon juice

¾ ounce honey syrup (page 5)

6 mint leaves, plus 1 sprig for garnish

4 thin cucumber slices

Combine the vodka, tea, lemon juice, honey syrup, mint leaves, and 3 cucumber slices in a shaker. Gently muddle, add ice, and shake vigorously. Strain into a double rocks glass over ice. Skewer the remaining cucumber slice with the mint sprig and perch them on the rim of the glass.

IN TAJIKISTAN'S TEAROOMS, it is considered rude to verbally refuse more tea. Once you've had your fill, simply turn your empty cup upside down, place it in front of you, and continue socializing.

THAILAND

One of Asia's—and the planet's—ultimate travel destinations, Thailand is a whirlwind of unforgettable nature excursions, nonstop beach parties and wild nightlife opportunities, treks to ornate Buddhist temples, and swanky spa experiences. Partaking in any one of these is enough to work up a mighty thirst. Thais appease theirs with a bevy of local beverages such as sato, a wine made with sticky rice, herbs, and spices, with a demand that greatly outpaces its limited releases. And SangSom, a sumptuous, oak-aged liquor with notes of coffee and coconut that's referred to as both a rum and a whiskey by locals, and is sipped on the daily from sunup to last call.

More popular still is Mekhong, Thailand's first industrially produced spirit, another rice and sugarcane–based "rum whiskey" with hints of vanilla and chile and a hue that resembles the infamously muddy river it's named after. It's grown in popularity so much that there's now a museum dedicated to exploring the liquor's history. But for more hands-on research, you're better off trying it in a Sabai Sabai, or the "Thai Welcome Drink," the country's official national beverage. This refreshing and peppery rickey riff offers a pleasurable cascade of uniquely complex booze, cool citrus, and basil-influenced spiciness that belies how easy and quick it is to whip one of these up. It's an elegantly addictive introduction to Thai flavors you'll want to keep going back to long after the initial introduction.

If Thai basil alone doesn't satisfy your lust for spice, try combining it with Thai chile, wasabi paste, and lemongrass in the Siam Mary. The vodka-heavy, tomato-tinged tornado was created at Bangkok's St. Regis Hotel to celebrate the eightieth birthday of its ancestor, the Bloody Mary, which was invented at the iconic bar of St. Regis's New York City location.

Sabai Sabai

Makes 1 drink

2 ounces Mekhong
1 ounce fresh lime juice
¾ ounce simple syrup (page 5)
Small handful of Thai basil leaves, plus 1 sprig for garnish
Club soda, to top
1 lime wedge, for garnish

Combine the Mekhong, lime juice, simple syrup, and Thai basil leaves in an ice-filled shaker. Shake vigorously and strain into a Collins glass over ice. Top with club soda. Garnish with the Thai basil sprig and the lime wedge.

Siam Mary

Makes 1 drink

3 thumbnail-size slices Thai chile

2 cherry tomatoes, halved

2 ounces vodka

Wasabi paste

4 ounces tomato juice

½ ounce fresh lemon juice

2 dashes Worcestershire sauce

Pinch of freshly ground coriander

Pinch of sea salt, for garnish

Pinch of cracked black pepper, for garnish

1 Thai basil sprig, for garnish

1 (6-inch) lemongrass stalk, for garnish

1 lime wedge, for garnish

Muddle the chile slices and cherry tomatoes in a shaker and add the vodka. Squeeze 3 pea-size dollops of the wasabi paste onto a spoon and use it to stir the vodka, chile, and tomatoes until dissolved. Add the tomato juice, lemon juice, Worcestershire, coriander, and ice. Shake vigorously and strain into a tall glass. Fill the glass with cracked ice. Sprinkle with the salt and pepper. Garnish with the Thai basil sprig, lemongrass stalk, and lime wedge.

TIMOR-LESTE

Timor-Leste declared independence from neighboring Indonesia in 2002, but the Southeast Asian nation occupying the eastern half of the island of Timor is much more culturally aligned with Portugal, another previous long-term colonizer. Portuguese sailors first arrived in the 1520s, setting up trading posts and exporting valuable sandalwood, wax, and later, coffee from the island's fertile shores, much as mainland-based Asian merchants had done in previous centuries. These business-minded Europeans left behind their language, religion (Timor-Leste is one of only two Asian states—along with the Philippines—whose predominant faith is Catholicism), and architectural stylings, all of which contribute to a fascinating melting pot that also includes significant Indonesian, Chinese, and indigenous Austronesian influences.

The Timorese's taste in spirits is also regionally unique. The country's most popular liquor, cachaça, is produced halfway around the world in Brazil, another former part of the Portuguese Empire. Yet thanks to a long history of importation (and the presence of Portuguese soldiers from other colonies stationed in Timor-Leste), the sugarcane-based firewater can be found in nearly every Timorese home, restaurant, and bar, where the cocktail du jour—as with Brazil—is the Caipirinha. For a Timorese spin on the South American classic, I've added locally cultivated ingredients like savory Thai basil and muddled orange both to provide an herbal, slightly spicy component and to up the drink's inherent fruitiness. The result is a tropical entanglement that's more relaxing than an afternoon spent by the Timor Sea.

Timorese Caipirinha

Makes 1 drink

2 ounces cachaça

¾ ounce simple syrup (page 5)

4 lime wedges

3 or 4 Thai basil leaves

2 thin orange slices

1 brown sugar cube

Combine all the ingredients in a shaker. Muddle thoroughly and fill the shaker with cracked ice. Shake 5 or 6 times and then pour the contents of the shaker into a double rocks glass.

TURKEY

Though a small portion of Turkey is geographically a part of Southeast Europe, including Istanbul (which would technically be that region's most populous city), most of its citizens consider themselves to be Middle Eastern, albeit with a much more Western, secularized lifestyle than their geographical neighbors. It's a transcontinental, cross-cultural balancing act that's been going on for millennia, from the Roman and Byzantine eras to the rise of the mostly Islamic Ottoman Empire to the establishment of the current republic by progressive statesman and military leader Mustafa Kemal Atatürk.

The melding of East and West is evident in Turkey's unique drinking culture. Though there are some restrictions about where and when alcohol can be consumed, and while nominally Muslim Turkish imbibers tend to put down far fewer drinks on average than Europeans, most cities and even small villages boast lively nightlife scenes, frequently fueled by the country's national beverage, raki. Similar in profile to other anise-flavored liquors like pastis, ouzo, and arak that are popular across the Mediterranean, this twice-distilled, grape-based spirit is often served mixed with chilled water to drinkers who follow a strict, centuries-old code of boozing etiquette that includes abstaining from imbibing until sundown and only drinking raki when it's served alongside meze, or small plates of food.

And while raki purists might scoff at the notion of their "lion's milk" in a cocktail, versions of the Swinging Sultan have been mainstays on Turkish bar menus for decades. Originally a Long Island Iced Tea–like blend of many liquors and orange juice, this modern iteration is closer to a cosmopolitan, with vodka, pomegranate juice, and orange liqueur adding a smooth contrast to raki's bitter, licorice-forward notes. It's a spiffy, citrusy mix of Eastern and Western that, like its country of origin, has an identity all its own.

THE TRADITIONAL TURKISH toast before consuming raki is long, but it's a good one: *En kötü günümüz böyle Olsun!*—meaning, roughly, "May our worst day be like this!" It's a testament to the raki drinker's philosophy of relaxation, savoring each sip, and enjoying deep conversations between good friends.

Swinging Sultan
Makes 1 drink

1½ ounces vodka

¾ ounce fresh lime juice

½ ounce curaçao

½ ounce pomegranate syrup (page 5)

1 barspoon raki

1 dash Angostura bitters

1 lime wedge, for garnish

Combine the vodka, lime juice, curaçao, pomegranate syrup, raki, and bitters in an ice-filled shaker. Shake vigorously and then strain into a coupe. Perch the lime wedge on the rim of the glass.

TURKMENISTAN

Before being annexed by Imperial Russia—and later, by its successor state the Soviet Union—in 1881, Turkmenistan played host to numerous conquering cultures thanks to its important location on the Silk Road. These include the Mongols, whose nomadic lifestyle is still practiced by many of today's Turkmen throughout the desert-rich, landlocked nation. Unlike their predecessors, however, these Central Asian roamers are subjected to some of the most bizarre laws on Earth, thanks to former dictator Saparmurat Niyazov. Men cannot grow long hair or beards until their seventieth birthday, ballet and Spandex are forbidden, and owning a black car, a dirty car, or a dog are all considered major crimes in the capital city of Ashgabat.

Despite its numerous unusual prohibitions, the Muslim-majority nation doesn't expressly ban drinking alcohol, and in fact, the country's national beverage, chal, is a fermented one. Made by mixing sour and fresh camel milk in a bag made of animal skin over several days, it's (unsurprisingly) not very prevalent outside of Central Asia. But some of Turkmenistan's other favorite refreshments—namely green tea and locally produced dessert wines—do have more of a global appeal. Based on the popular shot of the same name, the Green Tea Cocktail from Matthew Linzmeier conjures the earthiness of tea from the combination of Irish whiskey and plenty of fruity and citrusy notes. It's great as a sweet and fizzy after-dinner delight, or if you simply need to wash out the taste of spoiled camel juice.

Green Tea Cocktail

Makes 1 drink

1½ ounces Irish whiskey

1 ounce peach liqueur

½ ounce fresh lime juice

Club soda, to top

1 lime wedge, for garnish

Combine the whiskey, peach liqueur, and lime juice in a shaker. Add 1 or 2 ice pebbles, shake briefly, and pour into an ice-filled Collins glass. Top with club soda. Perch the lime wedge on the rim of the glass.

UNITED ARAB EMIRATES

A coalition of Arabian kingdoms ruled by absolute monarchs, the United Arab Emirates (UAE) is already a rather uncommon place, politically speaking. The outrageous contrast between its mostly barren and foreboding desert terrain and its wildly futuristic metropolises like Abu Dhabi and Dubai makes the UAE truly one of a kind. Dubai, in particular, is an architectural and technological marvel, home to dozens of manmade islands, luxurious villas, and the world's tallest building, the Burj Khalifa—which have made it a magnet for vacationing celebrities and young expats in search of business opportunities and the Middle East's best nightlife. Unlike the rest of the Arabian Peninsula, parched non-Muslims can choose from any number of watering holes, including several posh cocktail dens slinging progressive drinks that would feel at home on any Asian, American, or European bar.

Which is great, unless you fancy mingling with the locals. It's technically illegal for the UAE's approximately nine million citizens to partake in any booze-related festivities, so most Emiratis slake their thirst at cafés with a cup of Arabian coffee, or gahwa, traditionally served with dates. The few who choose to skirt the law often do so with a few sips of arak, the aniseed liquor that was a popular tonic throughout the Middle East until stricter forms of Islam came to dominate the region. The flavors of both beverages form a powerfully energetic bond in the Dubai in the Sky, adapted from a recipe by Corinne Mossati. Coffee liqueur and vodka mingle to smooth out some of arak's more astringent tendencies, making this caffeinated firecracker as appealing as a Dubai holiday—and far more affordable.

Dubai in the Sky

Makes 1 drink

1 ounce vodka

1 ounce freshly brewed espresso, chilled, or cold-brew concentrate

¾ ounce coffee liqueur, such as Mr. Black

½ ounce arak

¼ ounce simple syrup (page 5)

Pinch of freshly ground cardamom

Combine all the ingredients in an ice-filled shaker. Shake vigorously and then strain into a coupe.

United Arab Emirates / Dubai in the Sky (page 133)

UZBEKISTAN

Hydration is essential everywhere, but especially in a place like central Uzbekistan's Kyzylkum Desert, where temperatures can rise to 126 degrees Fahrenheit and where the dunes have been swallowing up unlucky—and underwatered—travelers since the earliest days of the Silk Road. For centuries, Uzbeks (and many other Asian and European peoples) have staved off thirst with kompot, a natural, nutrient-rich drink made by boiling seasonal fruits in large vats of water, infusing the mixture with sweeteners and a variety of herbs and spices, then chilling it. The vitamin-rich brew was essential before the advent of refrigeration and faster-than-horse transportation and is still a highly sought-after refresher in Uzbekistan, though perhaps less so in recent years due to the increasing availability of soft drinks and other bottled beverages.

Vodka, the former Soviet republic's liquor of choice, is in no danger of going out of style, however. It's traditionally drunk straight from porcelain teacups at family meals and larger gatherings where guests are expected to participate in endless speeches and toasts, consuming up to a pint of the neutral spirit in one sitting. If violent blackouts aren't your thing, try the Silk Road Punch for a less aggressive taste of Uzbekistan. The kompot portion of the drink comes from Paul Salopek, a journalist who crossed Central Asia on foot in the 2010s with Uzbek guide Azizbek Khalmuradov. Featuring the fruity goodness of apples, pears, and plums alongside basil's earthy and slightly floral notes, it's so healthy that mixing it with vodka only feels like the slightest of guilty pleasures.

Silk Road Punch

Makes 1 drink

4 ounces Uzbek Kompot (recipe follows)

2 ounces vodka

1 thin apple slice, for garnish

1 basil sprig, for garnish

Combine the kompot and vodka in a shaker. Shake without ice and then pour into a tall glass or mug filled with ice. Garnish with the apple slice and the basil sprig.

Uzbek Kompot

Makes 3 quarts

3 apples, cored and sliced

3 pears

6 to 8 large or 10 to 12 small plums, quartered and pitted

3 quarts water

1 cup sugar, plus more if needed

1 basil sprig

Combine all the ingredients in a large pot and bring to a boil over medium heat. This gentle heating takes about 45 minutes, during which time the fruit will begin infusing the water with color and flavor; just before the water reaches a boil, taste and add more sugar as desired. Reduce the heat to low, cover, and simmer for 5 minutes, then remove from the heat. Let cool to room temperature, covered, then transfer to a large jar or pitcher with an airtight lid and store in the refrigerator for up to 1 month. Before using, strain the liquid and discard the fruit.

REQUIRED HEAVY DRINKING at Uzbeki gatherings predates the vodka-loving Soviet era by many years. A British visitor to Uzbekistan in 1900 noted that his hosts would become totally distraught if he didn't consume at least a pint of brandy with every meal.

VIETNAM

In many respects, life in Vietnam—especially the countryside—looks much like it has for decades. Deep forests and Buddhist pagodas still define much of the landscape in this socialist country, where bicycle-riding farmers amble across rice paddies and stop at roadside stands selling traditional fish soups and homemade rice wines. But in the cities, particularly the capital Hanoi, there's a young and dynamic population brimming with modern ambitions and boasting a killer nightlife scene. Locals and tourists have their pick of countless sidewalk cafés serving adventurous eats, poolside bars, and cocktail lounges like Polite & Co, which has four hours of happy hour every day and sells bourbon shots for less than two dollars.

Wherever you decide to wet your whistle, there's a good chance you'll have the opportunity to try a Pho Cocktail, Hanoi's signature libation since 2012, when it was created by Pham Tien Tiep as his entry in a competition sponsored by spirits distributor Diageo. Combining spices like star anise, cinnamon, and cardamom from the world-famous Vietnamese noodle soup with gin, orange liqueur, and fresh citrus, it's a feast for both the nose and palate. And while Tiep's original presentation of the drink includes heating the spirits in a pitcher and running them through an elaborate tower of flaming metal cups, I prefer a slightly simplified, chilled adaptation from food and beverage writer Corinne Mossati. Her version includes fish sauce for some nice notes of umami and sriracha sauce for a rollicking kick, showcasing the amazing things that can happen when bartenders draw inspiration from their culinary surroundings.

Pho Cocktail
Makes 1 drink

2 ounces dry gin

¾ ounce fresh lime juice

¾ ounce Pho Spice Syrup (recipe follows)

½ ounce Cointreau

1 dash fish sauce

1 dash sriracha

1 cilantro sprig, for garnish

1 red Thai chile, for garnish

1 lime wedge, for garnish

1 star anise pod, for garnish

Combine the gin, lime juice, pho spice syrup, Cointreau, fish sauce, and sriracha in an ice-filled shaker. Shake vigorously and then strain into a double rocks glass over ice. Garnish with the cilantro sprig, Thai chile, lime wedge, and star anise.

Pho Spice Syrup

Makes 1 cup

3 green cardamom pods, cracked

1 cinnamon stick

1 star anise pod

1 cup sugar

1 cup water

In a small saucepan, toast the cardamom, cinnamon, and star anise over medium heat until they release their aroma, 1 to 2 minutes. Add the sugar and water and bring to a boil. Reduce the heat to low and simmer gently for 5 minutes. Remove from the heat and let cool for a couple of hours. Strain the syrup through a cheesecloth-lined fine-mesh sieve. Store in an airtight container in the refrigerator for up to 3 weeks.

LIQUORS CONTAINING whole insects or other creatures are common sights in Vietnamese souvenir shops. This includes Real Sea Horse Whiskey, a rare concoction that, true to its name, is infused with actual farm-raised seahorses and steeped for several months before bottling. It's consumed throughout Southeast Asia as an aphrodisiac and is said to relieve back and muscle pain. Similar medicinally minded whiskeys are available featuring snakes, scorpions, toads, or a combination of all three.

YEMEN

Following decades of civil wars and other domestic crises, Yemen isn't usually thought of as a prime Middle Eastern vacation destination. That said, the southernmost country—and only republic—on the Arabian Peninsula is home to quite a few awe-inspiring geological and architectural wonders, such as the biodiverse Socotra Archipelago, also known as the "Galapagos of the Indian Ocean," and other UNESCO World Heritage Sites like the Historic Town of Zabid and the Old Walled City of Shibam—"The Manhattan of the Desert"—famous for its impressively tall mudbrick buildings. Those who do get to take in any of these sites would be wise to toast to their beauty in the privacy of their hotel room (or better yet, on the flight home), as Yemeni police won't hesitate to make arrests for even the tamest public alcohol consumption.

Despite this culture of prohibition, more than a few Yemenis—particularly university students—take part in a vibrant underground booze trade, where liquor "dealers" make surreptitious house calls, serving their wares in unmarked plastic bags. Vodka rules the black market, usually Russian brands like Stolichnaya, sipped quickly and discreetly to avoid detection by the fuzz. If Yemenis had the opportunity to enjoy their tipples in a leisurely, stress-free environment, they'd be able to mix their hooch of choice with tasty native ingredients like hibiscus, several species of which only grow in Yemen. But you won't have to travel there to enjoy a Heavenly Hibiscus. This more herbaceous cosmo cousin, adapted from a recipe by food writer Brett Moore, is tart, fresh, and as vibrant as Yemen's fascinating and severely underappreciated landscape.

Heavenly Hibiscus

Makes 1 drink

2 ounces vodka

1 ounce fresh lime juice

¾ ounce Hibiscus Syrup (recipe follows)

½ ounce Cointreau

1 lime twist, for garnish

1 hibiscus flower, for garnish

Combine the vodka, lime juice, hibiscus syrup, and Cointreau in an ice-filled shaker. Shake vigorously and then strain into a sour glass. Place the lime twist in the glass and garnish with the hibiscus flower.

Hibiscus Syrup

Makes 1 cup

1 cup superfine sugar

1 cup water

3 (35-gram) hibiscus tea bags

Combine the sugar and water in a small saucepan and bring to a simmer over high heat, stirring until the sugar has completely dissolved. Remove from the heat and add the tea bags. Steep for 10 minutes, then remove and discard the tea bags. Store the syrup in an airtight container in the refrigerator for up to 1 week.

ICELAND

Norwegian Sea

SWEDEN

FINLAND

NORWAY

ESTONIA

UNITED KINGDOM

DENMARK

LATVIA

LITHUANIA

North Sea

IRELAND

NETHERLANDS

POLAND

BELGIUM

GERMANY

UKRAINE

FRANCE

ROMANIA

ITALY

SERBIA

Black Sea

BULGARIA

SPAIN

GREECE

Mediterranean Sea

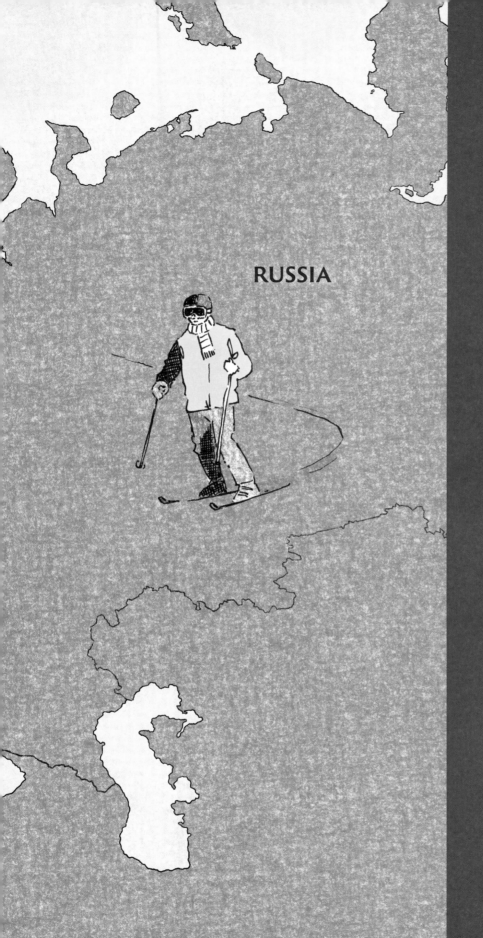

RUSSIA

EUROPE

ALBANIA

If you've been inside an Albanian home for more than a few minutes and no one's offered you a glass of raki, you might want to quickly figure out what you've done wrong. The exceptionally strong (40 to 80% ABV) fruit brandy—also called rakia—has been an essential component of hospitality in the Balkan country for nearly two centuries, as well as a staple at all manner of festivities, where it's usually served with meze, or small, Mediterranean-style appetizers. There's very little discrimination in terms of which fruits can be used in the copper-pot distillation process, but raki rrushi, or grape brandy, is the one you'll find most often at *meyhanes*, or traditional Balkan restaurants.

What you probably won't find on the menu is a raki-based cocktail. As has been the case since the spirit's invention, it's only served in shot glasses and any form of dilution—even a bit of water—is strictly discouraged. That's especially the case in the Skrapar region, which is famous for the quality of its grapes and its villagers' commensurate (some might say overblown) pride in their twice-distilled product. However, many heretical Albanian expats who have escaped this form of boozy tyranny use their country's hooch as a fiery yet sophisticated base in tried-and-true cocktail templates. The Raki Mule is one such creation. The combination of fresh lemon, ginger, muddled cucumbers, and soda does wonders to tone down the brandy's more aggressive qualities while keeping things a little spicy. At the very least, it's a much more palatable offering to guests than a full shot glass of straight-up Balkan firewater.

Raki Mule

Makes 1 drink

2 ounces Albanian raki, such as raki rrushi

¾ ounce ginger syrup (page 5)

½ ounce fresh lemon juice

3 thin cucumber slices

Club soda, to top

1 piece candied ginger, for garnish

Combine the raki, ginger syrup, lemon juice, and cucumber slices in an ice-filled shaker. Shake vigorously and then strain into an ice-filled Collins glass. Top with club soda. Skewer the piece of candied ginger with toothpicks and perch it on the rim of the glass.

WITH 654 COFFEE HOUSES per 100,000 residents, Albania boasts the most cafés per capita of any country in the world. Which is also a boon for raki drinkers, as many of these establishments become bars come early evening.

ANDORRA

Nestled in the Pyrenees mountains between France and Spain, the diminutive Principality of Andorra usually isn't considered one of the Iberian Peninsula's tourist hotspots. But this ancient microstate has more than enough unique features and historical quirks to include it on any European traveler's bucket list. Home to the highest elevated capital city on the continent—the popular ski resort and posh tax haven Andorra la Vella—the world's only constitutional elective diarchy is headed by two ceremonial "co-princes": the president of France and the bishop of Urgell in Catalonia, Spain—an odd throwback to the country's original feudal charter from 1278.

The dominant language here, like much of the surrounding region, is Catalan, though there are, as to be expected, significant Spanish, French, and even Portuguese cultural influences, all of which contribute to a fascinating—and delectable—melting pot as far as the food and drink scene is concerned. Al fresco diners can admire the striking mountain vistas while wolfing down plates of tapas, *cargols a la llauna* (garlic-basted snails), and *escudella* (a savory stew made with chicken, sausages, vegetables, and lentils), washed down with local brandies or Spanish sherries. Both spirits—as well as blanc vermouth, a popular French import—factor into Dan Greenbaum's The Andorra, first served at New York City's The Beagle. Blanche Armagnac, an unaged, fruity, and aromatic pisco-like distillate bursting with the flavors of nearby French vineyards, takes center stage, blending effortlessly with Manzanilla sherry's sharply floral bouquet. Like its namesake, this spirit-forward sipper is a lovely reminder of the magic that can happen when seemingly far-flung elements combine with just the right amount of balance—and ingenuity.

The Andorra

Makes 1 drink

1½ ounces blanche Armagnac

¾ ounce Manzanilla sherry

¾ ounce blanc vermouth

2 dashes orange bitters

1 orange twist, for garnish

Combine the Armagnac, sherry, vermouth, and orange bitters in an ice-filled mixing glass. Stir with a long-handled spoon for 20 to 30 seconds and then strain into a coupe. Place the orange twist in the glass.

Andorra / The Andorra (page 143)

AUSTRIA

Austrians get miffed when they're accidentally confused with their fellow German-speaking neighbors—the, um, Germans—but the two countries do share much more than a common language. Both ethnic Austrians and Bavarians can trace their ancestry to the Baiuvarii, a Germanic people who settled in Central Europe in the sixth century, and today the cultural similarities include a fondness for winter sports, wiener schnitzel, and a post-meal (or pre-meal) glass of schnaps, a vague term for a massive array of beverages including fruit brandies, herbal liqueurs, and infused neutral spirits. Yet while Austria's national cocktail, Jägertee, is widely enjoyed in both places and throughout much of the continent, it's a strictly local invention.

With its name originating from a combination of the German words for hunter (*jäger*) and tea (*tee*), this piping hot soother was originally sipped by wintertime sportsmen before heading out in the cold to stalk game animals. Today, the heartwarming (and super boozy) blend of spiced rum, fruit schnaps, red wine, orange juice, and black tea is more likely to be sold outside of mountain resorts to bone-chilled skiers and snowboarders and even comes in several prebatched forms. Like any cocktail, however, it's better when made from scratch. And if you want to be as authentic as possible, you'll need to procure yourself some Stroh Rum from one of Austria's preeminent producers of high-proof spirits. As an added bonus, it comes in a bottle meant to resemble a hunter's hip flask, just in case you're into making cold weather drinks and also providing fresh meat for your family.

Jägertee

Makes 1 drink

1 ounce spiced rum, such as Stroh Inländer 40

1 ounce Austrian schnaps, such as Prinz Obstler fruit brandy

1 ounce red wine

1 ounce loose black tea leaves

1 ounce fresh orange juice

1 lemon wedge

1 whole clove

¼ cinnamon stick

Sugar

In a small pot, combine the rum, schnaps, wine, tea, orange juice, lemon wedge, clove, and cinnamon stick and bring to a simmer over low heat. Simmer for 5 minutes, then strain into a mug (discard the solids) and stir in sugar to taste.

WHEN STROH STARTED producing rums industrially in the 1800s, the company had limited access to tropical ingredients like sugarcane molasses. To mimic the aroma and color of Caribbean rum, flavorings such as butterscotch, vanilla, and sugar beets were added to the batches. Today, while most Austrian rum is considered a "true rum" made from sugarcane by-products, Stroh's Inländer varieties are still infused with its traditional additives.

Austria / Jägertee (page 145)

BELARUS

Owing to its strict visa policies and authoritarian government under longtime president Alexander Lukashenko, Belarus is a relatively unknown entity, even to bordering states like Poland and Lithuania. Yet the nine million or so citizens of the former Soviet republic seem to enjoy a quality of life that's significantly better than their counterparts in most of the world's other highly insular countries. Unemployment is low thanks to a booming tech industry, public transportation is very reliable, crime is comparatively rare, and, with 40 percent of the land covered in forests, there's no shortage of fresh air and local vodka made with water drawn from pristine artesian wells.

Oftentimes that ever-present Eastern European liquor isn't enough for notoriously hard-drinking Belarusians. Many prefer to combine it with red wine and occasionally honey and spices like cinnamon, cloves, and nutmeg to create a Krambambula, a traditional cocktail so locally popular it now comes in prebatched, commercially produced versions. First introduced in the eighteenth century when Belarus was part of the Grand Duchy of Lithuania, the highly potent social staple was originally a party-pleaser for the nobility, as its spice component—imported from India and elsewhere in Asia—was a luxury few could afford. Today, it's the booze that will cost you; while vodka is the traditional spirit, feel free to co-opt whatever you have lying around the liquor cabinet. (Belarusians are also fond of using gin or rum.) Variety is the spice of life, especially when we're talking spiced booze.

Krambambula
Makes about 3 cups, to serve 6

1 cup red wine

2 cups vodka

3 whole cloves

3 allspice berries

3 whole black peppercorns

1 cinnamon stick

Pinch of freshly grated nutmeg

3 tablespoons honey syrup (page 5)

Pour the wine and 1 cup of the vodka into a medium pot. Crush the cloves, allspice berries, peppercorns, and cinnamon stick using a mortar and pestle or a coffee grinder and add them to the pot, along with the nutmeg. Bring to a boil over medium heat, stirring frequently. Reduce the heat to low and simmer for 10 minutes. Remove from the heat and let cool for 2 to 3 minutes. Add the remaining 1 cup vodka and the honey syrup. Cover and let stand for 5 minutes. Strain the infusion through 2 or 3 layers of cheesecloth into a large glass jar with a plastic lid. Cover and let stand in a dark place at room temperature for 8 to 10 days. Decant the mixture into a clean bottle and seal it. Store in the refrigerator for up to 3 months. Serve warm or chilled.

ACCORDING TO A 2019 STUDY, Belarussians consume the most alcohol worldwide at 14.4 liters per person per year, which is the equivalent of about 10 handles of vodka. Which sounds like quite a bit but averages out to less than a shot per day, well within the range of what's considered moderate drinking. It's also interesting to note that of the ten wealthiest countries by GDP, France consumes the most alcohol and has the highest life expectancy, whereas India, the driest country on the list, has the lowest.

BELGIUM

Belgium's inventiveness seemingly knows no bounds. Citizens of the small Western European kingdom are responsible for a mind-boggling number of innovations, from plastic, asphalt, and the internal combustion engine to inline skates, contraceptive pills, and the saxophone. Yet, according to Belgians, their biggest gift to the beverage community, jenever, has been unfairly credited to their northern neighbor, the Netherlands, which also claims the high-proof, juniper-infused malt wine as its national liquor.

That's in part due to the long-held tradition that attributes the invention of the spirit to seventeenth-century Dutch alchemist Franciscus Sylvius de Bouve. But evidence now suggests that authors from the Belgian region of Flanders had been describing the process of distilling jenever since at least the 1200s, with Antwerp-based Phillipus Hermanni writing the first definitive recipe in 1522. Regardless of which school of thought you choose to follow, there's no debate as to how Belgians (and many Dutch drinkers) like to down their traditional tipple—in shot form, filled to the brim, the first sip taken hands-free by bending over the table or bar and putting lips to the glass.

Ironically, there's nothing inherently Belgian about the Black Russian, the country's most famous cocktail creation. Attributed to bartender Gustave Tops, who first served the stripped-down White Russian variation at Brussels's Hotel Metropole in 1949, the mix of vodka and coffee liqueur has been a favorite of cream-averse caffeine freaks for decades. Sticking to the same philosophy, the Black Belgian substitutes jenever for an herbal finish that pairs best with a drier, zestier cold brew–based liqueur to keep things darker and broodier than a Belgian with a spirits-related chip on their shoulder.

Black Belgian

Makes 1 drink

1½ ounces Belgian jenever, such as Filliers 12 Year Oude Graanjenever

1½ ounces coffee liqueur, such as Mr. Black

Combine all the ingredients in a double rocks glass. Add ice and stir with a long-handled spoon for 5 or 6 seconds.

WHILE THERE ARE QUITE a few brands of Belgian jenever from which to choose, it's nothing compared to the mindbogglingly massive number of Belgian beers produced annually—with 304 active breweries in the country, it's possible to enjoy a Belgian beer every day for four years and never open the same bottle twice.

BOSNIA AND HERZEGOVINA

All the Balkan countries have well-earned reputations as booze-friendly locales. But spirits enthusiasts who have traveled extensively throughout the region tend to rank Bosnia and Herzegovina as the best place in those parts to grab a drink, citing the friendliness and laid-back, secular attitude of the locals, the inexpensive hooch, and the mesmerizing café views of ancient ruins and still-extant architectural achievements like the many Ottoman bridges sprawling across the country's rivers. Speaking of ancient, Bosnia's fertile soil and relatively mild climate have made it an ideal location for wine-making since the days of Roman occupation. Naturally, with the advent of distillation a millennium or so later, those grapes—as well as every other native Bosnian fruit—started being turned into rakia, the nation's ever-present brandy.

One of the most prevalent forms of rakia throughout the Balkans is slivovitz, which is made with plums and is a favorite of home distillers who churn out copious amounts of the powerful stuff in their backyards. This authentic taste of Bosnia and Herzegovina's terroir is also a lovely component in the Susina Sour, which was originally served at Portland, Oregon's Nostrana. In this flavorful quartet, gin and Grand Marnier provide the juniper and orange leading notes, while slivovitz and lemon juice form a powerful citrusy and fruity rhythm section. The original recipe calls for any plum brandy you can find, but infusing it with the true Bosnian stuff will have you and your drinking pals saying *Nazdravlje!*—"cheers," in the local parlance—after the first sip.

Susina Sour

Makes 1 drink

¾ ounce Grand Marnier

¾ ounce slivovitz

¾ ounce fresh lemon juice

¾ ounce honey syrup (page 5)

½ ounce London dry gin

1 brandied cherry, for garnish

1 rosemary sprig, for garnish

Combine the Grand Marnier, slivovitz, lemon juice, honey syrup, and gin in an ice-filled shaker. Shake vigorously and then strain into a coupe. Skewer the brandied cherry with the rosemary sprig and perch it on the rim of the glass.

BULGARIA

Existing as a distinct state for nearly 1,400 years, at an important geographical juncture between Eastern Europe and Asia, Bulgaria has, for centuries, been both an influencer of, and influenced by, the very different cultures that surround it. It was the birthplace of the Cyrillic alphabet that's primarily used by nearby Slavic countries like Ukraine and Russia. Most Bulgarians also speak Turkish and embrace some Middle Eastern customs, owing to their proximity to that region. But booze-wise, the hard-drinking Balkan country falls in line with its neighbors to the west like Serbia and Macedonia. The two predominant spirits are rakija, or brandy distilled with a variety of native fruits like plums and grapes, and mastika, an aggressively high-proof, aniseed liquor that's reminiscent of Greek ouzo, but with an even more intense nose.

When it's not being commandeered for lighter fluid, mastika gets the party going at Bulgaria's many beachside resorts along the Black Sea. Summertime revelers with a slightly lower tolerance, however, tend to opt for another local spirit, menta, a sweet liqueur infused with mint leaves (or mint extract) that runs at a manageable 15 to 25% ABV and comes in both clear ("white") and green varieties. Truly adventurous (or hangover-immune) Bulgarians combine mastika and menta in the Oblak—Bulgarian for "cloud"—an equal-parts sipper in which the former liquor's harsher qualities are reduced greatly by menta's herbal smoothness. But don't be fooled, this opaque blend still packs a formidable amount of alcohol in a relatively small package, so it's best to sip slowly, regardless of how hard the Eastern European vacation vibes are hitting.

Oblak

Makes 1 drink

1½ ounces mastika

1½ ounces menta

1 mint sprig, for garnish

Combine the mastika and menta in a double rocks glass. Add ice and stir with a long-handled spoon for 5 or 6 seconds. Place the mint sprig in the glass beside the ice.

CROATIA

Nineteenth-century poet Lord Byron once described the Croatian port city of Dubrovnik as "the pearl of the Adriatic." It's a sentiment that's shared by the millions of TV viewers who know its exquisite seaside architecture as the real-life setting for hundreds of *Game of Thrones* scenes. Croatia's appeal extends far beyond Dubrovnik's walls, however, as the former Yugoslavian republic's miles of dazzling blue shoreline, hundreds of untouched islands, gorgeous vineyards and olive groves, and stunning limestone cliffs have made the entire country a prime tourist destination. Visitors in need of washing down Croatia's famous seafood dishes and hearty meat stews can do so with pelinkovac, a wormwood-forward herbal liqueur that peaked in popularity in the early twentieth century and has lately been enjoying a major resurgence.

That's due, in large part, to the 2001 rediscovery of a pelinkovac recipe from noted chemist and distiller Franjo Pokorny that had been lost since World War II. Reformulated by the Badel 1862 spirits company and rebranded as Antique Pelinkovac, the slightly less intense modern version is balanced, bittersweet, and invitingly complex. Traditionally, the stomach-soothing digestif was sipped straight after large meals, taken as a nightcap, or included as a modifier in bracing, spirit-forward concoctions. More recently, it's been an inspiration to highly regarded bartenders like Meaghan Dorman, whose Thousand-Mile Coast is a tangy, herbaceous cooler that feels like summertime by the Adriatic Sea (from which its name derives), regardless of where you choose to shake one up.

Thousand-Mile Coast

Makes 1 drink

1½ ounces bourbon

1½ ounces fresh grapefruit juice

½ ounce Antique Pelinkovac

¼ ounce cinnamon syrup (page 4)

Club soda, to top

1 grapefruit slice, for garnish

Combine the bourbon, grapefruit juice, Antique Pelinkovac, and cinnamon syrup in an ice-filled shaker. Shake vigorously and then strain into an ice-filled Collins glass. Top with club soda. Perch the grapefruit slice on the rim of the glass.

WHEN IT COMES to alleviating the effects of a hangover, Croatians turn to ajvar. This traditional red pepper and eggplant spread is not only a delightful side dish but is also believed to have restorative properties, thanks to its rich vitamin and antioxidant content.

CYPRUS

Cyprus is a tale of two continents. The Mediterranean island lies only a few miles south of Turkey and west of Syria, placing it, geographically speaking, firmly in Western Asia. Yet, because of centuries of Greek influence and a recent stint as a British Crown colony, most Cypriots consider their republic a part of Europe—as does the European Union, which admitted Cyprus in 2004. Except for the Turkish-influenced northeastern corner of the county that's proclaimed itself to be an independent nation since 1983. Politics aside, most islanders appreciate the value of a good grape. Vineyards have existed in every region for thousands of years, with more than 20 grape varieties being cultivated today.

Many countries with impressive winemaking histories tend to produce some similarly inspiring brandies. Cyprus is no exception. With a tradition dating to the 1860s (when French pot stills were first brought to the island), Cypriot brandy often has a slightly lower alcohol content than cognac and Armagnac, a milder taste, and a sweet, caramel-forward finish. When not sipped straight, it's enjoyed as the base spirit in the country's national drink, the Brandy Sour, first served nearly a century ago in the resort village of Platres to the visiting King Farouk of Egypt. Created to mimic the appearance of iced tea—saving the booze-loving Muslim monarch from potential awkwardness—this tall refresher is more bitter than other sours due to the astringency of the island's locally grown lemons, as well as the use of squash, a concentrated citrus cordial. If you don't feel like making your own squash, there are plenty of prebatched options you can buy that make solid substitutes. Either way, it's a lot more fun than iced tea.

Cypriot Brandy Sour

Makes 1 drink

2 ounces Cypriot brandy, such as KEO VSOP

1 ounce Lemon Squash (recipe follows) or lemon cordial

2 dashes Angostura bitters

Club soda, to top

1 lemon wedge, for garnish

Combine the brandy, lemon squash, and bitters in a shaker. Add 1 or 2 ice pebbles, shake briefly, and then pour into an ice-filled Collins glass. Top with club soda. Perch the lemon wedge on the rim of the glass.

Lemon Squash

Makes ¼ cup

1 unwaxed lemon

1 to 2 tablespoons sugar

¼ cup water

Use a vegetable peeler to pare the yellow part of the lemon rind off in ribbons. Drop the lemon rind into a small saucepan and add the sugar and water (reserve the peeled lemon). Bring to a slow boil over medium heat. Reduce the heat to low and simmer for 1 minute, then remove from the heat and let cool. Squeeze the juice from the peeled lemon into an airtight container, then strain the lemon rind mixture through a sieve into the same container. Use immediately or cover and store in the refrigerator for up to 1 week.

CZECHIA

Sharing a drink with a good friend is one of the day's finest pleasures. Going on a quest with your best bud to create the perfect booze can be the adventure of a lifetime (if you don't kill each other in the process). Eighteenth-century Czech apothecary Josef Becher and his physician colleague Christian Frobrig went on one such mission in search of a therapeutic *eau de vie*, or "water of life," that would both cure ailments and raise the spirit. After years of trials and (very tipsy) tribulations, they debuted Becherovka, a secret mixture of twenty herbs, spices, and aromatic oils blended with the mineral-rich waters of the spa town of Karlovy Vary. Though its medicinal value is tenuous at best, it's still a beloved part of Czechia's drinking culture, and its recipe continues to be closely guarded by the Becher family, with only two members having knowledge of the complete formula at any time.

Featuring strong notes of cinnamon and clove, with a taste that's redolent of bittersweet herbs, baking spices, ginger, and orange peel, Becherovka is often served with tonic in a 1960s-era cocktail called a Beton ("concrete" in Czech). Since the brand's acquisition by spirits company Pernod Ricard, it's become widely available in the United States, where digestif devotees have begun implementing it as the foundation of crisp, refreshing libations like the Prague Smash. Created by Tad Carducci of the cocktail consultancy Tippling Brothers, this belly-soothing, (slightly) healthy pairing of Becherovka with fresh mint, citrus and pineapple would have made Josef Becher and Christian Frobrig proud (and quite a bit tipsier).

Prague Smash
Makes 1 drink

2 ounces Becherovka

1½ ounces pineapple juice

½ ounce fresh lemon juice

½ ounce simple syrup (page 5)

6 mint leaves, plus 1 sprig for garnish

1 thin pineapple slice, for garnish

Combine the Becherovka, pineapple juice, lemon juice, simple syrup, and mint leaves in an ice-filled shaker. Shake vigorously and then strain into a double rocks glass over cracked ice. Place the mint sprig and pineapple slice in the glass beside the ice.

AVERAGING MORE THAN 460 bottles a year per person, Czechs consume the most beer in the world by far. That's nothing new in one of the world's oldest drinking cultures, which is home to the earliest beer-centric monasteries, and where rudimentary brewing practices date to the fourth century BCE, when Czechia was first settled by Celtic tribes.

DENMARK

Depending on how you look at it, the Kingdom of Denmark is either one of the smaller countries in Europe, or its second largest. Its Scandinavian portion on the Jutland Peninsula and adjacent islands—what most people think of as "Denmark"—maxes out at around 16,500 square miles. But when combined with its island territories Greenland and the Faroe Islands, that number soars to more than 850,000. Either way, the Danish cocktail scene, centered in the capital Copenhagen and smaller cities like Aarhus, goes toe-to-toe with any major booze destination. The country's trendsetting bartenders, working at an exponentially increasing roster of delightful digs, are earning the highest marks at Nordic cocktail competitions and consistently busting out innovative craft drinks, many of which feature akvavit, the kingdom's traditional spirit.

Derived from the Latin *aqua vitae* or "water of life," this eau-de-vie (French for the same thing) has been distilled in just about every corner of Scandinavia since the fifteenth century. Akvavit gets its uniquely earthy and seedy flavor from a range of herbs and spices, primarily caraway and dill. When taken straight, its intense bouquet can be a bit divisive, but there's no doubt that the schnapps-like liquor is an interestingly herbaceous addition to cocktails when it's not trying to steal the show. Aurimas Mul from Copenhagen's K Bar wields this power exceptionally well in the Nordic Mule. Spicy, floral, and colder than the Greenlandic polar ice cap, with a dill finish that's more intriguing than overwhelming, this bubbly buddy has all the complexity of a Danish geography lesson. And in this case, that's a good thing.

THE DANISH have always had a famously relaxed attitude toward drinking, especially as it pertains to adolescents. Experimenting with alcohol as a teenager is not only encouraged, but considered an essential part of one's road to self-discovery. This period of life culminates in the week after Danes finish high school, when graduates are expected to go on a party adventure that includes several days and nights of extreme mandatory drunkenness and other traditional shenanigans.

Nordic Mule

Makes 1 drink

1½ ounces akvavit, such as Aalborg Taffel

¾ ounce elderflower liqueur

¾ ounce fresh lime juice

Ginger beer, to top

2 thin cucumber slices, for garnish

1 dill sprig, for garnish

Combine the akvavit, elderflower liqueur, and lime juice in a shaker. Add 1 or 2 ice pebbles, shake briefly, and pour into a large wineglass filled with cracked ice. Top with ginger beer. Skewer the cucumber slices with the dill sprig and perch them on the rim of the glass.

ESTONIA

Eastern and Western. Modern and ancient. Raucous and serene. Estonia's capital Tallinn is all of the above, a gem of a place that's unlike any other in Northern Europe. Its stone-walled Old Town is one of the best-preserved medieval cities in the world, with a wealth of architectural styles reflecting centuries of Livonian, German, and Russian rule. Today, it's a progressive high-tech hub that's spawned digital companies like Skype and Bolt.

It's also the birthplace of a fascinating Baltic liqueur, Vana Tallinn. Brought to life in 1960 by master distiller Ilse Maar and her team of mad scientists at the Liviko distillery, it's a combination of Jamaican rum and a proprietary blend of local herbs and spices. Maar described her creation as a protest against the overly sweet liqueurs that were saturating the market at the time and, true to her word, the 45% ABV spirit is intense and bitter, but with subtle notes of vanilla, toffee, and orange that make it a pleasantly complex, supremely sippable aperitif or digestif, as well as an excellent addition to mixed drinks.

And cocktail hunters visiting Tallinn's Old City don't have to walk far to find the latter. Every cobblestone block seems to have its own lauded spirits den, staffed with classically trained bartenders who like to shake up the status quo. Like Sigmund Freud Bar, where you're likely to find drink-slingers doling out proper classics alongside curious concoctions in ceramic kitty mugs, as well as the Tallinsker, an eye-openingly peaty ode to Vana Tallinn and Talisker whisky. Also featuring Frangelico, the smoky, nutty, and herbaceous revelation is somewhat like other Scotch Negroni variations, but, like its place of origin, is imbued with an Estonian uniqueness you've got to see (and taste) firsthand.

Tallinsker

Makes 1 drink

1½ ounces single-malt Scotch, such as Talisker 10 year

¾ ounce Vana Tallinn

¾ ounce Frangelico

1 orange twist, for garnish

Combine the Scotch, Vana Tallinn, and Frangelico in a double rocks glass. Add ice and stir with a long-handled spoon for 5 or 6 seconds. Place the orange twist in the glass beside the ice.

FINLAND

Though Finland's overall alcohol consumption has decreased slightly in the past decade or so—falling in line with Nordic neighbors like Norway and Sweden—having several drinks among friends is still seen by most Finns as one of the great social pleasures in this notoriously happy nation. That's held true since the Iron Age, when Viking ancestor cultures began brewing mead-like beverages for both fun and spiritual improvement. Light beer was the tipple of choice through the Medieval and Renaissance eras until, ironically, 1920s Finnish Prohibition, when liquor consumption increased drastically. Whatever your preferred spirit or brew, chances are that Finland's bars, especially in larger cities like Helsinki and Turku, will have plenty of it, with friendly bartenders eager to prepare your second round before you've finished your first.

Booze-related joviality occurred on a national scale during the 1952 summer Olympics in Helsinki. Event organizers wanted to create an easy-to-mix and easy-drinking libation that would appeal to a diverse crowd. Beverage maker Hartwall, also based in Helsinki, came up with the Lonkero, or Finnish Long Drink, a simple and fizzy refresher with just two ingredients—local gin and grapefruit soda. The spirited sensation immediately spread to every corner of the country, where it remains an unmitigated hit. As Finland's artisanal gin industry is now considered one of Europe's hottest, today's boozier versions of the Long Drink—one of which is balanced by lemon juice and grenadine—make for an even sexier and more satisfying sip. Down a few of these with the rowdiest Finns you can find, and you'll learn firsthand why Finland has sat atop the World Happiness rankings for the past decade-plus.

Finnish Long Drink

Makes 1 drink

2 ounces gin

1 ounce fresh grapefruit juice

½ ounce fresh lemon juice

¼ ounce grenadine or pomegranate syrup (page 5)

Grapefruit-flavored soda, to top

1 long grapefruit twist, for garnish

Combine the gin, grapefruit juice, lemon juice, and grenadine in a shaker. Add 1 or 2 ice pebbles, shake briefly, and pour into an ice-filled Collins glass. Top with grapefruit soda. Place the grapefruit twist in the glass beside the ice.

SINCE THE END of Finnish Prohibition in 1932, Alko, a government-operated beverage retailer, has been the sole legal distributor of hard alcohol in the country. From 1939 to 1940, the company also manufactured more than 450,000 Molotov cocktails that were used by the Finnish military in the Winter War against the Soviet Union.

FRANCE

In a country that many consider to be the planet's foremost culinary destination, where cooking and eating are considered sacred acts, it makes perfect sense that drinking is also a way of life for the French. The palpable adoration for all things boozy—at any time of day and in any social situation—has manifested itself in a seemingly infinite array of homegrown hooch, including iconic grape-based brandies like cognac and Armagnac, liqueurs that run the gamut from pleasantly dry and fruity cordials (Cointreau, Grand Marnier) to brightly floral infusions (St-Germain, crème de violette) to bracing and herbal elixirs (Chartreuse, Suze) to anise-forward aperitifs (pastis), various vermouths, and Champagne, the massively popular sparkling wine from the region of the same name.

Thanks to its pervasive café culture and its people's penchant for innovation, France's cocktail history is nearly as impressive as its spirits selection. In the early twentieth century, the epicenter of the drinks scene was—unsurprisingly—in Paris, specifically Harry's New York Bar, which was manned for many years by legendary Scottish bartender and writer Harry MacElhone (1890–1958), alleged inventor—or at least popularizer—of all-time France-inspired classics like the sidecar and French 75. Both sour variations employ lemon and cognac (though in recent decades gin has become a more popular ingredient in the latter), a template for slightly newer drinks that combine multiple French ingredients.

Like the Champs-Élysées, a lovely after-dinner tipple sharing its name with the touristy Paris avenue, which first appeared in Nina Toye and Arthur H. Adair's *Drinks—Long and Short* (1925). Its potent and almost mystically herbaceous qualities come from the addition of green Chartreuse, one of two liqueurs produced in the village of Aiguenoire by Carthusian monks who follow a secret recipe of 130 herbs, roots, and flowers that dates to the early seventeenth century. Likewise, the D'Artagnan (page 160), an explosively citrusy French 75 riff that uses Armagnac—cognac's multi-grape, oak barrel–aged cousin—and ratchets up the "Frenchness" by including Grand Marnier, a brandy-backed liqueur infused with essence of bitter orange. While its origin is indeterminate, its name certainly derives from the eponymous fourth Musketeer in Alexandre Dumas's novel *The Three Musketeers* (the character's native Gascony is also the birthplace of Armagnac).

Predating the opening of Harry's New York Bar by more than a century, France's oldest cocktail, the Kir Royale (page 160), is still one of the country's most popular creations, both at home and abroad. That's due in part to the effortlessness with which it can be made, by simply topping a half ounce of crème de cassis—a slightly sweet blackcurrant liqueur—with Champagne. Bright and gorgeous, it's an eye-catching complement to any party, with just enough berry-infused complexity to delight the palates of even the most discerning bubbly enjoyers.

We would be remiss not to include a drink featuring pastis, France's contribution to the pantheon of aniseed liquors. First produced in the early twentieth century after the enactment of a nationwide ban on the similarly flavored absinthe (see page 194), it's commonly sipped in the form of a Ricard (page 160), also known as the "milk of Marseilles." Named for Paul Ricard, who first commercialized pastis in 1932, the blend of that spirit, cold water, and grenadine has all the vibes of an afternoon at a French café, minus the croissants and charmingly pretentious waiter.

Champs-Élysées

Makes 1 drink

1½ ounces cognac

¾ ounce fresh lemon juice

½ ounce green Chartreuse

½ ounce simple syrup (page 5)

2 dashes Angostura bitters

1 lemon twist, for garnish

Combine the cognac, lemon juice, Chartreuse, simple syrup, and bitters in an ice-filled shaker. Shake vigorously and then strain into a coupe. Place the lemon twist in the glass.

D'Artagnan

Makes 1 drink

1½ ounces fresh orange juice

½ ounce Armagnac

½ ounce Grand Marnier

Champagne, to top

1 lemon twist, for garnish

Combine the orange juice, Armagnac, and Grand Marnier in an ice-filled shaker. Shake vigorously and then strain into a coupe. Top with Champagne. Place the lemon twist in the glass.

Kir Royale

Makes 1 drink

½ ounce crème de cassis

Champagne, to top

1 lemon twist, for garnish

Pour the crème de cassis into a Champagne flute. Top with Champagne. Place the lemon twist in the glass.

Ricard

Makes 1 drink

1 ounce pastis, such as Pernod

1 dash grenadine

5 ounces cold water

Crushed ice

Combine the pastis and grenadine in a highball glass and then add the water. Add a small bit of crushed ice and stir until the ice dissolves, 10 seconds or so.

GERMANY

If your conception of Germany is one big Oktoberfest tent where everyone's dressed in traditional attire, munching brat-wurst, and swigging giant beers while dancing to polka music, you might be slightly disappointed upon visiting. Except for the beer part, that is. Germans generally save the lederhosen for special occasions, but their love of hops is an everyday affair. One of the top beer-consuming countries in the world, Germany also produces and exports a fabulous array of sudsy favorites, from light and golden pilsners and lagers to fruity hefeweizens and dark and brooding bocks. Even the most popular traditional German "cocktails" are basically just beers with something added to them, like the Diesel (equal parts beer and Coca-Cola), the Bananenweizen (wheat beer topped with banana nectar), or the Radler (light beer mixed with lemonade).

That's not to say that Germans don't enjoy a more spir-ited approach to drinking. The country's most beloved hard alcohol brand is Jägermeister (which translates to "Master Hunter"), a notorious, slightly sweet digestif made with fifty-six herbs and spices like citrus peel, licorice, poppy seeds, and ginseng. One glance at its distinctive green bottle is enough to strike fear into the livers of countless former collegiate weekend warriors who did a few too many Jäger Bombs—the sinister act of dropping a shot of Jägermeister into a glass of Red Bull and chugging it—but there are better ways to experience this unique spirit. The classiest is probably the MasterMix, a martini variation in which the standard gin or vodka base is swapped out for Jägermeister and blessed with a hint of bitters, creating a wonderfully complex counter-point to dry vermouth's delicate notes. And, unlike the Jäger Bomb, there's no accompanying caffeine jitters and sense of impending doom.

Germans are also fond of schnapps, a word that can refer to any strong spirit, though it most often applies to fruit bran-dies and neutral spirits infused with spices, herbs, and syrups. One of the most recognizable brands is Rumple Minze, an overproof peppermint schnapps that's become popular in places like Lake Tahoe, where no après-ski session is complete without a Rumplesnuggler (page 161). The bone-warming blast of Baileys, Rumple Minze, and hot chocolate is perfect after a day of exploring the German Alps, or while watching a documentary about them from the comfort of your couch.

MasterMix

Makes 1 drink

2 ounces Jägermeister

1 ounce dry vermouth

1 dash Angostura bitters

1 brandied cherry, for garnish

Combine the Jägermeister, vermouth, and bitters in an ice-filled mixing glass. Stir with a long-handled spoon for 25 to 30 seconds and then strain into a coupe. Place the brandied cherry in the glass.

Rumplesnuggler

Makes 1 drink

1½ ounces Baileys Irish Cream

1 ounce Rumple Minze peppermint schnapps

6 ounces Homemade Hot Chocolate (page 27) or prepared hot chocolate of your choice

Whipped cream, for serving

Fill a large mug with hot water to warm it, then discard the water. Pour the Baileys, Rumple Minze, and hot chocolate into the mug and stir briefly. Float some whipped cream on top.

A GERMAN WEDDING tradition dictates that the groomsmen should "kidnap" the bride the night before the ceremony and escort her to a bar of their choosing, leaving clues for the groom to find her. Only once the groom has found her and bought his friends a round of drinks will the bride be returned to her future husband.

Rumplesnuggler

GREECE

One taste of Greece's national spirit, ouzo, and chances are you'll form a strong opinion about the powerful, clear liquor. Either consumed straight up or with a bit of added water that makes it cloudy, its fiery anise notes and subtle hints of clove and cardamom make an immediate impact on the palate. What isn't so clear is how the drink came to be. Some sources suggest that it began as a version of tsipouro, an un-aged brandy made by monks on Mount Athos since the fourteenth century. Others claim the silk-producing town of Tirnavos as its place of origin, or the island of Lesbos, where its production is centered today.

Discovering ouzo's true birthplace is far less important to Greeks than simply enjoying what many consider an essential part of their cultural patrimony. The versatile social lubricant is sipped with small plates of food and in the company of good friends, used to toast newlyweds and newborns, applied to aching joints as a folk remedy, or simply taken whenever the need arises to slow down and better appreciate the day.

Trying to impress a member of an older generation or an anise traditionalist with an ouzo-based cocktail, however, is a dangerous game, as blending the spirit with any modifiers other than water might be taken as a crime against Greece itself. That said, ouzo's somewhat astringent flavor does form an interesting contrast with light, fruity, and herbal ingredients in drinks like the Strawberry Ouzito. The mojito riff has become a staple at many of Greek's storied island resorts with its impeccable summertime mix of strawberries, mint, lime, and sugar. Sitting under a glorious sunset with one of these in hand, preferably staring out at the sea, and it's easy to agree with the Greek saying "Ouzo makes the spirit."

Strawberry Ouzito

Makes 1 drink

2 ounces ouzo

1 ounce fresh lime juice

¾ ounce simple syrup (page 5)

2 or 3 strawberries, halved, plus 1 whole strawberry for garnish

Crushed ice

1 mint sprig, for garnish

Combine the ouzo, lime juice, simple syrup, and halved strawberries in a shaker. Muddle gently, then dump into a double rocks glass. Fill the glass two-thirds with crushed ice, add a straw, and top with more crushed ice. Garnish with the whole strawberry and mint sprig.

IT'S EXTREMELY rare to see a person drinking alone in Greece. From the earliest days of antiquity, partaking of alcohol has been considered a communal activity that often lasts for hours. Which is why, when a group of Greeks finds a suitable spot at a taverna or café, they don't just say that they've found a table; rather, they're "renting" it for as long as it takes to get the vibes right.

HUNGARY

Often considered Hungary's national spirit, Unicum was nearly erased from history due to volatile twentieth-century politics. The closely guarded blend of forty herbs and spices was created in 1790 by József Zwack, the Royal Physician to the Habsburg Court, and was manufactured by his descendants until World War II, when the family factory was obliterated by German bombs. Escaping Hungary's post-war communist regime, the Zwacks fled to the Bronx with their top-secret recipe, leaving millions of Hungarians desperately thirsting for the 80-proof digestif. Those cravings were finally satiated in 1988 when József's great-grandson Péter Zwack returned to his homeland and resumed production of the deeply bitter, medicinal liqueur that's been compared to other syrupy, murky spirits like Fernet-Branca, Amaro Averna, and Jägermeister.

Unicum allegedly received its name shortly after its creation, when Holy Roman Emperor Joseph II tasted the distinctly bold mixture and exclaimed, *"Das ist ein Unikum!"* ("That is unique!"). Joseph is also the nominal inspiration for the Emperor Cocktail, a relatively delicate introduction to Unicum's intense notes of pine, eucalyptus, angelica root, and oak (that comes from the barrels in which it's aged). Softened and sweetened by vermouth and curaçao, it's guaranteed to be one of the more intriguing Manhattan variations you'll ever try. In recent years, several "milder" versions of Unicum have become available in the United States, but if you want the authentic experience, go with the original recipe.

Emperor Cocktail

Makes 1 drink

1½ ounces Unicum
⅔ ounce sweet vermouth
1 teaspoon curaçao
1 orange twist, for garnish

Combine the Unicum, sweet vermouth, and curaçao in an ice-filled mixing glass. Stir with a long-handled spoon for 20 to 30 seconds and then strain into a coupe. Place the orange twist in the glass.

ICELAND

Iceland is known as a tourist hotspot for the unprecedented beauty of its fjords, mountains, waterfalls, and glaciers. But besides some volcanoes and geothermal springs, there really isn't much in the way of heat on this windswept rock in the middle of the North Atlantic Ocean.

To keep warm on frigid winter (and summer) nights, the descendants of Iceland's Viking settlers distill Brennivín, a distinct schnapps inspired by the aquavit that was first brought to the island's shores in the 1600s by Danish traders. Made from a fermented mash of potatoes and flavored with native caraway seeds, the savory, subtly sweet, and uniquely herbal blend is known as "the Black Death," due to both the color of its foreboding label and its effect on overenthusiastic Nordic tipplers who have been pounding the stuff nonstop since Icelandic prohibition was partially repealed in 1935.

The locals traditionally enjoy Brennivín served as a nearly freezing shot, often accompanied by small chunks of *Hákarl* (fermented shark meat). If rancid fish isn't your thing, the clear spirit's surprisingly savory botanicals lend themselves to a wide variety of cocktails, like the Thor's Hammer, which I created in 2015 on a trip to Iceland to calm my nerves after nearly falling off the Langjökull glacier. A brisk, viscous, old-fashioned-esque sipper, it also highlights liqueurs from regions of Europe that were popular Viking raid locations.

If you're looking for something a little lighter, brighter, and citrusy, try the I Wanna Be a Dog, a boldly herbaceous riff on a Last Word from the bartenders at Slippbarinn, Iceland's premier cocktail spot in the heart of downtown Reykjavík.

Thor's Hammer
Makes 1 drink

2 ounces Brennivín

¼ ounce Amaro CioCiaro

¼ ounce Licor 43

2 dashes Angostura bitters

1 lemon twist, for garnish

Combine the Brennivín, Amaro CioCiaro, Licor 43, and bitters in a rocks glass. Add ice and stir with a long-handled spoon for 5 or 6 seconds. Place the lemon twist in the glass beside the ice.

I Wanna Be a Dog
Makes 1 drink

1½ ounces Brennivín

¾ ounce fresh lime juice

½ ounce green Chartreuse

½ ounce Thyme Syrup (recipe follows)

1 thyme sprig, for garnish

Combine the Brennivín, lime juice, Chartreuse, and thyme syrup in an ice-filled shaker. Shake vigorously and strain into a coupe. Garnish with the sprig of thyme.

Thyme Syrup
Makes 1 cup

1 cup water

1 small bundle thyme sprigs

1 cup sugar

Combine the water and thyme in a small saucepan and bring to a boil. Reduce the heat to low and simmer for 15 minutes. Add the sugar and stir until it has dissolved completely. Remove from the heat and let cool for 20 minutes, then strain. Store the syrup in an airtight container in the refrigerator for up to 1 week.

Thor's Hammer

IRELAND

Chances are your first—and perhaps only—experience with Irish whiskey happened during a night of youthful exuberance, when downing a small ocean's worth of Jameson or Tullamore Dew shots seemed like a good idea. But to brush off this noble and ancient spirit as simply a shooter would be doing it a great injustice. One of the oldest distilled liquors—the first recorded derivation of the word "whiskey" comes from the Irish *uisce beatha*, or "water of life"—it was originally made by monks who acquired pot stills on trips to southern Europe and brought them back to Ireland as early as 1000 CE. Prized for its smooth finish—especially in comparison to its spiritual cousin, Scotch—Irish whiskey rose in popularity until the late 1800s, when production reached its zenith and the Emerald Isle's native hooch was considered by many to be the world's preeminent dark liquor.

Due to several factors—imbibers' changing tastes, the temperance movement, the Irish Revolution, and so on—Irish whiskey experienced a drastic downturn in popularity during the early twentieth century, to the extent that, by 1966, there were only two licensed distilleries producing it. One of the cocktails credited with keeping interest in the spirit alive during this dark age was the Irish Coffee, a still-popular mixture of whiskey, coffee, sugar, and cream with an origin that's cloudier than an early spring hike in the Irish countryside. According to some sources, it was born in the 1940s at the restaurant of a rural airbase where a chef named Joe Sheridan would offer it to customers as a preflight pick-me-up. Others point to American travel writer Stanton Delaplane, who popularized the recipe in his home city of San Francisco in the 1950s after claiming to have witnessed it being made in a different Irish airport.

Throughout its long history, Irish whiskey has traditionally been sipped neat, taken as a shooter, or nipped from a flask to ward off the chill of a long winter's night. One of the few Irish whiskey–based cocktails to achieve worldwide prominence during the tail end of the spirit's heyday is the Tipperary. Purportedly stemming from in the county of the same name, it first appeared in print in Harry Johnson's 1882 edition of his *New and Improved Bartenders' Manual* (and later, with slightly altered specifications, in Harry McElhone's *ABC of Mixing Cocktails*), with the original recipe calling for equal parts whiskey, green Chartreuse, and sweet vermouth. The following modern version from Milk & Honey adds orange

bitters and dials down the Chartreuse and vermouth to play up Irish whiskey's characteristic smoothness while retaining its boldly herbaceous, slightly fruity backbone.

Irish Coffee

Makes 1 drink

2 teaspoons Demerara sugar

4 ounces strong brewed coffee, hot

1½ ounces Irish whiskey

Whipped cream, for serving

Fill a large mug or heat-safe glass with hot water to warm it, then discard the water. Put the sugar in the warm mug or glass. Add the coffee and whiskey and stir until the sugar has dissolved. Float some whipped cream on top.

Tipperary

Makes 1 drink

1½ ounces Irish whiskey

¾ ounce green Chartreuse

¾ ounce sweet vermouth

2 dashes orange bitters

1 orange twist, for garnish

Combine the whiskey, Chartreuse, vermouth, and bitters in an ice-filled mixing glass. Stir with a long-handled spoon for 25 to 30 seconds and then strain into a coupe. Place the orange twist in the glass.

THE LARGEST POT STILL to ever exist was built in the early 1800s at the Old Midleton Distillery in Midleton, County Cork, Ireland. Measuring a whopping 31,618 gallons, it was nearly twice the size of the largest pot still in operation today, which is located at the nearby New Midleton Distillery.

ITALY

"When in Rome, do as the Romans do."

That phrase, attributed Saint Ambrose, the fourth-century Catholic bishop of Milan, is still wise advice for lovers of boozy beverages visiting Italy's capital city—or anywhere else in the country for that matter. Social drinking has seemingly always been an integral part of life on the Apennine Peninsula, whether involving famously full-bodied Italian wines, vermouths, mild after-dinner sippers like Amaretto and Frangelico, or the countless herbaceous liqueurs known collectively as amari (whose singular form, *amaro*, translates to "bitter" in Italian). Taken both to stimulate the appetite and settle the stomach after a large meal, these liquid cornerstones of the Italian diet have been produced throughout the country since the 1200s and get their bold and botanical-rich flavors by infusing neutral spirits with locally grown ingredients like citrus peels, spices, flowers, roots, and herbs that vary widely depending on their regional origin.

Whether you prefer your aperitivo light and breezy like Aperol, bitter and fruity like Campari, bittersweet and vegetal like Cynar, nutty and viscous like Averna, or intensely medicinal like Fernet-Branca, there's at least one amaro to suit every palate (and probably several). The best method of introduction to any of these complex sippers is to try them straight or on the rocks, but once you've found one that works for you, use it as a base in one of Italy's most iconic cocktails, the Spritz. While the version featuring Aperol achieved its greatest fame in the 2010s, this airy, bubbly, and endlessly versatile cocktail format—whose name comes from the German word for "splash"—has been sipped since the 1800s, when Austrian soldiers stationed in Northern Italy's Veneto region would dilute their tipples with soda water. The modern version, which also includes Prosecco, a sparkling white wine that's a ubiquitous presence at Italian meals, is the perfect way to enjoy amari in their myriad forms.

Another Italian classic that's risen to the pantheon of beverage royalty in the twenty-first century is the Negroni (page 168). A descendant of the Americano, which features Italian sweet vermouth and Campari topped with club soda, the cocktail was purportedly invented in the late 1910s at Caffè Casoni in Florence, when a member of the aristocratic Negroni family asked a bartender to strengthen his go-to aperitivo by substituting the club soda with gin. In its more than one hundred years, the bitter yet refreshing—and super easy-to-mix—sipper has become a favorite of bartenders and spawned innumerable variations that have become stars in their own right, such as the Negroni Sbagliato (see note, page 168) and the White Negroni. The former's recent popularity is thanks in large part to *House of the Dragon* actor Emma D'Arcy, whose shout-out to the drink in an interview caused a viral sensation—and chaos among the thousands of bartenders who had to immediately memorize its specs.

Amari might get most of the headlines, but they're far from the only local spirits enjoyed by Italians on the regular. Like grappa, a grape-based pomace brandy known for its digestive properties and throat-searing potency (up to 70% ABV). When combined with limoncello, an opposingly sweet and citrusy liqueur made from the zest of Femminello Santa Teresa lemons, it becomes a slightly more laid-back, intriguingly flavorful base in the Grapparita (page 168), an Italian twist on the margarita that was first mixed up in Alfredo's of Rome in New York in the early 2000s. The following adaptation is sour, foamy, and supremely summery, perfect for exploring Italy's fascinating terroir in glass form.

Spritz

Makes 1 drink

2 ounces amaro of choice

3 ounces Prosecco

Club soda, to top

1 thin orange slice, for garnish

Fill a large wineglass with cracked ice. Pour the amaro into the glass, followed by the Prosecco. Add a straw and top with club soda. Place the orange slice in the glass.

Negroni

Makes 1 drink

1 ounce gin

1 ounce Campari

1 ounce sweet vermouth

1 orange twist, for garnish

Combine the gin, Campari, and vermouth in a double rocks glass. Add ice and stir with a long-handled spoon for 5 or 6 seconds. Garnish with the orange twist.

Negroni

NOTE: To make a **Negroni Sbagliato**, simply substitute Prosecco for the gin.

White Negroni

Makes 1 drink

1½ ounces gin

¾ ounce Suze

¾ ounce white vermouth, such as Carpano Bianco

1 grapefruit twist, for garnish

Combine the gin, Suze, and vermouth in a double rocks glass. Add ice and stir with a long-handled spoon for 5 or 6 seconds. Garnish with the grapefruit twist.

Grapparita

Makes 1 drink

1½ ounces grappa

1 ounce limoncello

¾ ounce fresh lemon juice

¼ ounce simple syrup (page 5)

1 egg white

1 lemon wedge, for garnish

Combine the grappa, limoncello, lemon juice, simple syrup, and egg white in a shaker. Shake without ice for 5 or 6 seconds to emulsify the egg white, then add ice and shake vigorously. Strain into a coupe. Perch the lemon wedge on the rim of the glass.

BEFORE 2006, Campari achieved its distinctive ruby hue by adding cochineal, the crushed-up wings of *Dactylopius coccus*, a parasitic insect related to beetles. While purists have decried the switch to artificial coloring, it's been lauded by vegetarians and people who prefer not to have bugs in their amaro of choice (even though many of them had probably been drinking and eating cochineal for years without caring about the ingredients).

LATVIA

Traveling through the Baltic region, you're guaranteed to cross paths with a few bottles of Riga Black Balsam liqueur. Latvia's national drink, the secret blend of twenty-four roots, berries, herbs, spices, and resinous plant extracts called balsams is named after the country's picturesque capital city, where it was created as a tonic by apothecary Abraham Kunze in 1752. Kunze allegedly used his patented elixir to cure Russian empress Catherine the Great, who had fallen ill on a trip to Riga, for which he was granted exclusive production and inheritance rights to the Black Balsam recipe. Which, according to tradition, is only known to one "head liquor master" and two apprentices at any given time.

Latvians go crazy for the forebodingly acetone-smelling, intensely bittersweet, coffee-black mélange, adding it to syrups, hot chocolate, ice cream, and various medicinal tonics, mixing it with fruit juices, or just shooting it straight. For those who find the original recipe a tad overstimulating, there are also fruitier varieties like Black Balsam Currant that, by adding Nordic blackcurrant juice, smooths out some of Black Balsam's funkier elements—including gentian, Valerian root, sweet flag root, ginger, oak bark, Saint-John's-wort, and buckbean leaves—without oversweetening the final product. At around 60 proof, Black Balsam Currant is also a fairly potent base in flavorful spirit-forward concoctions like the Black Latvian Cocktail. Adding gin and maraschino liqueur creates a bonanza of botanicals that stays balanced while highlighting some of Black Balsam's more delicate ingredients like honey, caramel, and blueberries, which also function as a nifty garnish (and accompanying happy hour snack).

Black Latvian Cocktail

Makes 1 drink

1½ ounces Black Balsam Currant

¾ ounce dry gin

¾ ounce maraschino liqueur

2 blueberries, for garnish

1 rosemary sprig, for garnish

Combine the Black Balsam Currant, gin, and maraschino liqueur in a double rocks glass. Add ice and stir with a long-handled spoon for 5 to 6 seconds. Skewer the blueberries with the rosemary sprig and perch them on the rim of the glass.

HARD-PARTYING visitors looking to get rowdy in Latvia might be a bit disappointed. Despite its location in notoriously booze-friendly Eastern Europe, the country is one of the region's lightest drinking nations, with less than 3 percent of the population claiming to overindulge on a weekly basis.

LIECHTENSTEIN

Whether due to favorable personal and corporate tax rules or an overabundance of valuable natural resources, many of the world's smallest countries are also some of the richest. But the 62-square-mile Principality of Liechtenstein, a mountainous, German-speaking remnant of the Holy Roman Empire sandwiched between Austria and Switzerland, is ridiculously wealthy even by microstate standards. A former billionaire tax haven and current financial services hotspot, this miniscule economic powerhouse has been ruled, since 1719, by the House of Liechtenstein, whose current head, Prince Hans-Adam II, is so popular that his subjects voted overwhelmingly to expand his constitutional powers in a 2003 referendum.

After a long day of crushing the global markets, shredding pristine Alpine ski slopes, or praising their monarch (and his son, Hereditary Prince Alois, who now manages the country's day-to-day affairs), the principality's business-savvy citizens have no shortage of local beverage options to take the edge off. Winemaking has been a major part of the culture for more than 2,000 years, with one hundred vineyards still in operation, including the prince's own Hofkellerei, or Court Vineyard. The oldest distillery, Telser, has been producing tasty fruit brandies since the nineteenth century, and more recently, a highly regarded single-malt whisky aged in pinot noir barrels. Created in 2019 at Liechtenstein's embassy in Washington, DC, to celebrate the country's tricentennial, the Imperial Rickey 300 highlights homegrown ingredients such as sparkling wine and elderflowers, which grow wild throughout the Alps. The addition of Applejack symbolizes the similarities between American and Liechtensteinian distilling and, more importantly, adds a welcome bit of fruitiness to this deliciously floral and bubbly number.

Imperial Rickey 300

Makes 1 drink

1 ounce applejack
½ ounce elderflower liqueur
½ ounce fresh lemon juice
3 ounces dry sparkling wine, such as Hofkellerei des Fürsten von Liechtenstein FL Brut
1 lemon twist, for garnish

Combine the applejack, elderflower liqueur, and lemon juice in an ice-filled shaker. Shake vigorously for 15 seconds, then strain into a Champagne flute and top with the sparkling wine. Place the lemon twist in the glass.

LITHUANIA

Like its fellow Baltic nations Estonia and Latvia, Lithuania's cultural identity has fluctuated greatly over the years. The epicenter of the Grand Duchy of Lithuania, which at one time was the largest state in Eastern Europe, it was later partitioned between Hapsburg Austria, Prussia, and the Russian Empire. Following several decades of Soviet control, the country assumed its current status as a basketball-crazy independent republic, known for its bucolic countryside and well-preserved ancient architecture.

Lithuanians' drinking preferences have followed a comparably circuitous path. For centuries, the traditional drink of choice was midus, a kind of honey wine like other meads found throughout medieval Europe. Occupying Germans and Russians introduced beer and vodka, respectively, which still account for the majority of the country's alcohol consumption. For more discerning drinkers, the collapse of the Iron Curtain and easier access to once-exotic spirits and ingredients has given rise to a blossoming cocktail scene, led by several innovative bartenders working in and around the capital city of Vilnius. One of these, Robertas Janovskis, based at Vilnius's Sweet & Sour, won the 2013 Lithuanian Bacardí Legacy competition with his recipe for the Lithuanian Daiquiri. In this adaptation, white rum mingles nicely with lime juice, lemongrass, and basil—increasingly popular ingredients in Lithuanian cooking—and raspberries, which grow just about everywhere in the country's prolific woodland areas. Now that's a boozy path worth taking.

Lithuanian Daiquiri

Makes 1 drink

1 ounce fresh lime juice

¾ ounce simple syrup (page 5)

½ fresh lemongrass stalk

2 ounces light rum, such as Bacardí Carta Blanca

5 basil leaves

4 raspberries

Combine the lime juice, simple syrup, and lemongrass in a shaker. Muddle, then add the rum, basil, and 3 raspberries. Add ice, shake vigorously, and strain into a coupe. Skewer the remaining raspberry with a toothpick and place it on the rim of the glass.

THE CONCEPT of a honeymoon is believed to have developed in Eastern and Northern Europe during midus's Lithuanian heyday in the fifth century CE. Newly married couples, having been gifted the honey wine at their wedding, would drink it after their first "moon" together as an aphrodisiac that was said to help with conception.

Lithuania / Lithuanian Daiquiri (page 171)

LUXEMBOURG

Nearly the same size as Rhode Island, the Grand Duchy of Luxembourg still more than manages to hold its own among Western Europe's mightiest players. The tiny powerhouse is the richest country in the world, thanks to its highly profitable banking, steel, and industrial sectors, as well as its recent success as one of the continent's biggest audiovisual and communications centers. When well-heeled Luxembourgish professionals want to celebrate closing another deal, they might open a bottle of quetsch, a native plum liqueur that's also produced in nearby Alsace. But most opt for the local bubbly, crémant de Luxembourg, a dry, aromatic sparkling wine with a soft, velvety finish.

That exceptional smoothness makes a lovely addition to fizzy drinks. And there are plenty of those to be had in Luxembourg's capital, Luxembourg City, which features an impressive coterie of cocktail bars specializing in everything from impeccably balanced classics to tiki standbys to playful and progressive inventions. Though one of those dens of deliciousness, Tailors Concept, has unfortunately been shuttered, one of its signature libations, the Tailor at Home, serves as one inspiration for the Grand Duke, which shares its name with the title of Luxembourg's hereditary monarchs. Airy, herbal, and decadently topped off with the finest adult grape juice in the country, the high-class tipple is the gin-based representation of an average Luxembourger's ultra-posh lifestyle.

Grand Duke

Makes 1 drink

1 ounce gin

½ ounce fresh lime juice

½ ounce Rosemary Syrup (recipe follows)

Crémant de Luxembourg, to top

1 rosemary sprig, for garnish

Combine the gin, lime juice, and rosemary syrup in an ice-filled shaker. Shake vigorously and then strain into a coupe or Champagne flute. Top with Crémant de Luxembourg. Place the rosemary sprig in the glass.

Rosemary Syrup

Makes ½ cup

½ cup superfine sugar

½ cup water

2 rosemary sprigs

Combine the sugar and water in a medium saucepan and bring to a boil, stirring until the sugar has completely dissolved. Place the rosemary sprigs in a heatproof container with a lid. Pour the hot syrup into the container, cover with the lid, and let stand for a few hours or up to overnight to infuse. Remove the rosemary sprigs, cover, and refrigerate for up to 1 week.

MALTA

Some countries have evidence of culture stretching far into antiquity. Then there's Malta. Containing 10 UNESCO World Heritage Sites, including several gigantic megalithic temples that are said to be some of the oldest freestanding structures on the planet, this 122-square-mile Mediterranean archipelago was home to an impressively complex civilization when most of Europe was populated by scattered tribes of hunter-gatherers living much like they had during the Stone Age. Malta's more recent history is just as fascinating. Occupied by eleven foreign powers in the past 2,000 years, including the Romans, Aghlabids, Normans, and, of course, the British, Maltese society is an incomparable mix of customs, traditions, and languages.

Malta is also the birthplace of bajtra, one of the Mediterranean's most curious and enchanting liqueurs. Derived from the fruit of the prickly pear cactus, which was introduced to the islands from the Americas and grows exceptionally well in the Maltese climate and soil, the bloodred nectar is prized locally and abroad for its delicate, slightly sweet, melon-like flavor. Usually served chilled and enjoyed as an aperitif, it also makes a delightful base in cocktails like the Girgentina Spritz. Named after one of Malta's indigenous grapes, the bubbly beauty is the signature drink at Maldonado Bistro on the island of Gozo. Brisk, airy, with the perfect hint of citrus, it's an ideal companion for kicking back in Malta's famously balmy climate, or wherever (and whenever) the need for smooth summertime vibes arises.

Girgentina Spritz

Makes 1 drink

1½ ounces bajtra

½ ounce fresh lime juice

½ ounce simple syrup (page 5)

Maltese sparkling wine, such as Girgentina Frizzante (if unavailable, use Prosecco), to top

Club soda, to top

1 thin orange slice, for garnish

1 mint sprig, for garnish

Combine the bajtra, lime juice, and simple syrup in a shaker. Add 1 or 2 ice pebbles, shake briefly, and pour into a large wineglass filled with cracked ice. Top with sparkling wine and club soda. Place the orange slice and mint sprig in the glass.

MOLDOVA

Not too familiar with Moldovan history? That's to be expected, considering that this landlocked, Romanian-speaking republic in Eastern Europe has only been an independent entity since 1991, having existed as a vassal state of the Soviet Union, Romania, Imperial Russia, and the Ottoman Empire for most of the past 700 years. It's been one of Europe's most productive wine regions for much longer than that, going back thousands of years, when Moldova's vineyards supplied generations of hard-partying ancient Greeks and Romans.

Today, the country's many imbibers—who, along with nearby Belarusians, consume more alcohol per capita than anywhere else—can choose from a wealth of locally grown and globally renowned wine varieties, from whites like Chardonnay, Pinot Gris, and Riesling, to popular reds like Merlot and Cabernet Sauvignon, as well as several sparkling options. Unfortunately, wine tourism isn't big here (due to internal political strife and regional instability, Moldova is the least-visited country in Europe), but thanks to a vibrant export market, Moldovan wines are widely available online and wherever oenophiles can be found.

When it comes to local spirits, Moldovan distillers are, unsurprisingly, all about the grapes, which they turn into divin, a properly strong, high-quality brandy that has been favorably compared to some of France's best cognacs. A grape-forward take on Giuseppe González's bourbon–based modern classic, the Moldovan Beekeeper is an old-fashioned riff that's ideal for showcasing divin's light, floral bouquet and complex aromatics, with just enough added herbaceous sweetness and a pleasantly intriguing finish. So smooth, it'll have you advocating for peace in Eastern Europe just so you can personally high-five the craftspeople behind its underappreciated base liquor.

Moldovan Beekeeper

Makes 1 drink

2 ounces Moldovan divin, such as Kvint VSOP 5 year

1 barspoon honey syrup (page 5)

2 dashes Angostura bitters

1 dash absinthe

Pinch of sea salt

1 lemon twist, for garnish

Combine the divin, honey syrup, bitters, absinthe, and salt in a rocks glass. Add ice and stir with a long-handled spoon for 5 or 6 seconds. Place the lemon twist in the glass beside the ice.

ACCORDING TO GUINNESS World Records, the Milestii Mici wine cellar in Moldova is the world's largest, containing nearly two million bottles in its vaults, with the most sought-after bottles selling for around 480€ each.

MONACO

The adage "Make the most of what you have" could have easily been written about Monaco. This uber-swanky Mediterranean principality has maxed out every inch of its 0.81-square-mile territory with Michelin-starred restaurants, extravagant spas, haute couture shops, a world-class Formula One racecourse, and plenty of docking options for the most outrageously opulent yachts. Ruled by the House of Grimaldi since 1297 and a former vassal state of the Genoese Republic, the Crown of Aragorn, Napoleonic France, and the Kingdom of Sardinia, the planet's most densely populated country took its first steps to becoming Europe's preeminent playground for the rich and famous when it legalized gambling in 1846.

Today's high rollers flock to Monte Carlo, an administrative area synonymous with the posh nightlife centered around its massive casino, a world-famous gaming den where libations of every variety flow as freely as the euros. And though Monaco's lone distillery produces a tasty liqueur made from carob fruit (carob being the country's national tree), you're more likely to be served a posh classic cocktail like the aptly named Monte Carlo, which first appeared in David A. Embury's *The Fine Art of Mixing Drinks* (1948). A sumptuous blend of rye whiskey—a nod to American actress Grace Kelly, who married Monaco's Prince Rainier III and whose son Albert II currently sits the throne—and Bénédictine from neighboring France, this herbaceous old-fashioned variation will make you feel like a billion bucks, even if your bank account says otherwise.

Monte Carlo

Makes 1 drink

2 ounces rye whiskey

½ ounce Bénédictine

2 dashes Angostura bitters

1 lemon twist, for garnish

Combine the rye, Bénédictine, and bitters in a rocks glass. Add ice and stir with a long-handled spoon for 5 or 6 seconds. Place the lemon twist in the glass beside the ice.

MONTENEGRO

Though it's one of Europe's smaller countries by area, Montenegro boasts an incredibly diverse collection of landscapes. Visitors to the tourist-friendly Balkan nation can expect to encounter gorgeous peaks (Montenegro literally means "black mountain"), pristine bays, massively deep canyons, and some of the largest lakes on the continent. In every Montenegrin region, the village café is the primary social hub, the go-to place for conversation, strong coffee, and, in the evenings, a bar scene fueled by local wines, wormwood-infused pelinkovac, and rakija, the national spirit. This ferociously strong fruit brandy is generally the only kind of alcohol socially gregarious Montenegrins will drink at their homes, where a generously poured shot is considered a standard gesture of welcome to guests.

No matter how impressive you consider your own mixological skillset, or what other interesting ingredients you may have on hand, it's best to avoid mixing up a rakija-based cocktail for your Montenegrin hosts, unless you want that feeling of welcome to disappear faster than an anti-communist activist in the former Yugoslavia. Like most Balkans, the folks here are absolute purists when it comes to their sacred hooch—it's neat or nothing. If you're tasked with entertaining a slightly less dogmatic crowd, Montenegrin rakija—and particularly šlivovica, the most common, plum-based variety—is a nice starting point for the Blossom Caresser, a fruity flip that takes inspiration from the creepily named Bosom Caresser, a silky pre-Prohibition dessert beverage with a similarly orange-forward finish.

Blossom Caresser

Makes 1 drink

1½ ounces šlivovica or a comparable plum brandy

¾ ounce fresh orange juice

½ ounce curaçao

¼ ounce pomegranate syrup (page 5)

1 egg yolk

1 thin orange slice, for garnish

Combine the šlivovica, orange juice, curaçao, pomegranate syrup, and egg yolk in a shaker. Shake without ice for 5 or 6 seconds to emulsify the egg yolk, then add ice and shake vigorously. Strain into a coupe. Perch the orange slice on the rim of the glass.

NETHERLANDS

Today, the Kingdom of the Netherlands is known for its picturesque windmills, tulip fields, innovative dike system, canals, and coffeeshops that don't sell coffee. Prior to the creation of the current monarchy in 1815, the Dutch Republic earned a somewhat notorious reputation as a leader in global commerce, establishing colonies and trading posts on every continent and jockeying with rival European powers for the control of goods and resources.

You'd have to go back much further still to trace the origins of the Netherlands's greatest contribution to the drinks world. Specifically, the late Middle Ages, when physicians in what was then the Holy Roman Empire began distilling *moutwijn* (malt wine) in pot stills and adding juniper berries to mask its otherwise unpalatable taste. The result was jenever, best known as a direct precursor to English gin. It was originally prescribed as a medicinal tonic until the late sixteenth century, when its consumer base shifted from the sick and dying to the kind of folks who like to party until they feel that way. Over the years, as production methods improved, grains like barley, wheat, and rye were added to the distillation process, birthing the distinctive spirit that's still enjoyed throughout the Low Countries and wherever the Dutch have roamed.

To appreciate the complex flavors and aromas of this woody and smoky liquor, it's best to keep things simple, cocktail-wise. Enter the Holland Razor Blade. First appearing in Charles H. Baker Jr.'s *The Gentleman's Companion* (1939), the refreshing, sporty, and spicy sour variation carefully mingles citrus, botanicals, malt, and pepper, with just enough sweetness to make it sing. Doctor recommended or not, a daily dose of one or two of these will do the body good.

Holland Razor Blade

Makes 1 drink

2 ounces jenever

¾ ounce fresh lemon juice

¾ ounce simple syrup (page 5)

Pinch of cayenne pepper

Combine the jenever, lemon juice, and simple syrup in an ice-filled shaker. Shake vigorously and strain into a stemmed cocktail glass. Top with the cayenne pepper.

A RENAISSANCE-ERA English nickname for a hangover was a "Dutch headache," due to the prevalence (and frequent overindulgence) of jenever in that country.

Netherlands / Holland Razor Blade (page 179)

NORTH MACEDONIA

What's in a name? Apparently a great deal, as evidenced by North Macedonia's testy, decades-long dispute with neighboring Greece over what it could call itself. Originally known as the Republic of Macedonia when it broke from Yugoslavia in 1991, the landlocked Balkan nation only forms one part of the historical region of Macedonia, which was named after the ancient Greek kingdom of Macedon. Northern Greeks—who also call themselves Macedonians, but only in the geographic and non-ethnic sense—were livid that another group was staking a claim to the moniker, as well as, according to them, appropriating symbols of Greek culture like Alexander the Great and the Star of Vergina. After twenty-five years and numerous economic embargos, the ethnic Macedonians finally relented, putting an end to a saga that's confusing enough to warrant downing a few glasses of mastika, North Macedonia's national spirit.

But make sure you check the bottle's country of origin first. Mastika made in Greece is an entirely different liqueur (ugh, names) that's flavored with mastic, a resin with a pine or cedar-like taste gathered from a small evergreen tree. Whereas the North Macedonian version is a wine distillate that's infused with ingredients like meadow honey and aniseed essential oil, as well as a proprietary blend of other aromatic plants. Some of the most respected beekeepers in the Balkans, North Macedonians prefer to spruce up their brandy of choice with a bit of extra honey and club soda to soften and sweeten mastika's sharp and fragrant notes. It's referred to simply as Macedonian Honey, but free to call it whatever you like; some names just aren't worth the fuss.

Macedonian Honey

Makes 1 drink

1½ ounces North Macedonian mastika, such as Grozd Strumica

½ ounce honey syrup (page 5)

Club soda, to top

1 lemon wedge, for garnish

Combine the mastika and honey syrup in an ice-filled Collins glass. Top with club soda. Perch the lemon wedge on the rim of the glass.

NORWAY

If you're planning a trip to Norway, bring clothes you don't mind getting dirty. The Scandinavian kingdom is all about the outdoor life: skiing, fishing, hiking, cycling, or simply taking in the countless islands, mountains, and fjords that contribute to this Nordic paradise's unparalleled wow factor. There isn't much time for "ass-sitting," as the locals call it, but when traditionalist Norwegians take a break from their active lives, they do it with a glass of akevitt. The caraway- and dill-infused liquor has a noble history in the country, dating back to the early Renaissance, when monks and other medical "professionals" prescribed it as a cure-all and distilled it using everything from herbs and berries to elk hooves and snake blood.

None of the ninety or so varieties of akevitt produced in Norway today contain such wild ingredients; generally, you'll find some combination of things like juniper, fennel, star anise, angelica root, bitter orange, and jasmine, to name a few. And unlike similar spirits from Sweden and Denmark, the Norwegian version is made with potatoes. With so much character in the spirit, akevitt-based cocktails should be kept relatively straightforward. The Arctic Summer is a four-ingredient stunner that incorporates cloudberry preserves—a Norwegian homage of sorts to Sasha Petraske's gin-based Cosmonaut—as well as a hint of citrus to keep things balanced, while still letting the akevitt remain the star of the show. Herby, juicy, and jammy, it's versatile enough to thrill the palate from brunch to last call. Whenever you choose to enjoy it, know that snake blood is strictly optional.

Arctic Summer

Makes 1 drink

1½ ounces Norwegian akevitt, such as Linie Aquavit

¾ ounce fresh lemon juice

½ ounce Aperol

1 heaping spoonful cloudberry preserves

1 dill sprig, for garnish

Combine the akevitt, lemon juice, Aperol, and cloudberry preserves in an ice-filled shaker. Shake vigorously and then strain into a coupe. Place the dill sprig on the rim of the glass.

WHEN TRAVELING in Scandinavia, it's customary to raise a glass and let out a hearty *Skål!*—a toast to friendship, wealth, and health that translates as "shell," "bowl," or "skull"—while making steady eye contact with your pals. The tradition dates to the time when Vikings from Norway and elsewhere would allegedly sip from the hollowed-out heads of their fallen enemies while keeping a mistrustful eye on their drinking company.

POLAND

Poland is often considered to be one of Europe's most homogenous societies. And though ethnic Poles do make up around 97 percent of the population, recent waves of immigration from both nearby countries and from outside the continent have begun to diversify things a bit. Culturally, there's been a shift, especially among younger generations, from traditional Eastern European values to a more open environment where formerly frowned-upon Western traditions like Halloween and Valentine's Day are now mainstream.

Where alcohol is concerned, however, things have remained pretty much the same for centuries. As in, it's all about the vodka. Polish pharmacists were infusing overproof neutral spirits with herbs and berries for medicinal purposes as early as the 1400s, and these powerful, usually homemade liqueurs, or nalewki, are still popular, especially during holiday celebrations. Industrial vodka production—using both grains and potatoes as distillates—peaked in the 1960s and '70s, when the industry was so widespread that the value of Poland's currency on international markets was determined by the price of a bottle.

Today, globally recognized Polish vodka brands like Chopin and Belvedere are lauded for their smoothness and purity. But flavor-wise, the country's most interesting export has got to be Żubrówka, or bison grass vodka. Infused with its namesake plant, it has a pale-yellow hue, a faint aroma of freshly mown hay, and a subtly floral finish. Locally, it's enjoyed both neat and as part of Poland's most popular cocktail, the Szarlotka. Designed to mimic the taste of apple pie (Poland is Europe's leading apple grower) and sharing the same name, the easy-to-mix blend of Żubrówka, apple juice, and cinnamon brings the vodka's uniquely grassy and earthy notes to the forefront, while adding the perfect amount of sweetness and a hint of spice to this surprisingly complex tipple.

Szarlotka

Makes 1 drink

4 ounces unfiltered apple juice

2 ounces Żubrówka

¼ ounce cinnamon syrup (page 4)

Pinch of freshly ground cinnamon, for garnish

Combine the apple juice, Żubrówka, and cinnamon syrup in a shaker. Add 1 or 2 ice pebbles, shake briefly, and pour into a tall glass filled with ice. Sprinkle with the cinnamon.

THE STRONGEST commercially available spirit in the world—coming in at a blistering 192 proof—is Poland's *spirytus rektyfikowany* (rectified spirit). This ultra-harsh, grain-based firewater is mostly used as a base in homemade herbal and fruit liqueurs or for medical purposes. It's never a good idea to shoot anything that's 96 percent pure alcohol, but those brave (read: idiotic) souls who have done it have likened the experience to getting drop-kicked in the face by an angry blackbelt.

PORTUGAL

As one of the first seafaring powers during the so-called European Age of Discovery that began in the 1400s, Portugal contributed greatly—and somewhat inadvertently—to the global spread of distilled liquors. Introducing sugarcane to its newly conquered African and South American territories, Portuguese farmers literally planted the initial seed that would eventually give rise to now-ubiquitous beverages like aguardente, rum, and cachaça. The country's signature domestic spirit, however, wouldn't appear for another few centuries, when vintners in the Douro Valley began fortifying their wines with neutral grape liquors to create port. Named for the coastal city of Porto, the rich, dense, and slightly sweet aperitif can be made from more than one hundred varieties of grapes that, depending on how they're aged and fermented, are turned into several different styles, such as tawny, ruby, rosé, and white, which all have unique flavor and color characteristics.

While the world's most admired dessert wine is delightful on its own, port has been featured in cocktails since the first major mixed drinks craze of the mid-1800s, when the Coffee Cocktail—a combination of cognac, ruby port, egg, sugar, and nutmeg that, according to mixological godfather Jerry Thomas, visually resembles its caffeinated namesake—first appeared in Thomas's seminal *Bar-Tenders Guide* (1862). A simplified version, the Port Flip, debuted a couple decades later and eventually overtook its predecessor in popularity. With a luscious and silky mouthfeel, ratcheted-up dessert vibes thanks to a whole egg and a dash of sugar, and the freedom to use whatever style of port your palate prefers, it's not hard to see why.

Port Flip

Makes 1 drink

2 ounces port

¼ ounce simple syrup (page 5)

1 egg

Pinch of freshly grated nutmeg, for garnish

Combine the port, simple syrup, and egg in a shaker. Shake without ice for 5 or 6 seconds to emulsify the egg, then add ice and shake vigorously. Strain into a coupe. Sprinkle with the nutmeg.

ROMANIA

When discussing Romania's many intriguing cultural and geographical highlights—from its picturesque Black Sea coastline to its large population of nomadic Romani people to the famously mysterious and vampire-friendly Transylvania region—plums usually don't make the list. But they should, because the country is the European Union's largest grower of the juicy purple fruits, with 80 percent of the yearly crop transformed into Romania's national spirit, țuică. Prepared using traditional methods like copper stills and a wood or charcoal fire source, the tangy, vibrant brandy is served as an appetite-inducing shot before all meals and at every conceivable social event. And though there are several unaged and aged varieties produced on an industrial level, this great source of liquid pride is more commonly distilled at home, with Romanians churning out up to 200 liters per family per year.

Thanks to its highly productive orchards, Romania also exports a number of other fruit-based alcohols, including apricot liqueur. That spirit's intensely fruity, semisweet notes make an excellent dancing partner for tuica's mildly astringent and subtly spicy elements in the Transylvania Tango, a sidecar riff that's bold, beautiful, and 100% Romanian. It's named after the fictional birthplace of undead icon Count Dracula (who was inspired by real-life fifteenth-century Prince Vlad the Impaler, an occasional resident of the region), but this bloodred, fruit-forward powerhouse's flavors are much better appreciated by those with living palates.

Transylvania Tango

Makes 1 drink

1½ ounces țuică

1 ounce apricot liqueur, such as Saber Elyzia

½ ounce fresh lemon juice

4 dashes Angostura bitters

1 lemon twist, for garnish

Combine the țuică, apricot liqueur, lemon juice, and bitters in an ice-filled shaker. Shake vigorously and strain into a coupe. Place the lemon twist in the glass.

RUSSIA

While there's still a bit of a kerfuffle over vodka's exact geographical origins, it's been the spirit of choice for the Russian people since at least the 1400s, when it was used as medicine for everything from the common cold to impotency. As has long been the case, today's Russians consume more of the neutral, grain- or potato-based liquor than anyone else in the world, both by total volume and per capita, with long-standing—and some might say, rather aggressive—vodka-related traditions remaining a cornerstone of everyday social interactions.

It's a testament to the global perception about Russia's powerful relationship to vodka that the two most popular cocktails referencing the country—the White Russian and Moscow Mule—were created by bartenders in California and New York, respectively. It's also an indication of the lack of a real cocktail culture in the planet's largest nation. Like the older generations in most Eastern European countries, Russians of a certain age scoff at the idea of anything other than vodka taken in shot form. But younger imbibers, particularly in urban areas, have embraced the entire gamut of cocktails inspired by their homeland, including the From Russia with Love, adapted from a recipe by Nebojsa Kutlesic, head bartender at London's Skylon restaurant. A highly floral take on the Moscow Mule, it's bold and bracing like a Siberian winter and smooth enough to entice more than a few vodka-only purists.

From Russia with Love

Makes 1 drink

1½ ounces vodka

¾ ounce ginger syrup (page 5)

½ ounce elderflower liqueur

½ ounce fresh lime juice

Club soda, to top

1 piece candied ginger, for garnish

Combine the vodka, ginger syrup, elderflower liqueur, and lime juice in a shaker. Add 1 or 2 ice pebbles, shake briefly, and pour into an ice-filled Collins glass. Skewer the piece of candied ginger with toothpicks and perch it on the rim of the glass.

VLADIMIR THE GREAT of Kievan Rus (the Slavic kingdom that eventually became Russia) was confronted with the choice of converting his formerly pagan lands to Christianity or to Islam around the year 980 CE. He chose Christianity, citing Islamic prohibitions on alcohol, and allegedly said, "Drinking is the joy of all Rus. We cannot exist without that pleasure."

SAN MARINO

"If it ain't broke, don't fix it" is a phrase that applies both to certain cocktail recipes and countries like San Marino. Both the oldest sovereign state and oldest constitutional republic, this landlocked microstate was founded in 301 CE and has had the same form of government since the thirteenth century, which seems to be working out nicely for its roughly 33,000 citizens. San Marino is among the wealthiest countries in Europe with some of its healthiest and long-lived people. And, despite having less than twenty-four square miles of semi-mountainous territory, there's a sizable wine-making region devoted to Biancale, a grape variety used in several dry, aromatic whites.

The Sammarinese also make mistrà, a triple-distilled, anise-forward liqueur that shares the name of nearly identical spirits produced in surrounding Italy. It's sipped straight or splashed on San Marino's other favorite beverage, the espresso, to enhance its flavor. For better or worse, the current standard-bearer for booze and cocktail collaboration is the Espresso Martini, which, unlike most tried-and-true classics, has a neutral vodka base that's ripe for tinkering. That's where the Marino Martini comes in. Sharing the same coffee and coffee liqueur template, it's embellished with a licorice aroma, spicy nuances, and a pleasantly dry finish, thanks to mistrà's infusions of both green and star anise. This is one eye-opening libation that all caffeine cronies should try at least once, regardless of their convictions about its predecessor.

Marino Martini

Makes 1 drink

1 ounce mistrà, preferably Mistrà di San Marino

1 ounce vodka

1 ounce freshly brewed espresso, chilled, or cold-brew concentrate

½ ounce coffee liqueur

½ ounce simple syrup (page 5)

Combine all the ingredients in an ice-filled shaker. Shake vigorously and strain into a coupe.

SERBIA

Making rakija—the Serbo-Croatian name for any high-proof brandy that's distilled from fermented fruit—is an age-old tradition in every former Yugoslavian republic, as well as in most of Eastern Europe. You might be tempted to assume that all of these are more or less the same, flavor-wise, but please don't say that to a Serbian if you value your physical health. The stiff-sipping spirit is the liquid heart and soul of this Balkan nation, with just about every family going to great pains to preserve its secret, generations-old recipe. Šljivovica, or plum rakija, is the most popular, cheapest, and strongest version; however it's not hard to find the clear liquor distilled with everything from peaches, apricots, or grapes to figs, quinces, and juniper berries.

All of these versions and more can be sampled at Rakija Fest, an annual celebration of the fruity phenomenon that pops off every September in Belgrade, the capital city. But if you visit during the colder months, you're more likely to be offered the national hooch in the form of a steamy Vruca Rakija ("hot brandy"), a Serbian toddy of sorts that's especially prevalent around the holidays and a requirement after the ceremonial Christmas Eve burning of the Yule log. There are countless variations, each probably well-guarded by someone's grandmother, but the simplest form of the drink—šljivovica, caramelized sugar, and hot water—is also one of the tastiest options.

Vruca Rakija

Serves 8 to 10

½ cup sugar

1½ cups šljivovica

3 cups water

Put the sugar in a heavy-bottomed medium stainless-steel pot. Heat over medium heat, stirring occasionally, until the sugar liquefies and turns a light brown color. Immediately remove from the heat and add the šljivovica and the water. Return the pot to medium heat and cook, stirring continuously, until the mixture comes to a boil and the sugar has completely melted. Remove from the heat. Serve hot in heat-safe glass mugs.

SLOVAKIA

The now-extinct House of Hapsburg is remembered today as a cautionary story about the devastating consequences of multigenerational royal inbreeding. In its heyday, however, the dynasty was a powerful political and economic force, ruling over much of Western and Central Europe until the late 1700s and facilitating the exportation of products like Slovakia's borovička to every corner of its empire. The clear or golden-hued brandy, which originated in the sixteenth century in the county of Liptov, gets its name from the Slovak word for juniper, *borievka*, and is flavored with that plant's berries. With a flavor that's similar to gin but slightly more intense, the liquor was an immediate hit in cities like Vienna and Budapest, though certainly not as much as in its own country, where International Juniper Brandy Day on June 24 is a major annual event.

While Slovaks like their borovička, which ranges from 35 to 70% ABV, straight and unadulterated, they also incorporate it, and any similar fruit brandies they can find, in some truly unique concoctions. None is as wild as the Hriatô, a traditional cold-weather potation sold on city streets that's been described as the world's only authentic bacon cocktail. This pork-infused caloric Clydesdale, appearing on the *Bake Your Slovak Roots* blog, adds fruity booze and honey to the simmering bits of swine for a sweet and salty shooter that's neither an aperitif nor a digestif but a meal itself. Be sure to consume it quickly, because, according to the recipe, the fat in this hot drink "sets really quickly." It goes without saying that vegetarians are going to want to sit this one out.

Hriatô

Makes 1 drink

1 small cube of lard or unsalted butter

1 strip thick-cut bacon, finely diced

½ ounce honey

2 ounces fruit brandy, such as slivovitz

Melt the lard in a medium saucepan over medium heat. Add the bacon and cook until crispy, 5 to 7 minutes. Add the honey and let the mixture bubble for 30 seconds. Add the brandy, reduce the heat to low, and simmer for 1 minute; do not let the mixture boil. Remove from the heat. Serve hot in a mug or heat-safe glass.

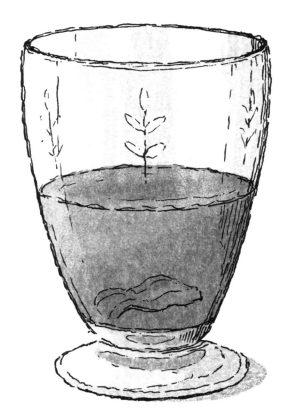

SLOVENIA

Western European countries like France, Italy, and Spain have long been considered to be some the world's premier wine cultivators. To the north, the Germans are just as famous for their dedication to brewing beer. And in many of the eastern Slavic states, potent spirits like vodka and brandy are a vital part of the cultural consciousness. Slovenia's advantageous location at the crossroads of all three regions has made it a prime destination for aficionados of just about every boozy tradition, with a powerfully diverse wine-making industry, an excellent selection of traditional local lagers and adventurous craft beers, lively liqueurs including Jägermeister-like pelinkovac, and fruit-based schnapps—or rakijas—such as borovnica (blueberry), medica (honey), and viljamovka (pear).

The most popular of these tangy powerhouses is slivovka—also known as slivovitz—which is infused with local plums and is synonymous with the most raucous nights spent in the company of friends—and the poor decision-making that tends to follow such festivities. That stigma is mainly due to Slovenians' (and most Europeans') propensity for shooting it neat, quickly, and often. But when sipped slower as part of a flawlessly balanced Slivopolitan, the damage is minimal, and the tastefulness is exponentially improved. Created by Dushan Zaric, cofounder of long-standing New York cocktail bar Employees Only, this citrusy sidecar/cosmopolitan variation is a revelation for plum lovers—as it also features plum puree alongside the plum brandy—and anyone intrigued by how delightful a notoriously hangover-producing spirit can be when surrounded by the right components.

Slivopolitan
Makes 1 drink

1½ ounces slivovitz

1 ounce Cointreau

¾ ounce plum puree

½ ounce fresh lime juice

1 plum slice, for garnish

Combine the slivovitz, Cointreau, plum puree, and lime juice in an ice-filled shaker. Shake vigorously and then double-strain into a coupe. Perch the plum slice on the rim of the glass.

SPAIN

"If penicillin can cure those who are ill," quipped Scottish physician and Nobel-prize-winning microbiologist Sir Alexander Fleming, "Spanish sherry can bring the dead back to life." It's a particularly impressive statement, given that none of Spain's many other contributions to global culture and art—the Spanish language, the Sagrada Família basilica, the Alhambra Gardens, *Don Quixote*, Pablo Picasso's paintings—have seldom been imbued, even facetiously, with the power of resurrection.

A fortified wine made from white grapes that grow in the vineyard-crazy region of Andalusia, sherry has been produced for nearly 1,300 years, when Moorish conquerors introduced distillation techniques to the region. Since then, this nutty, fruit-forward spirit has been linked to some of the most notorious moments and figures in Spain's history. Like Christopher Columbus, who loaded copious casks on his Spanish-funded voyages to the West Indies. Or sixteenth-century privateer Sir Francis Drake, who sacked the port of Cádiz during the Anglo-Spanish War and brought 2,900 barrels of sherry back to England, where it's still much beloved by British tipplers of all stripes.

Today, sherries come in a wide variety of flavors and styles, from light and dry Manzanilla and fino to caramel-like amontillado to molasses-dark and sweet Pedro Ximénez. Whatever your preference, the Sherry Cobbler—a fruity favorite of the low-ABV set since the 1810s—is a supremely refreshing way to enjoy all the grapey goodness while treating yourself to a healthy dose of vitamin C. The following version adds a dollop of Spain's popular herbal liqueur, Licor 43, for an even more authentic Iberian experience. It probably won't raise the dead, but it's just the thing for when a nasty hangover—or life in general—has got you feeling like a walking corpse.

THE SHERRY COBBLER was instrumental in popularizing one of the nineteenth century's most important inventions—drinking straws—which were originally made of actual straw, wood, or even macaroni.

Sherry Cobbler

Makes 1 drink

2 ounces Spanish sherry

½ ounce simple syrup (page 5)

¼ ounce Licor 43

1 lime wedge

1 lemon wedge

1 orange slice

1 strawberry, halved

1 blackberry

Crushed ice

1 mint sprig, for garnish

Combine the sherry, simple syrup, Licor 43, and fruit in a shaker. Muddle and pour into a tall glass. Fill with crushed ice, add a straw, and garnish with the mint sprig.

SWEDEN

Sweden has long been recognized as a bastion of progressive ideologies, a place that champions gender equality, and the birthplace of some of the most killer pop acts, from ABBA to Ace of Base. That's not to say that Scandinavia's oldest and most populous country isn't greatly steeped in its own heritage. Holidays like Midsommar that date back to the Viking age are still widely celebrated, as are old-school drinks like punsch, an aromatic liqueur dating to the eighteenth century, and glögg, a mulled drink consisting of red wine, sugar, orange zest, and spices. For an extra kick, the latter is often splashed with local akvavit that's made with dill, caraway, and, in most Swedish varieties, fennel and coriander, and is frequently served as a festive shot.

While it's not hard to find a well-made libation here, especially in the larger cities, Swedish cocktail tastes tend to be as traditional as the local spirits. Most menus play it safe with old-fashioneds, daiquiris, piña coladas, and the like, though there are some bartenders who have begun tinkering with these well-worn templates in new and intriguing ways. Like Maria Hallhagen, based at Paradiso in Stockholm's up-and-coming Södermalm neighborhood, whose Tjolahopp puts a floral, fragrant, and 100% Swedish spin on the classic Negroni. With a dual base of akvavit and gin—which, thanks to a boom in local distilleries, has become the spirit of choice for many Swedes—as well as hefty notes of elderflower, another favorite local flavor, it's got a nose that's fresher than the chorus of "Gimme! Gimme! (A Man After Midnight)" and a mildly bitter and refreshing finish to get any Midsommar party jumping faster than the opening bars of "I Saw the Sign."

Tjolahopp

Makes 1 drink

¾ ounce Campari
¾ ounce elderflower liqueur
½ ounce akvavit
½ ounce dry gin
1 strip of lemon peel

Combine the Campari, elderflower liqueur, akvavit, and gin in a double rocks glass. Add ice and stir with a long-handled spoon for 5 or 6 seconds. Express the oils from the lemon peel over the rim of the glass and then discard the peel.

FROM 1919 TO 1955, Swedish drinkers had their alcohol consumption regulated by the Bratt System. Every citizen of legal drinking age was given a booklet called a motbok, in which every alcohol purchase was recorded and stamped. When a certain number of bottles had been purchased, the motbok's owner would have to wait until the following month to buy more booze. Imbibers could purchase a nearly unlimited amount of wine, but liquor was capped at less than 2 liters per month.

SWITZERLAND

Since emerging as a confederacy within the Holy Roman Empire in 1291, Switzerland has been a hub of innovation. The landlocked Alpine country was the first to explore political concepts like direct democracy and armed neutrality and was the birthplace of widely used inventions like the Swiss Army knife, Velcro, white chocolate, and LSD. Perhaps the most controversial Swiss creation is absinthe, the exceptionally high-proof spirit (up to 75% ABV) with a distinctive, licorice-like flavor and verdant hue—thanks to a mixture of green anise, sweet fennel, and other herbs—and alleged hallucinogenic properties due to trace amounts of the chemical thujone.

Originally distilled in the Neuchâtel region in the late 1700s, the "green fairy" gained special prominence among Europe's late-1800s and early-1900s bohemian set, particularly in cities like Paris, and was a favorite of painters like Vincent van Gogh and Henri de Toulouse-Lautrec and writers like Lewis Carroll and Oscar Wilde. And though it was banned in much of Europe and the United States by 1915—due to fears by art-hating conservative busybodies about its (unproven) harmful effects—it's experienced a resurgence since the 1990s, when food and beverage laws became far less tyrannical.

In the cocktail world, absinthe has played a role in countless classics like the Sazerac, Corpse Reviver No. 2, and Pan American Clipper. Due to the intense, in-your-face nature of its botanicals, it's usually used like bitters, a sidekick ingredient meant to highlight and embellish other flavors in drinks. But it does occasionally take center stage in boozy numbers like the Absinthe Suissesse ("Swiss Absinthe"), an old-school New Orleans brunch favorite with a nutty, minty, and creamy bouquet that, despite its full ounce and a half of the green fairy, still maintains a balanced finish that's both sweet and refreshing.

Today's bartenders have continued to find new and exciting ways to incorporate absinthe's intensely bittersweet, licorice-like notes into unexpectedly delicious potations. Like the Matterhorn, adapted from a recipe that appeared in *Bohemian Mixology: Alternate Spirits & Modern Cocktails* (2022) by British photographer and writer David Jordan Melia. Bracing, spicy, herbaceous, citrusy, and minty, there's something in this mountainous ode to the Swiss countryside for everyone.

Absinthe Suissesse

Makes 1 drink

1½ ounces absinthe

1 ounce heavy cream

½ ounce crème de menthe

½ ounce orgeat

1 egg white

1 dash orange blossom water

Combine all the ingredients in a shaker. Shake without ice for 5 or 6 seconds to emulsify the egg white, then add ice and shake vigorously. Strain into a highball or Collins glass.

Matterhorn

Makes 1 drink

¾ ounce absinthe

¾ ounce Amaro Montenegro

¾ ounce ginger syrup (page 5)

¾ ounce fresh lime juice

2 dashes mint bitters

1 mint sprig, for garnish

Combine the absinthe, Amaro Montenegro, ginger syrup, lime juice, and bitters in an ice-filled shaker. Shake vigorously and strain into a double rocks glass over ice. Place the mint sprig in the glass beside the ice.

PERHAPS THE MOST famous American absinthe devotee, Ernest Hemingway is also the creator of the Death in the Afternoon cocktail, which first appeared in celebrity-penned compilation *So Red the Nose, or Breath in the Afternoon* (1935). The two-ingredient slammer is famed both for its mind-numbing potency and Hemingway's charmingly exacting recipe: "Pour one jigger absinthe into a Champagne glass. Add iced Champagne until it attains the proper opalescent milkiness. Drink three to five of these slowly."

Absinthe Suissesse

UKRAINE

If anything, recent military conflicts have illustrated just how fundamentally valuable Ukraine is to both its longtime antagonist, Russia, and its neighbors to the west—but that importance is nothing new for Europe's second-largest country. Often described as living in the continent's "breadbasket," Ukrainian farmers harvested virtually all the Soviet Union's wheat during the communist era and still supply grains to neighbors like Moldova, as well as to developing countries in Africa and Asia, accounting for nearly 20 percent of global wheat exports. For centuries, the country has also been the world's biggest exporter of sunflower products and a noted producer of vodkas that are, unsurprisingly, distilled with wheat.

When sipped straight from a chilled bottle, the Slavic nation's favorite liquor is lauded for its smoothness and purity, but Ukrainian imbibers prefer to gussy up their booze with all manner of herbs, fruits, roots, and berries. One of the most popular of these infusions (known as horilka) is khrenovykha, which introduces horseradish, lemon, and honey to the neutral spirit. The Kyiv Hornet, named for Ukraine's capital, converts that spicy and sweet flavor profile into cocktail form. Featuring horseradish-infused vodka based on a recipe from Dylan Prime that appeared in the *New York Times*, the drink is reminiscent of other citrus- and honey-backed classics like the Bee's Knees and Gold Rush, but with a funky, salty, and fiery complexity befitting one of the world's most complicated socio-political environments.

VODKA, WHICH TRANSLATES to "little water" in several Slavic languages, is not just useful for making bad decisions, it's also great for your hair. Mixing a tablespoon of vodka with a cup of water and pouring it over your head as part of a deep conditioning routine can help eliminate frizz, soothe an itchy scalp, and reduce dandruff, leaving your locks shinier and more luscious.

Kyiv Hornet

Makes 1 drink

Celery salt, for rimming the glass
1 lemon wedge, for rimming the glass
2 ounces Horseradish-Infused Ukrainian Vodka (recipe follows)
¾ ounce fresh lemon juice
¾ ounce honey syrup (page 5)

Spread some celery salt over a small plate. Run the lemon wedge around the rim of a double rocks glass, then dip the rim into the celery salt to coat. Fill the glass with ice and set aside. Combine the vodka, lemon juice, and honey syrup in an ice-filled shaker. Shake vigorously and then strain into the prepared glass.

Horseradish-Infused Ukrainian Vodka

Makes one 750ml bottle

2 ounces fresh horseradish root (see Note)
1 (750ml) bottle Ukrainian vodka, such as Nemiroff Delikat
2 tablespoons whole black peppercorns
1 tablespoon celery seed

Peel the horseradish and cut it into fine shreds with a vegetable peeler. Pour 1 cup of the vodka into a separate container and set aside. Using a funnel, add the peppercorns and celery seeds to the vodka bottle. Add the horseradish, then top off the bottle with the reserved vodka. Cover and let stand at room temperature for 24 hours. Strain the vodka through a fine-mesh sieve and return it to the bottle for storage. It will keep indefinitely.

NOTE: When prepping the fresh horseradish, be sure to work in a well-ventilated area, as the strong fumes can be irritating.

UNITED KINGDOM

It's impossible to understate, for better or worse, the United Kingdom's vast influence on global culture and politics for the past several centuries. Once the seat of a London-based empire that controlled huge territories on every continent, the British Isles' predominant language and legal system are still spoken and practiced by billions of people today, including citizens of the fifteen Commonwealth realms who acknowledge the British monarch as their (mostly) symbolic head of state.

That worldwide reach has made England's native liquor, gin, one of the planet's most well-known spirits. A grain distillate flavored by juniper and other botanicals, it's a descendant of the malty and medicinal jenever that had been produced in Belgium and the Netherlands since the early Renaissance era, and, by the middle of the eighteenth century, was the beverage of choice at more than half of London's abundant drinking establishments. While distillation methods became more refined in its home country—thanks to the introduction of pot stills—gin's popularity surged among British sailors in the form of a gin and tonic, one of the earliest British mixed drinks, whose quinine content was crucial for fending off malaria while delivering a smooth, sea-leg-settling buzz.

Subsequent years gave rise to several now-classic gin-based libations birthed in the UK, such as the Gimlet, John Collins, Vesper Martini, and the Dubonnet Cocktail, a combination of fortified wine and London dry gin that was a favorite of Queen Elizabeth II. But no drink is perhaps as quintessentially British as the Pimm's Cup (page 198). Created in the early 1800s by restaurateur James Pimm and served at his London oyster bar, the mouthwatering punch traditionally features a gin-infused herbal liqueur—eventually trademarked as Pimm's No. 1—various muddled fruits, and either citrusy soda or ginger ale. Considered by many to be the kingdom's official summertime refresher, it's the most popular cocktail at events like the Henley Royal Regatta, Chelsea Flower Show, Glyndebourne Festival Opera, and the Wimbledon tennis tournament, where tens of thousands of Pimm's Cups are quaffed by spectators each year.

The combination of gin and fruit has continued to inspire British drink slingers well into the modern era. One of these is Dick Bradsell, best known as the creator of the Espresso Martini, whose 1980s stint at Fred's Club in London also led to the invention of the Bramble (page 198). Named for the bush that blackberries grow on and inspired by classic drinks like the Gin Fix, this icy refresher is both sour and slightly sweet thanks to crème de mûre, a blackberry liqueur. In the early 2000s, bartenders at places like New York's Milk & Honey began tweaking Bradsell's recipe by substituting the liqueur for freshly muddled blackberries. Both recipes are delightful—and delightfully simple—examples of contemporary British mixology.

England isn't the only constituent country in the UK with its own signature liquor. The whiskies produced in Northern Ireland, Wales, and Scotland are far older than gin, and, in the case of Scotch, nearly as globally popular. That peaty spirit, made with malted barley since the late 1400s, is the base in what is perhaps Europe's earliest mixed drink, the Athol Brose (page 200). A sweet and smoky blend of Scotch, honey, and cream that's been around since at least 1475, it's attributed to John Stewart, 1st Earl of Atholl, who allegedly trapped one of his enemies by filling a well with the tempting concoction. The definitive modern version, as described in Charles H. Baker Jr.'s *The Gentleman's Companion* (1939), has become Scotland's unofficial holiday tipple.

The only UK constituent country located outside the island of Great Britain, Northern Ireland shares many cultural similarities with its southern neighbor, the Republic of Ireland, including its ancient history of whiskey making. Distilleries on both sides of the border use virtually the same ingredients and techniques, meaning that brands such as Belfast's Bushmills—distilled in County Antrim since 1784—are simply considered Irish whiskeys, regardless of their country of origin. One thing for which Northern Ireland can take sole credit is the invention of ginger ale, which was first whipped up by Belfast apothecary Thomas Cantrell in the 1850s. That spicy and fizzy flavor profile combines with local whiskey in the Belfast Buck (page 200), a lovely gingery highball that's equally satisfying to Irish aficionados of any political persuasion.

Unlike in other UK whisky-producing regions, Wales's ancient distilleries had completely disappeared by the early twentieth century due to a particularly vociferous temperance movement. That changed in 2000 with the opening of the Penderyn Distillery, which, like most of the modern Welsh operations that have sprung up in recent decades, produces several varieties of single-malt, barrel-aged whiskies that are similar in style to Scotch, but with a lighter, sweeter, and fruitier flavor profile. Penderyn is also the preferred base in the Large Coal (page 200), a belly-warming, boilermaker-like concoction that's sipped in cold weather and is a nod to Wales's longtime mining industry.

Pimm's Cup

Makes 1 drink

2 ounces Pimm's No. 1

3 thin cucumber slices

1 lemon wedge

1 lime wedge

1 thin orange slice

1 strawberry, halved

1 blackberry

1 brandied cherry

Lemon-lime soda, to top

1 mint sprig, for garnish

Combine the Pimm's, 1 cucumber slice, the lemon wedge, lime wedge, orange slice, strawberry, blackberry, and brandied cherry in a shaker. Muddle, then pour into a Collins glass. Add ice and top with the lemon-lime soda. Skewer the remaining 2 cucumber slices with the mint sprig and perch them on the rim of the glass.

Bramble

Makes 1 drink

2 ounces London dry gin

1 ounce fresh lemon juice

2 teaspoons simple syrup (page 5)

Crushed ice

½ ounce crème de mûre

1 lemon wedge, for garnish

1 blackberry, for garnish

Combine the gin, lemon juice, and simple syrup in an ice-filled shaker. Shake vigorously and then strain into a double rocks glass filled with crushed ice. Slowly drizzle the crème de mûre over the top of the drink. Garnish with the lemon wedge and blackberry.

Fresh Bramble

Makes 1 drink

2 ounces London dry gin

¾ ounce fresh lemon juice

¾ ounce simple syrup (page 5)

5 blackberries

Crushed ice

Combine the gin, lemon juice, and simple syrup in a shaker. In a double rocks glass, muddle 4 blackberries, then fill the glass two-thirds of the way with crushed ice. Add the contents of the shaker and top with more crushed ice. Garnish with the remaining blackberry.

Pimm's Cup

Athol Brose

Makes 1 drink

2¼ ounces Scotch

½ ounce honey syrup (page 5)

Whipped cream, for serving

Combine the Scotch and honey syrup in an ice-filled mixing glass. Stir with a long-handled spoon for 30 seconds and then strain into a coupe. Float some whipped cream on top.

Athol Brose

Belfast Buck

Makes 1 drink

2 ounces Irish whiskey from Northern Ireland, such as Bushmills

¾ ounce ginger syrup (page 5)

½ ounce fresh lime juice

Club soda, to top

1 piece candied ginger, for garnish

Combine the whiskey, ginger syrup, and lime juice in a shaker. Add 1 or 2 ice pebbles, shake briefly, and pour into an ice-filled Collins glass. Top with club soda. Skewer the piece of candied ginger with toothpicks and perch it on the rim of the glass.

Large Coal

Makes 1 drink

4 ounces stout beer, such as Guinness

2 ounces Welsh whisky, such as Penderyn Legend

Fill a double rocks glass with hot water to warm it. Warm the beer in a medium saucepan over low heat until it begins to froth; don't let it come to a boil. Discard the water from the glass. Pour the whisky into the glass, followed by the warm beer.

VATICAN CITY

At 121 acres—about four city blocks—the world's smallest sovereign state is barely a speck on any map. But make no mistake, Vatican City means serious business. Specifically, the business of tending to the spiritual needs of more than 1.3 billion baptized Catholics scattered around the globe. Thanks to their support—and hefty donations—this ancient enclave in the middle of Rome remains a formidable political entity under the rule of the last absolute monarch in Europe, Pope Francis I.

In addition to being the official residence of a few hundred clergy members, diplomats, Swiss Guards, and a handful of laypeople, the Vatican is also home to some truly jaw-dropping works of art, from the frescoes in the Sistine Chapel and the ornate Renaissance architecture of Saint Peter's Basilica to the approximately 70,000 publicly displayed works at the Vatican Museums. And if modern practices are any indication, at least some of that creativity was encouraged by a beverage or three. Though there's only one museum bar in the entire country, the Vatican's citizens consume more wine per capita than any other nation—an impressive 76 bottles a year per person.

This love of the grape also partially fuels Mikki Kristola's divinely crushable Vatican City cocktail, which features blanc vermouth, a slightly sweet and delicate fortified wine. Adding to the bubbly sipper's refreshing complexity is Suze, a bitter, gentian-based liqueur produced in France (which was the home of several popes in the 1300s) and readily available at any decent Roman spirits shop. While this rickey riff has a low enough alcohol content to keep you on reasonably good behavior during a trip to one of the world's most solemn locales, it's probably best to swear off the booze completely if you're able to score a rare audience with His Holiness.

Vatican City
Makes 1 drink

1 ounce Suze
1 ounce blanc vermouth
1 ounce fresh lime juice
¾ ounce simple syrup (page 5)
Club soda, to top
1 grapefruit twist, for garnish

Combine the Suze, vermouth, lime juice, and simple syrup in a shaker. Add 1 or 2 ice pebbles, shake briefly, and pour into a Collins glass filled with ice. Top with club soda. Place the grapefruit twist in the glass beside the ice.

North
Pacific
Ocean

CANADA

UNITED
STATES

MEXICO

THE
BAHAMAS

CUBA

BELIZE

JAMAICA

HONDURAS

GUATEMALA

EL SALVADOR

NICARAGUA

PANAMA

*North
Atlantic
Ocean*

BERMUDA

**BARBADOS
TRINIDAD AND TOBAGO**

NORTH
AMERICA

ANTIGUA AND BARBUDA

Lying at the meeting point of the Caribbean Sea and the Atlantic Ocean, Antigua and Barbuda, at 170 square miles, is one of the smallest nations in the world. Size isn't everything, however, as this multi-isle segment of the Leeward Islands is chock-full of gorgeous nature, mouthwatering eats, and tempting boozy beverages. Visitors to Antigua (the country's largest island at 14 by 11 miles) can spend the day relaxing at one of several hundred beaches or working up a thirst on a hike to the top of Mount Obama—once called Boggy Peak but renamed in 2009 in honor of the former US president—and quenching it with several highly regarded local rums produced at Antigua Distillery in the capital city of St. John's.

Whether you fancy a simple liquid lunch or a feast of regional delicacies like grilled lobster, saltfish, sweet potato dumplings, or fungie, a national dish that's similar in texture to Italian polenta, Uncle Roddy's is the place to be. Located on the southwest coast of the second-largest island Barbuda, this popular solar-powered beach bar and restaurant is known for both its seafood and its signature cocktail, the Barbuda Smash. The base is Antigua Distillery's impeccably smooth English Harbour five-year-old rum, a molasses-based spirit aged in oaken casks with lovely notes of vanilla and cinnamon. Combined with diced coconut and classic Caribbean modifiers pineapple, lime, Cointreau, and bitters, it's a potent personification of this proud and occasionally neglected slice of the tropics.

Uncle Roddy's Barbuda Smash

Makes 1 drink

1 tablespoon finely diced fresh coconut

3 ounces pineapple juice

2 ounces English Harbour Antigua Rum 5 Year

1 ounce Cointreau

½ ounce fresh lime juice

2 dashes Angostura bitters

1 lime wedge, for garnish

Put the coconut in a tall glass and fill the glass two-thirds of the way with ice. Combine the pineapple juice, rum, Cointreau, and lime juice in a shaker. Add 1 or 2 ice pebbles, shake briefly, and pour into the glass. Add the bitters and top with more ice. Perch the lime wedge on the rim of the glass.

THE BAHAMAS

US astronaut Scott Kelly once claimed that the Bahamas "is the most beautiful place from space," an opinion that's been echoed by many of his colleagues. Those who have been lucky enough to observe the turquoise waters and pink sand beaches of this archipelagic nation up close will find it hard to disagree with the sentiment, especially with an icy rum-forward beverage in hand(s). Like the rest of the Caribbean, the sugarcane-based spirit has played a prominent role in the country's history since the seventeenth century, when pirates would quaff bottles while evading colonial authorities on its approximately 3,000 islands, cays, and islets. In the 1920s, the Bahamas' proximity to Florida made it a prime location for rum runners looking to profit from Prohibition and provide thirsty Americans with a blessed respite from sobriety.

Today, that tradition is carried on by numerous local producers, most notably Paradise Island's John Watling's Distillery, which dates to 1789 and still churns out four types of harmoniously smooth aged rums. And while these might not be as globally fashionable as varieties from nearby Cuba or Jamaica, they shine in the Bahamas' plethora of home-grown tropical classic cocktails, of which the Bahama Mama is undoubtedly the biggest star. Dueling coconut and dark rums make blissful peace in this stress-melting smoothie that's enthusiastically enjoyed by both locals and tourists. But beware, as this sweet and summery liquid candy does have a bit of an edge that, combined with a few too many hours in the sun, might have you feeling as spacey as an astronaut.

Bahama Mama

Makes 1 drink

1½ ounces coconut rum

½ ounce aged rum

1 ounce pineapple juice

1 ounce fresh orange juice

½ ounce pomegranate syrup (page 5)

1 lime wedge

Crushed ice

1 thin orange slice, for garnish

1 brandied cherry, for garnish

Combine the rums, pineapple juice, orange juice, pomegranate syrup, and lime wedge in a shaker. Gently muddle the lime wedge and then pour the contents of the shaker into a tall glass. Fill the glass two-thirds of the way with crushed ice, add a straw, then top with more crushed ice. Garnish with the orange slice and brandied cherry.

BARBADOS

It's no secret that the Caribbean is the preeminent rum-producing region in the world, with virtually every major island distilling its own commercially produced and home-made varieties. But only Barbados is considered the birthplace of the sugar-based spirit. The island nation's robust industry dates to the early seventeenth century, when a group of Jewish immigrants fleeing persecution in South America was able to successfully cultivate sugarcane and harness the magic of its boozy biproduct. Barbados's legendary Mount Gay distillery is the world's oldest, having operated continuously since at least 1703 and producing rums that, like most Bajan varieties, are highly regarded for their crisp and aromatic flavors and bold finishes, as well as being excellent base spirits in all manner of mixed drinks.

Speaking of cocktails, Barbados is also responsible for one of the oldest forms of the Swizzle, a family of tall coolers that are all about booze, citrus, bitters, and lots of ice. The Barbados Rum Swizzle, which dates to the early 1800s, sticks to the script: a straightforward accompaniment of lime juice, sugar, and Angostura bitters that allows the rum's best qualities to shine through and show why Bajans—and spirits lovers across the globe—can't get enough of their country's liquid gold. If you do want to get a little fancier, feel free to add a cocktail umbrella as a secondary garnish in honor of Barbados's other wildly famous export, the singer and business mogul Rihanna. We won't judge!

For a boozier take on Barbados's signature spirit, there's no bigger bang for your buck than the Corn 'n' Oil. This classic and highly potent team-up of Caribbean flavors—molasses, falernum, citrus, and a mountainous heaping of bitters—has been tantalizing Bajan palates since the 1700s. It's sometimes said, erroneously, that the "oil" in the drink's name refers to the blackstrap rum—often from St. Croix or Jamaica—that appears in modern recipes. But if you value historical accuracy, it's crucial—and in my humble opinion, tastier—to use a rum from the island where it all started.

Barbados Rum Swizzle

Makes 1 drink

2 ounces aged Barbados rum

1 ounce fresh lime juice

¾ ounce simple syrup (page 5)

Crushed ice

4 dashes Angostura bitters

1 mint sprig, for garnish

Combine the rum, lime juice, and simple syrup in a shaker. Pour into a tall glass filled two-thirds of the way with crushed ice. Add the bitters and stir briefly with a swizzle stick. Add a straw and fill the glass to the top with crushed ice. Garnish with the mint sprig.

Corn 'n' Oil

Makes 1 drink

2 ounces aged Barbados rum

½ ounce falernum, such as John D. Taylor's Velvet Falernum

1 lime wedge

10 dashes Angostura bitters

Combine all the ingredients in a double rocks glass. Gently muddle the lime wedge. Add ice and stir with a long-handled spoon for 5 or 6 seconds.

WHEN THINGS are getting spicy at the end of a hot date, Bajan couples might opt for a nightcap of dehydrated sea moss mixed with milk and sugar, a drink that's said to increase romantic "energy" for both men and women.

BELIZE

Although Belize's interior—mountainous, densely jungled, and full of ancient Mayan ruins—aligns with those of its Central American neighbors, its picturesque beaches, stress-melting seaside resorts, and rum-centric drinking culture give much of the country an unmistakably Caribbean flair. But unlike most of those islands, rum production here is a recent affair, only dating to the 1950s, when Belizean landowners realized that their abundant sugarcane crops could be put to a much nobler purpose than simply sweetening food. Today, the local industry is dominated by Travellers Liquor, producers of several varieties of gold and white rums, including the fantastically popular Kuknat coconut rum, which is synonymous with Belize's easy-living ethos.

Perhaps the tastiest way to enjoy Kuknat's notes of natural coconut essence, butterscotch, oak, and vanilla is in a Dragon Fruit Mojito. Served at the Lodge at Chaa Creek, a popular inland vacation destination and nature reserve, the colorful mix of coconut rum, dragon fruit, lime, and mint features ingredients that grow in abundance in Belizean forests. And despite its fierce mythological moniker, this glass of liquid sunshine is about as peaceful on the taste buds as possible. It's the perfect sweet and fruity companion for any climate, though it's best enjoyed with toes firmly entrenched in the tropical sand.

Dragon Fruit Mojito
Makes 1 drink

5 or 6 mint leaves, plus 1 sprig for garnish

2 small (1-inch) squares dragon fruit

1 brown sugar cube

2 ounces Belizean coconut rum, such as Travellers Kuknat rum

1 ounce fresh lime juice

¾ ounce simple syrup (page 5)

Cracked or crushed ice

Club soda, to top

1 lime wedge, for garnish

Muddle the mint leaves, dragon fruit, sugar cube, rum, lime juice, and simple syrup in a Collins glass. Fill the glass two-thirds of the way with cracked or crushed ice, add a straw, and top with club soda. Perch the lime wedge on the rim of the glass and place the mint sprig in the glass beside the ice.

CANADA

Despite its famously blistering winters, pristine but mind-numbingly desolate landscapes with few populated areas, high taxes, and a language demarcation between French-speaking Quebec and the rest of its provinces, Canada is known for being home to some of the most genuinely friendly people on the planet. Maybe it's the booze. Whether they're getting rowdy at a hockey game, toasting to the latest Drake album release, or washing down a hearty bowl of poutine in subzero temperatures, Canadians consume far more alcohol per capita than the global average, slightly above their American neighbors.

When they're feeling especially patriotic, imbibers from British Columbia to Newfoundland opt for their country's unofficial national drink, the Caesar, a concoction that's as quirky (and some might say as foul) as an episode of *Trailer Park Boys*. Created in 1969 by Calgary restaurateur Walter Chell to re-create the flavors of a Venetian spaghetti and seafood dish, this Bloody Mary–style mix of vodka, clam broth, tomato juice, Worcestershire sauce, and spices was an Immediate smash hit and quickly found its way onto bar menus around the country. Today, the juice company Mott's—maker of Clamato—claims that 350 million Caesars are consumed annually, mostly north of the Canadian border. It might sound a little weird, but the unique blend of brine, heat, and umami is worth a (slap)shot.

If you're in the mood for something more traditional, break out some Canadian rye whisky. A grain-based spirit with a slightly higher corn content than its American cousin, it's been distilled since the eighteenth century and peaked in popularity during the 1920s and 1930s, when thirsty Yanks were forced to look beyond their borders for a decent dram. One of the best cocktails from that era, the Toronto (page 210), is an homage to Canada's most populous city, which was forced to suffer through its own (mildly enforced) alcohol ban from 1916 to 1927. It first appeared in print in Robert Vermeire's *Cocktails: How to Mix Them* (1922) as the Fernet Cocktail—due to the inclusion of that notoriously aggressive, menthol-like Italian amaro as a modifier—before receiving its current, city-specific moniker in David A. Embury's *The Fine Art of Mixing Drinks* (1948). Whatever you want to call it, Canadian rye's vegetal freshness and gentle palate subtly accented by Fernet-Branca's distinctive bite makes for a deliciously complex sipper that all whisky lovers will want to have in their repertoires.

Caesar

Makes 1 drink

Celery salt, for rimming the glass

1 lime wedge, for rimming the glass and garnish

4 ounces Clamato

1½ ounces vodka

2 dashes Worcestershire sauce

2 dashes Tabasco sauce

Prepared horseradish, to taste

1 celery stalk, for garnish

1 cucumber spear, for garnish

Spread some celery salt over a small plate. Run the lime wedge around the rim of a tall glass, then dip the rim into the celery salt to coat. Add ice and set aside (reserve the lime wedge for garnish). Combine the Clamato, vodka, Worcestershire, Tabasco, and horseradish in an ice-filled shaker. Shake gently for 5 to 10 seconds and strain into the prepared glass. Place the celery stalk, cucumber spear, and lime wedge in the glass.

Toronto (page 210)

Toronto

Makes 1 drink

2 ounces Canadian rye whisky

¾ ounce Fernet-Branca

¼ ounce simple syrup (page 5)

2 dashes Angostura bitters

1 orange twist, for garnish

Combine the whisky, fernet, simple syrup, and bitters in an ice-filled mixing glass. Stir with a long-handled spoon for 25 to 30 seconds and strain into a coupe. Place the orange twist in the glass.

JOINING AN EXCLUSIVE cocktail club sounds like a swanky proposition. But there's nothing posh about the Sourtoe Cocktail Club, based at the Downtown Hotel's Sourdough Saloon in Dawson City, Yukon Territory. The only requirement for membership is finishing a Sourtoe Cocktail, which consists of an ounce of alcohol and a mummified human toe that must touch your lips before you finish the booze. The gnarly concoction debuted in 1973, when a Dawson City local found a 1920 bootlegger's toe preserved in moonshine and proceeded to drop it in his shot of whiskey as a dare. Since then, more than 100,000 people have accepted the challenge, which features a rotation of preserved toes donated by their former owners.

COSTA RICA

Since the earliest days of Spanish and Portuguese influence in the Western Hemisphere, distillers in virtually every Central and South American country have been making aguardiente ("firewater"), a generic term for boozy beverages ranging between 29 and 60% ABV and derived from a wide variety of sources. The tropical paradise of Costa Rica is no exception. From its tranquil Caribbean and Pacific shores to the mountainous jungles between, locals and tourists alike enjoy guaro, the country's national liquor, a potent aguardiente made with sugarcane with a taste that's been described as somewhere between vodka and white rum.

While the production of homemade hooch is rampant—which, unfortunately, has led to several poison-related fatalities in recent years—the only "official" guaro is distilled by Fábrica Nacional de Licores (the National Liquor Factory) and marketed as Guaro Cacique (30% ABV) and Cacique Superior (35% ABV). Both brands, though occasionally difficult to find outside of Central America, are globally respected for their smoothness and purity. Which is a huge deal for eco-friendly Costa Ricans. Their unofficial motto, *pura vida*, literally translates to "pure life," and can be used as a greeting, a farewell, an expression of agreement or thanks, or simply a phrase encapsulating the nation's naturally laid-back, environmentally conscious culture.

Pura Vida is also the name of a super juicy, punch-like concoction that's been a popular staple at Costa Rican resort bars for decades. Guaro's mostly neutral flavor lends itself well to embellishment with sharp notes of orange and pineapple, playful citrusy bubbles, and a balancing hint of pomegranate. If vacation vibes are what you're seeking today—and really, who isn't?—this tropically succulent beauty should be at the top of your to-do list.

Pura Vida

Makes 1 drink

1½ ounces Guaro Cacique

½ ounce Cointreau

½ ounce fresh orange juice

½ ounce pineapple juice

¼ ounce pomegranate syrup (page 5)

Lemon-lime soda, to top

1 lime wedge, for garnish

Combine the Guaro Cacique, Cointreau, orange juice, pineapple juice, and pomegranate syrup in a shaker. Add 1 or 2 ice pebbles, shake briefly, and pour into a tall glass filled with ice. Top with the lemon-lime soda. Perch the lime wedge on the rim of the glass.

CUBA

The places with the highest quality sugarcane tend to produce some of the best rums, and Cuba is no exception. Sugar production started early in the Caribbean's largest island country, with Spanish farmers from the Canary Islands setting up the first plantations in 1511. It wasn't long before the indigenous peoples and Africans who were forced to toil there were turning sugarcane's by-product—molasses—into a homemade aguardiente that quickly gained popularity among Cubans of all social strata; some of whom began refining the often-abrasive firewater into the former Spanish colony's first rums.

International recognition for the spirit first came in the mid-1800s, when Facundo Bacardí developed a technique that eliminated impurities from sugarcane molasses, giving birth to an incredibly clean and smooth light rum. And while Bacardí's descendants fled Cuba during the 1950s socialist revolution, the adherence to impeccable distilling continues today with Havana Club, a joint venture between the Cuban government and Pernod Ricard that's been one of the most sought-after rum brands for decades.

Cuba's cocktail tradition is no joke, either. The birthplace of both the mojito and the daiquiri—two drinks that more than a few professional tipplers place in their cocktail Mount Rushmore—it was also the longtime home of Ernest Hemingway, who claimed to have invented several libations like the Hemingway Daiquiri while sitting at hallowed Havana haunts like El Floridita and Sloppy Joe's Bar. All three of these aforementioned libations are the spiritual precursors for the Old Cuban, a modern classic from Pegu Club's Audrey Saunders that was first served in 2001 at the dawn of the current cocktail renaissance. Minty, limey, bubbly, and decadently smooth, it's one of the classiest ways to experience Cuba's forbidden nectar, which hasn't been available for purchase in the United States for decades, as any American scouring foreign airports for a last-minute purchase at the duty-free shop knows all too well.

As anyone who's spent enough time around a bottle of Havana Club will tell you, citrus isn't a requirement in Cuban rum-based concoctions. Bartenders have crafted plenty of spirit-forward libations with the spirit over the years, the most renowned being the El Presidente, named after Mario Garcìa Menocal, who led Cuba for most of the 1910s. Especially popular among American tourists during Prohibition, the cheerful, well-balanced, Manhattan-esque sipper has been tweaked considerably since its heyday. The following recipe attempts to re-create the essence of the original by using equal parts rum and semidry blanc vermouth, with just enough curaçao for a finish that's fruity, but not overpoweringly so.

And of course, we'd be remiss not to include the classics, like the Daiquiri and the Mojito.

Hemingway Daiquiri

Makes 1 drink

1½ ounces light Cuban rum, such as Havana Club 3 Años

1 ounce fresh grapefruit juice

¾ ounce maraschino liqueur

½ ounce fresh lime juice

1 brandied cherry, for garnish

Combine the rum, grapefruit juice, maraschino liqueur, and lime juice in an ice-filled shaker. Shake vigorously and then strain into a coupe or sour glass. Drop the brandied cherry into the glass.

Old Cuban

Makes 1 drink

1 ounce aged Cuban rum, such as Havana Club 5 Años

½ ounce fresh lime juice

½ ounce simple syrup (page 5)

2 dashes Angostura bitters

Small handful of mint leaves, plus 1 leaf for garnish

Champagne, to top

Combine the rum, lime juice, simple syrup, bitters, and mint in an ice-filled shaker. Shake vigorously and strain into a coupe. Top with Champagne. Garnish with the mint leaf.

Old Cuban

El Presidente

Makes 1 drink

1½ ounces aged Cuban rum

1½ ounces blanc vermouth

¼ ounce curaçao

1 dash grenadine

1 orange twist, for garnish

Combine the rum, vermouth, curaçao, and grenadine in an ice-filled mixing glass. Stir with a long-handled spoon for 20 to 30 seconds and strain into a coupe. Place the orange twist in the glass.

Daiquiri

Makes 1 drink

2 ounces Cuban rum

1 ounce fresh lime juice

¾ ounce simple syrup (page 5)

1 lime wedge, for garnish

Combine the rum, lime juice, and simple syrup in an ice-filled shaker. Shake vigorously and then strain into a coupe. Perch the lime wedge on the rim of the glass.

Mojito

Makes 1 drink

2 ounces light Cuban rum, such as Havana Club 3 Años

1 ounce fresh lime juice

¾ ounce simple syrup (page 5)

5 or 6 mint leaves, plus 1 sprig for garnish

1 sugar cube

Crushed ice

Combine the rum, lime juice, simple syrup, mint leaves, and sugar cube in a shaker. Muddle gently and pour the contents of the shaker into a tall glass. Fill the glass two-thirds of the way with crushed ice. Add a straw and top with more crushed ice. Garnish with the mint sprig.

DOMINICA

Immediately upon touching down at Dominca's only international airport, you'll understand why the nation's nickname, "the Nature Isle," is more than well-earned. Covered by miles and miles of untouched jungle, it's a sanctuary for highly endangered species like the sisserou parrot and a playground for hikers looking to check out intimidatingly powerful waterfalls, soothing sulfur springs, and volcanically produced oddities like the Boiling Lake, a massive bubbling gash in the earth that looks like it would be more at home on the moon than in the Caribbean.

The country's high-proof "bush rum" culture is as wild as the ambiance. Tiny ramshackle street bars dot the few populated areas, each infusing home-distilled firewater with a range of medicinally minded infusions of local herbs like *chook chook* (culantro), *pueve* (pepper), and cannabis that are said to aid in digestion, lower cholesterol, and even function as a natural alternative to erectile dysfunction pills. Just one small distillery, Macoucherie, located near the beach town of Mero, offers thirty-six distinct versions of its 96-proof barrel-aged rum.

Other establishments focus on crafting tropical drinks that highlight the island's impressive array of indigenous and introduced fruits. Like Local Paradise, also located in Mero, a seaside bar famous for its selection of sweet local delicacies and infused potations. One of its signature libations, the Mero Beach Colada, is beloved by natives and tourists alike, and for good reason. Combining locally distilled rum, coconut cream, and the juices of readily available fruits like guava, papaya, and passion fruit, it's the best way to beat the tropical heat and a sweet and a trusty chaser for Dominica's notoriously mind-bending bush rum shots.

Mero Beach Colada

Makes 1 drink

1 lime wedge

2 ounces Dominican white rum, such as Macoucherie White Rum

1 ounce Coco López

1 ounce guava juice

½ ounce papaya juice

Crushed ice, for serving

½ ounce passion fruit juice

Pinch of freshly grated nutmeg, for garnish

Muddle the lime wedge in a shaker. Add the rum, Coco López, guava juice, papaya juice, and ice. Shake vigorously and then strain into a tall glass filled two-thirds of the way with crushed ice. Add a straw and top with more crushed ice. Sprinkle with the nutmeg.

DOMINICAN REPUBLIC

Like most Caribbean locales, much of the land that would become the Dominican Republic was converted into sugarcane plantations shortly after the arrival of Europeans in the fifteenth century. Unlike other nearby territories, however, that industry was largely extinct by the seventeenth century thanks to constant slave revolts and frequent pirate raids on port cities like Santo Domingo that made interisland trade nearly impossible at times. Most Dominican farmers fled the volatile coastline for the country's interior, where they switched to cattle ranching, stunting any nascent rum production for decades.

And while the country's rums, though quite tasty, are still not as highly regarded as, say, Cuba's or Puerto Rico's, the Dominican Republic proudly lays claim to one of the oldest distilled spirits in the Caribbean, Mamajuana. Originally a mixture of European liquors like brandy and traditional herbal teas brewed by the indigenous Taíno people, it quickly gained fame throughout the Americas as both a powerful medicine and an aphrodisiac, a reputation that persists today, although most Dominicans drink it solely for recreational purposes.

There are countless Mamajuana recipes, most of which infuse dark rum, red wine, and honey with a variety of herbs, spices, and bark from plants like *palo de Brasil* (brazilwood), *bohuco pega palo* (princess vine), and *uña de gato* (cat's claw). Some of these can be extremely hard find outside Latin America, so Dominicans living in places like the United States, including writer Carlos Matias, have developed their own versions made with easy-to-obtain ingredients that still simulate the traditional flavors of their homeland. Matias's Mamajuana, adapted from a recipe that first appeared in *Bon Appétit*, is chock-full of spicy standbys like cloves and anise, paired with eucalyptus and basil for a brisk, warming, and savory blend that may not inspire physical love, but always makes for a good time.

NOTE: You can adjust the ratios of the rum, red wine, and honey, if desired.

Mamajuana
Makes 1 (750ml) bottle

8 hibiscus petals

6 dried basil leaves

5 whole cloves

5 star anise pods

5 cinnamon sticks

5 allspice berries

4 dried eucalyptus leaves

2 tablespoons chicory root

1 (2-inch) piece fresh ginger

1 to 1½ cups Dominican dark rum, such as Brugal Añejo

1 to 1½ cups red wine

¼ cup honey

Combine the hibiscus petals, basil leaves, cloves, anise stars, cinnamon sticks, allspice berries, eucalyptus leaves, chicory root, and ginger root in an empty 750ml liquor bottle or 1-quart jar. Fill the bottle with the rum, red wine, and honey. Let the mixture steep for 1 month, shaking the bottle every few days to encourage extraction. Serve neat or over ice.

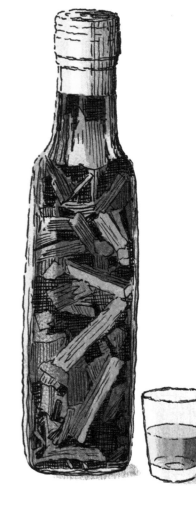

EL SALVADOR

Like the rest of Central America, El Salvador is a study in both collision and confluence. The region's smallest country by area was a prominent tributary of the Mayan Empire for nearly a thousand years—as evidenced by the still-impressive remnants of the ancient city of Chalchuapa—before its local customs and flavors were either obliterated or absorbed by conquering Spaniards during the colonial era. That biculturalism is most salient in Salvadorean Spanish, with its unusual number of indigenous words and phrases; in the country's cuisine that introduces Old World meat and seafood dishes to native spices, beans, and corn; and in popular beverages like horchata.

The name for this milky, cinnamon-infused drink comes from the Latin *hordeata*, derived from *hordeum*, meaning "barley." Consumed in North Africa as early as the eleventh century and possibly long before that, precursors of horchata became popular in Spain during the Muslim conquest and eventually found their way onto ships bound for the New World. In much of Latin America, it's now made with white rice instead of the tiger nuts that are used in the African and Spanish versions, along with various local spices. But Salvadoreans prefer their drink with freshly ground morro seeds from the calabash tree, which give the cloudy concoction a slightly sweeter, nuttier vibe, as well as a delightful warming finish when spiked with guaro, the local aguardiente, in a Dirty Horchata. These golden nuggets of plant-based goodness can be hard to track down outside of Central America, so feel free to buy pre-mixed horchata powder, which is readily available online. Just don't tell your Salvadorean amigos.

Dirty Horchata

Makes 1 drink

4 ounces whole milk
1½ ounces guaro
½ ounce coffee liqueur
1 tablespoon horchata de morro powder
Simple syrup (page 5)

Combine the milk, guaro, coffee liqueur, and horchata de morro powder in an ice-filled shaker. Shake vigorously and then strain into a double rocks glass over ice. Add simple syrup to taste.

GRENADA

Whether due to a lack of direct flights or a 2004 hurricane that temporarily wiped out its tourist industry, Grenada is one of the least-visited places in the Caribbean. And those who do find their way to this unspoiled, densely forested oasis—nicknamed "the Spice Isle" for its vast nutmeg, mace, and vanilla plantations—tend to like it that way. As there are very few population centers scattered across the country's main eponymous island and its two much smaller neighbors, Carriacou and Petite Martinique, it's possible to take hours-long jungle hikes, walk miles of pristine white-sand beaches, and enjoy diverse wildlife such as the critically endangered Grenada dove, all with little to no disturbance.

But if you'd like to experience Grenada's highly regarded, notoriously hard-to-find rums, you might want to make some friends. Distilleries like the fabled River Antoine, which has been churning out extremely high-proof bottles since 1785, sell so much of their supply to locals that they're unable to export any. Even if you can't manage the trip, or get on any Grenadians' good sides, you can still experience some of the country's signature flavors with its most popular tropical beverage, the Calabash Cocktail. This bodacious blend of rum, lime, and blue curaçao also features both Grenadian nutmeg syrup and grated nutmeg—which is totally on brand, as, amazingly, Grenada produces around 20 percent of the world's supply of the versatile spice. It's pure Caribbean bliss, with just the right amount of pungency to make it as interesting as the hidden gem from which it originates.

Calabash Cocktail

Makes 1 drink

1½ ounces Grenadian white rum, such as Clarke's Court Superior Light Rum
¾ ounce blue curaçao
¾ ounce fresh lime juice
¾ ounce Nutmeg Syrup (recipe follows)
Crushed ice
Pinch of freshly grated nutmeg, for garnish
1 lime wedge, for garnish

Combine the rum, curaçao, lime juice, and nutmeg syrup in a shaker. Pour into a tall glass filled two-thirds of the way with crushed ice. Add a straw and top with more crushed ice. Sprinkle with the nutmeg and perch the lime wedge on the rim of the glass.

Nutmeg Syrup

Makes about 2 cups

2 cups water
1 cup Demerara sugar
3 whole nutmeg seeds, halved

Combine all the ingredients in a saucepan. Bring to a light boil over medium heat, then reduce the heat just enough to keep it at full simmer (with small, gentle bubbles breaking the surface, not a rolling boil). Simmer for 30 minutes, until the syrup is thick enough to coat the back of a spoon. Remove from the heat and discard the nutmeg. Let cool completely, then pour into a large glass jar or bottle with a lid. Cover and store in the refrigerator for up to 1 month.

GUATEMALA

Like much of Central America, Guatemala's spirits scene is dominated by sugarcane-based beverages, but it wasn't always that way. For thousands of years, Mayans brewed cusha, a corn-based, fermented drink that they would use in rituals where shamans would drink it and spit it over participants to heal whatever ailed them. For many modern imbibers, getting hocked on doesn't sound like the best time, which is why, although cusha continues to be produced in indigenous communities, most Guatemalans prefer aguardiente or rum. And when it comes to the latter spirit, it doesn't get much better than Ron Zacapa Centenario.

Introduced in 1976 to celebrate the hundredth anniversary of the eastern Guatemalan village of Zacapa, this undeniably silky blend of rums aged six to twenty-three years is the result of unique stabilization and maturation techniques invented by local chemist Alejandro Burgaleta. The unusually high elevation of the factory in which it's produced creates a naturally cold environment that reduces evaporation during the aging process, also adding to its overall smoothness.

It's a no-brainer to use Zacapa in any number of spirit-forward libations like the Zegroni, created in 2011 by Taiwan's Mark Huang as his entry in a world bartending competition, which he won. Unlike its equal-parts predecessor, the Negroni, the amount of rum is ramped up here to fully appreciate Zacapa's unique flavor profile, with just enough of the trademark bittersweetness that happens when an Italian vermouth and herbal aperitif get together. A lovely testament to the long-standing global appeal of Guatemala's most important boozy export.

Zegroni

Makes 1 drink

1½ ounces Zacapa No. 23 Rum

¾ ounce sweet vermouth

¾ ounce Campari

1 orange twist, for garnish

Combine the rum, sweet vermouth, and Campari in a double rocks glass. Add ice and stir with a long-handled spoon for 5 or 6 seconds. Place the orange twist in the glass beside the ice.

GETTING SPIT on by a cusha-swilling shaman might actually be preferable to drinking the stuff—and far safer. Not only do cusha producers frequently use cow dung as a fermentation accelerator (yummy), but the unregulated hooch is often so strong that it can cause numerous health problems, including permanent blindness.

HAITI

Haiti has always done things a bit differently than its fellow independent Caribbean states. It's the only country created after a successful slave rebellion and the first predominantly Black republic in the world, the birthplace of Haitian Vodou and its unique beliefs in ancestral spirits and zombies, and home to a singular style of art that marries African, European, and indigenous island influences. Its locally produced hooch, clairin, also has several interesting characteristics that set it apart from most of the region's other sugarcane spirits. Like rhum Agricole from French islands Martinique and Guadeloupe—and unlike molasses-based Caribbean rums—the cane juice is fermented with yeast before distillation, resulting in a liquor that's raw, funky, and vegetal with an identity that's wholly its own.

For Haitians, clairin is much more than just booze. It's a cultural emblem, a liquid personification of the country's terroir, independent mindset, music, and people, as well as an indispensable part of Vodou ceremonies and national holidays. That proud tradition extends to cocktails with the Ti' Punch Kreyòl, a simple, outstanding mix of clairin, lime, and cane syrup that's considered an all-time Caribbean classic. The following recipe scales down the latter two ingredients to the bare minimum in order to fully appreciate clairin's grassy, rustic charm. However, in Haiti, it's often served *chacun prépare sa propre mort* (French for "each prepares their own death") where the bartender provides the ingredients and glassware but lets each drinker build their own to their taste. So feel free, like Haitian revolutionary leader Toussaint Louverture, to embrace liberation and fix this delicious sipper however you see fit.

Ti' Punch Kreyòl

Makes 1 drink

2 ounces clairin

¼ ounce cane syrup

1 lime wedge

Combine the clairin and cane syrup in a rocks glass. Squeeze the juice from the lime wedge into the glass, then run the peel side of the wedge around the rim of the glass and drop it into the glass. Add ice and stir with a long-handled spoon for about 10 seconds.

THERE ARE MORE than ten times the number of micro-distilleries in Haiti than the rest of the Caribbean combined (between 500 and 600, compared to fewer than 50). Most of these countryside establishments are little more than small shacks housing stills that provide enough rhum for a single village, or even just a small neighborhood.

HONDURAS

Upon arriving in Honduras in 1502, Christopher Columbus gave the country its current name, which means "depths" in Spanish, because of the unusually deep waters off its coast. That depth also applies to the Central American republic's countless natural and historical spectacles—hundreds of Mayan ruins, the largest reef system in the Western Hemisphere, more than 700 bird species including the endangered scarlet macaw—as well as its numerous varieties of indigenous alcohol. Like chicha, a fermented drink made with maize that was brewed throughout pre-Columbian America. Or coyol wine, a moonshine distilled from the sap of the coyol palm that's famous for causing brutal hangovers despite its relatively low ABV.

You likely won't find either of those tipples without making the trek to Honduras, but the country's most popular industrially produced booze, guaro, is now widely available outside of Central America. Identical to the aguardientes produced in nearby countries like Nicaragua and Costa Rica, it's a clear, strong, and somewhat neutral spirit that lends itself nicely to traditional Honduran cocktails such as Ponche de Piña, a kind of hot piña colada, and Rompopo, the nation's undisputed favorite wintertime concoction. Luxuriously creamy, the eggnog-style punch—adapted from a multi-serving recipe by Suellen Pineda—also has a pleasant nuttiness thanks to a "healthy" dollop of peanut butter and a rich, starchy, and mildly spicy mouthfeel, making it a welcome addition to any holiday get-together. And it can be the star of yours, as long as you've got an hour to spare during the most stressful time of the year.

THE EXACT SCIENCE behind coyol wine's proclivity for morning-after disasters is somewhat of a mystery. One popular theory suggests that exposure to the sun while drinking activates enzymes in the body that cause far more intoxication than ingesting the fermented beverage's relatively minuscule alcohol content. So if you must indulge, do it under the cover of darkness.

Rompopo, Honduran-Style

Serves 6 to 8

3 tablespoons cornstarch

4¼ cups cold whole milk

2 (12-ounce) cans evaporated milk

1 cinnamon stick

5 or 6 whole cloves

½ teaspoon pure vanilla extract

6 large egg yolks

1 cup sugar

1 tablespoon peanut butter

12 ounces aged or white rum

Freshly grated nutmeg, for garnish

In a measuring cup, dissolve the cornstarch in ½ cup of the whole milk and set aside. In a medium saucepan, combine the remaining 3¾ cups whole milk, the evaporated milk, cinnamon stick, and cloves and bring to a boil over high heat, stirring continuously. Reduce the heat to medium-low, add the cornstarch mixture, and stir vigorously with a wooden spoon until the spiced milk thickens. Remove from the heat, stir in the vanilla, and let cool to room temperature.

Meanwhile, in a large bowl, beat the egg yolks with a hand mixer on high speed until they turn a pale yellow color, 4 to 5 minutes. Add the sugar and peanut butter and beat until the mixture is well combined.

Pass the cooled milk mixture through a strainer to remove the cloves and cinnamon stick. Return the milk mixture to the saucepan and, while stirring continuously, very slowly pour in the egg mixture. Cook over medium heat, stirring continuously, for 7 to 10 minutes. Remove from the heat and let cool completely. Add the rum and refrigerate until chilled.

Serve in large mugs, garnished with the nutmeg.

JAMAICA

Funky. Spicy. Complex. One-of-a-kind. Those are just a few of the adjectives that describe Jamaica's vibrant culture, food, and music scenes. Not coincidentally, they're the same words spirits writers use when praising the island nation's inimitable contributions to the world of sugarcane-based booze. Bursting with notes of oak, caramel, pineapple, bananas, rubber, spice, and molasses, barrel-aged Jamaican rums are considered by many to be the best tasting, perfect for sipping straight or blended into any of the copious punches and cocktails that encapsulate the country's laid-back tropical ethos.

This distinctive flavor profile can be attributed both to Jamaica's limestone-rich soil and the use of pot stills, which arrived with English colonizers in the seventeenth century. The distillation process, which includes fermenting molasses in casks called puncheons before going into the still, makes for a heavier, more robust spirit that beautifully captures the essence of its unique terroir. Which is why brands like Smith & Cross, Appleton Estate (the second oldest rum distillery in the world), and Wray & Nephew are some of the most sought-after bottles on the global market.

Jamaican rum's worldwide popularity means that many cocktails featuring it were created elsewhere, but there are several palate-catching potations with origins on the island. The wildest of these is probably the Sea Cat Punch, which combines rum, boiled octopus ("sea cat" in the local parlance), rum cream, crushed peanuts, and protein powder. For a more accessible—and seafood-free—introduction to Jamaica's legendary hooch, the Planter's Punch is a better bet. Named for the sugarcane farmers who set up shop shortly after Christopher Columbus "discovered" Jamaica in 1494 and a favorite of Caribbean imbibers since the 1800s, it's tall, bright, and limey, and, more importantly, works exceedingly well with any Jamaican rum you can find.

While making for an exceptional standalone base, Jamaican rum's funkiness—or *hogo*, as it's known on the island—has long lent itself to collaboration with many other spirits, such as cognac in the Pineapple Milk (page 223), which appeared in Charles H. Baker Jr.'s *Jigger, Beaker and Glass: Drinking Around the World* (1895), a rare flip that's equal parts creamy, fruity, and yolky. Similarly, the Soursop Margarita (page 223), variations of which have been appearing on food and drink blogs in recent years, mixes tequila and Jamaican white rum with the tangy and sweet Caribbean fruit of the same name for an equally pleasing result.

Planter's Punch

Makes 1 drink

2 ounces Jamaican rum

1 ounce fresh lime juice

¾ ounce simple syrup (page 5)

4 dashes Angostura bitters

1 teaspoon grenadine

Club soda, to top

1 lime wedge, for garnish

Combine the rum, lime juice, simple syrup, bitters, and grenadine in a shaker. Add 1 or 2 ice pebbles, shake briefly, and pour into an ice-filled Collins glass. Top with club soda. Perch the lime wedge on the rim of the glass.

Pineapple Milk

Makes 1 drink

1½ ounces fresh pineapple juice

1 ounce Jamaican rum

1 ounce cognac

¾ ounce cane syrup

1 ounce heavy cream

1 egg

Combine all the ingredients in a shaker. Shake without ice for 5 or 6 seconds to emulsify the egg, then add ice and shake vigorously. Strain into a tall glass.

Soursop Margarita

Makes 1 drink

2 ounces soursop juice

½ ounce fresh lime juice

1 ounce tequila

¾ ounce Jamaican white rum, such as Wray & Nephew

½ ounce simple syrup (page 5)

1 dash Angostura bitters

1 lime wedge, for garnish

Combine the soursop juice, lime juice, tequila, rum, simple syrup, and bitters in an ice-filled shaker. Shake vigorously and then strain into a double rocks glass over ice. Perch the lime wedge on the rim of the glass.

Planter's Punch (page 221)

MEXICO

For more than 9,000 years, agave has been much more than just a plant to Mexicans. Prized by ancient cultures for its alleged divine properties, the sharp-leafed monocots (also known as magueys) have been used in medicine, food, textiles, and, since the introduction of distillation techniques by Spanish colonizers in the sixteenth century, some of the world's most treasured spirits. Made from extracted juices found in the mature heart (*piña*) or center of the plant, these liquors are commonly referred to as mezcals, of which there are more than thirty varieties that vary widely in taste, from smoky and earthy to fruity and peppery. Tequila, the most popular of these, is specifically derived from the blue agave plant and comes in an impressively wide array of styles and flavors.

Agave-based spirits are synonymous with the margarita, the world's most-ordered cocktail, which, in its original basic form, is a combination of tequila, triple sec, and lime juice. However, according to historical sources, the early twentieth-century drink was most likely created in the United States, in either California, Texas, or Syracuse, New York, where it was advertised in the 1930s as a Tequila Daisy.

For an undeniably authentic Mexican tipple, there are few tastier options than the Paloma (page 225). Originating, aptly, in the town of Tequila, Mexico, at La Capilla cantina, the lime-and-grapefruit-infused refresher is the country's official national drink and the most frequently served cocktail there. It takes its name from the popular 1860s folk song "La Paloma" ("The Dove") and flows liberally during the September 16 national holiday celebrating Mexico's victory over Spain in the 1821 War of Independence. But this light, fizzy, and delicious ode to native Mexican flavors is a perfect pick-me-up on any day of the year (and twice a day, when necessary). And while the earliest versions of the Paloma employed tequila, using smokier mezcals as the base has become an equally permissible, if not more popular, option.

While they're often associated with citrusy concoctions, both varieties of Mexico's signature hooch—as many spirit-forward aficionados profess—are ripe for exploration in a boozier, stripped-down fashion, letting the liquor speak for itself. It doesn't get more agave-heavy than the Oaxaca Old-Fashioned, invented in 2007 by Philip Ward of New York's Death & Co as an homage to the Mexican state that proudly holds the unofficial title of mezcal capital of the world. Simple yet sophisticated, smoky and serene, it's the perfect way to explore Mexico's terroir with no frills attached.

Long before the invention of mezcal, Mexico's Indigenous peoples were brewing pulque, a milky fermented beverage made from the sap of the agave plant. The viscous and sour, low-ABV brew—which the Aztecs called "the drink of the gods"—was used mostly in religious ceremonies until after the Spanish conquest, when it transitioned to its current status as a secular everyday tipple. Peaking in popularity in the late nineteenth century, pulque was ultimately replaced by beer as the after-work drink of choice, though it's experienced a bit of a renaissance recently, making its way into cocktails like the El Chacal (Spanish for "The Jackal") from Mexican American bartender Luis Gil, which augments pulque's uniquely grassy and fizzy flavor profile with lime, citrus, ginger, and agave.

Mexico's distinctively vibrant cuisine—like its spirits culture—has rapidly spread across the globe in recent decades. One Mexican delicacy that hasn't caught on with most international foodies, however, is the chapulín, a species of grasshopper found throughout Central America that indigenous peoples like the Aztecs have been consuming for thousands of years. Distinctively smoky and nutty, it's an excellent flavor enhancer in Luis Gil's cocktail of the same name (see page 226), which also features uniquely tangy Cholula hot sauce and native guajillo and piquín peppers—a spicy and savory Mexican culinary adventure in a glass.

Paloma

Makes 1 drink

2 ounces tequila or mezcal

1 ounce fresh grapefruit juice

½ ounce fresh lime juice

½ ounce simple syrup (page 5)

Pinch of sea salt

Club soda, to top

1 thin orange slice, for garnish

Combine the tequila, grapefruit juice, lime juice, simple syrup, and salt in a shaker. Add 1 or 2 ice pebbles, shake briefly, and pour into an ice-filled Collins glass. Top with club soda. Place the orange slice in the glass beside the ice.

Oaxaca Old-Fashioned

Makes 1 drink

1½ ounces reposado tequila

½ ounce mezcal

1 teaspoon agave nectar

1 dash Angostura bitters

1 orange twist, for garnish

Combine the tequila, mezcal, agave nectar, and bitters in a rocks glass. Add ice and stir with a long-handled spoon for 5 or 6 seconds. Place the orange twist in the glass beside the ice.

El Chacal

Makes 1 drink

2 ounces pulque

¾ ounce fresh lime juice

½ ounce fresh orange juice

⅜ ounce ginger syrup (page 5)

⅜ ounce agave nectar

Pinch of freshly grated cinnamon, for garnish

Combine the pulque, lime juice, orange juice, ginger syrup, and agave nectar in an ice-filled shaker. Shake vigorously and then strain into a double rocks glass over ice. Garnish with the cinnamon.

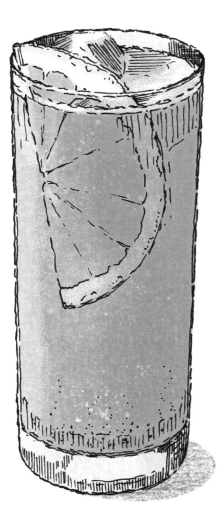

Paloma

Chapulín

Makes 1 drink

Grasshopper Salt (recipe follows), for rimming the glass

1 lime wedge, for rimming the glass

2 ounces mezcal

1 ounce fresh lime juice

¾ ounce simple syrup (page 5)

4 dashes Cholula hot sauce

3 thin cucumber slices

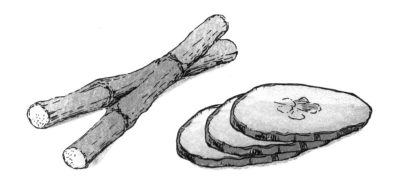

Spread some grasshopper salt over a small plate. Run the lime wedge around the rim of a coupe, then dip the rim into the grasshopper salt to coat; set aside. Combine the mezcal, lime juice, simple syrup, hot sauce, and cucumber slices in an ice-filled shaker. Shake vigorously and then strain into the prepared coupe.

Grasshopper Salt

Makes about 8 ounces

4 ounces dried grasshoppers (chapulínes), such as Plazita Gourmet Marinated Grasshoppers

2 dried guajillo peppers

5 to 7 dried piquín peppers

1 ounce fresh lime juice

Sea salt

Combine the grasshoppers and peppers in a medium saucepan and toast over medium-low heat for 3 to 5 minutes. Do not let them burn. Transfer to a blender, add the lime juice and salt to taste, and blend thoroughly. Transfer the mixture to a baking sheet and spread it out evenly. Set aside to dry at room temperature for several hours, then store in an airtight container at room temperature for up to 1 week.

GRASSHOPPERS and moth larvae are far from the only critters whose essences have been infused into Mexican booze. The gnarliest of these animal-based libations might be the Aragog Cocktail from Romeo Palomares at Luciferina Bar in Juárez. Named for the fictional spider from the Harry Potter books and featuring mezcal, cachaça, pisco, and a drop of tarantula venom, the drink was known to cause tongue and throat numbness that would last for hours. Luciferina closed in 2017, so you'll need to find a competent venom extractor if your goal is to pick this (literal) poison.

NICARAGUA

In Central America, Costa Rica gets most of the headlines where environmentalism is concerned. But over the past few years, Nicaragua has also been taking massive strides to protect its impressive natural resources. Programs to promote sustainability for farmers and ranchers, conservation-related education, and ecotourism opportunities are flourishing in this small country whose biodiversity is second only to Brazil's Amazon Rainforest.

That commitment to green living is evident in the business practices of Nicaragua's premier spirits company, Flor de Caña. The distillery's array of cocktail-friendly and sip-worthy rums are the first spirits to be declared carbon neutral and fair trade certified, made with all-natural ingredients and enriched by soil and mineral water from the San Cristóbal Volcano, the tallest and most active in the country.

Aged in bourbon barrels for an exceptionally smooth, oaky finish, Flor de Caña's rums make an excellent base in an El Macuá, which was dubbed the country's official national drink in 2006 following a nationwide cocktail competition. Created by Dr. Edmundo Miranda Saenz, a native of Granada, the first European city on mainland America, the mixture of juices from local produce like guava, oranges, and lemons is Nicaraguan-jungle lush, with a fresh burst of eco-friendly rum that's about as guilt-free as any high-proof alcohol can be. Named after a local bird whose orange and yellow feathers match the drink's color, this fruity crowd-pleaser will have you flying higher than a volcanic peak.

El Macuá

Makes 1 drink

1½ ounces Nicaraguan white rum, such as Flor de Caña 4 Year Extra Seco

1 ounce guava juice

1 ounce fresh orange juice

½ ounce fresh lemon juice

⅓ ounce simple syrup (page 5)

1 thin orange slice, for garnish

1 candied cherry, for garnish

Combine the rum, guava juice, orange juice, lemon juice, and simple syrup in an ice-filled shaker. Shake vigorously and then strain into a tall glass filled with ice. Perch the orange slice on the rim of the glass and drop the candied cherry into the drink.

PANAMA

Even if you're unfamiliar with the famous palindrome "A man, a plan, a canal, Panama," you're probably hip to what it refers to. The Panama Canal, an artificial waterway that connects the Atlantic and Pacific Oceans and divides North and South America, was a world-altering boon for global maritime trade when it was completed in 1914 by a group of American engineers and mostly Panamanian workers, and it's still a vital route for today's commercial vessels. But Panama is much more than just a stopover for boat traffic. The narrow, serpentine nation boasts an insane amount of biodiversity (estimated to be three times higher than that of the United States, Canada, and Europe combined); the greatest relief pitcher in baseball history, Mariano Rivera; and seco, a sugarcane-based aguardiente that's the country's national liquor.

Thrice-distilled and sold at 35% ABV, the clear, neutral spirit was invented by the Varela family in 1908, during the canal's construction, and is still made by them today, with Varela Hermanos producing around one million cases of their brand of seco, Seco Herrerano. Its smooth and unobtrusive nature allows for mingling with any number of juiced and muddled fruits. Two of these—strawberries and lemons—do most of the palate tickling in the Seco Sour, a locally popular potation that's as cool and summery as the breeze from either of Panama's oceans. Theodore Roosevelt, one of the driving forces behind the Panama Canal, often discussed his "eager pride" at the achievement. You might feel a similar sentiment after successfully whipping up—and eagerly sipping—one of these too-easily-quaffed refreshers.

Seco Sour

Makes 1 drink

2 ounces Seco Herrerano

¾ ounce fresh lemon juice

¾ ounce Strawberry Syrup (recipe follows)

1 halved strawberry, for garnish

Combine the Seco Herrerano, lemon juice, and strawberry syrup in an ice-filled shaker. Shake vigorously and then strain into a coupe. Skewer the strawberry with toothpicks and perch it on the rim of the glass.

Strawberry Syrup

Makes 1 cup

1 cup water

1 cup superfine sugar

2 cups quartered strawberries

Combine the water and sugar in a saucepan and heat over medium-high heat, stirring, until the sugar has dissolved. Add the strawberries and bring to a boil. Boil for 10 minutes, then reduce the heat to medium-low and simmer until the strawberries are mushy and the sauce is thick, about 10 minutes. Strain the syrup into a lidded bottle and let cool. Seal the bottle and store in the refrigerator for up to 1 week.

TODAY, seco is respected throughout the Americas as an excellent base for cocktails, though it wasn't always that way. Like mezcal in Mexico, it was originally considered cheap countryside booze, consumed by farmers who would only drink it mixed with milk or coconut milk, a concoction known as *seco con vaca,* or "seco with cow."

SAINT KITTS AND NEVIS

For many Caribbean territories, including the tiny nation of Saint Kitts and Nevis, most of the past few hundred years has been one big identity crisis. Originally the home of several indigenous tribes like the Kalinago and Igneri peoples, this pair of volcanic islands was visited by Christopher Columbus, who claimed them for Spain and allegedly inspired the naming of Saint Kitts (officially Saint Christopher). Starting in the 1620s, the islands were passed back and forth every few decades between the French and the British, usually after some violent conflict, before finally gaining independence in 1983 and becoming the smallest sovereign state—by area and population—in the Western Hemisphere.

The one constant during centuries of upheaval was the sugarcane industry, which was, until recently, the islands' only source of income. Where there's ideal sugar growing conditions, there's usually great rum, and Saint Kitts and Nevis has produced some great varieties, including Cane Spirit Rothschild (known locally as CSR), a clear, overproof firewater said to be so pure that it was impossible to get a hangover from drinking it, even in amounts that would discombobulate the most debauched pirate.

Until its distillery shut down in 1998, CSR was also the preferred base spirit of Saint Kitts and Nevis' national drink, the Ting with a Sting. It's about as simple as a cocktail gets—overproof white rum topped with Ting, a sweet and tart, grapefruit-forward soda from Jamaica that's popular throughout the Caribbean. But this zesty, sneakily potent vacation favorite is packed with a unique blend of citrusy island flavors, making it the perfect way to cool down on a hot day.

Ting with a Sting

Makes 1 drink

2 ounces overproof white rum, such as Wray & Nephew

Ting or comparable grapefruit-flavored soda, to top

1 lime twist, for garnish

Pour the rum into a Collins glass filled with ice. Top with Ting. Place the lime twist in the glass beside the ice.

Saint Kitts and Nevis / Ting with a Sting (page 229)

SAINT LUCIA

Of the 195 countries featured in this book, Saint Lucia is the only one named after a woman. But that's far from the only thing that makes this Eastern Caribbean island nation special or puts it on countless travelers' bucket lists. Dominated by dense rainforests and the jaggedly breathtaking Pitons, it's the only home of the endangered Saint Lucia parrot, has more Nobel Prize winners per capita than any other country, and was a frequent port of call for the infamous pirate Blackbeard. More importantly for rum lovers, it's a veritable slice of boozy heaven, with dozens of distilleries operating across the island, including the tiny Roseau Valley, which produces twenty-one distinct varieties of rum in an area with barely more than 200 inhabitants.

Most visitors to Saint Lucia get their first taste of the local spirit after it's been blended with copious local fruit juices and sweeteners. And that can be great. But if you're looking for a stiffer, unapologetically rum-centric tipple, you can't do much better than the St. Lucian, which was originally stirred up by bartender Brad Smith at Latitude 29, New Orleans's famed tiki den. A sophisticated, spirit-forward nod to Saint Lucia's super-popular rum punches, its notes of orange and cinnamon—a spice that's found in many of the island's signature dishes—as well as the smooth and stimulating flavors of Amaro Averna, bring out the best in the deeply citrusy and herbal elements that are common features of most Saint Lucian aged rums. This invigorating old-fashioned-esque sipper will have you dreaming of future nights spent in paradise. Or, more immediately, fixing yourself a second round.

St. Lucian

Makes 1 drink

2 ounces Saint Lucian dark rum, such as Hamilton St. Lucia 5 Year

1 ounce Clément Créole Shrubb

½ ounce Amaro Averna

¼ ounce cinnamon syrup (page 4)

1 dash chocolate bitters

1 orange twist, for garnish

Combine the rum, shrub, amaro, cinnamon syrup, and bitters in a double rocks glass. Add ice and stir with a long-handled spoon for 5 or 6 seconds. Place the orange twist in the glass beside the ice.

SAINT VINCENT AND THE GRENADINES

Sometimes names can be misleading. For instance, you'd think that the small, mostly uninhabited islands neighboring Saint Vincent would be rife with pomegranates, considering that the word "grenadine" originates from the French word *grenade*, which means, you guessed it, pomegranate. However, these specks of land were actually named by Christopher Columbus as an homage to Granada, Spain. That might be a bummer for lovers of both the red fruit and pomegranate-based grenadine syrup, but this gorgeous archipelagic nation still has plenty to offer, including endless beach-related activities, volcano hikes, the oldest botanical gardens in the Western Hemisphere, and a staggering number of local rums.

The most prominent distillery in the country, St. Vincent Distillers Ltd, puts out several highly regarded varieties, including Captain Bligh XO, which is aged for up to ten years in ex-bourbon casks and is lauded for its distinctive vanilla nose and oaky finish. If you prefer (or dare) to drink like the locals, grab a bottle of the company's 169-proof Sunset Very Strong, named the best overproof rum at the 2016 World Rum Awards. Sipping something that diabolically strong on its own can lead to immediate feelings of regret, so it's best to mix it up as part of one of St. Vincent Distillers's signature cocktails, the Sunset Rum Punch. In this slightly toned-down version of the original recipe, a healthy dose of pineapple, orange, and yes, pomegranate combine to mask Sunset Very Strong's harshest attributes, leaving only light notes of molasses and raisins. But don't get it twisted—drink more than one or two of these potent potables and the sunset will be coming for you much earlier than expected.

Sunset Rum Punch

Makes 1 drink

1½ ounces Sunset Very Strong rum or comparable overproof rum

¾ ounce Sparrow's Premium rum or comparable aged rum

1 ounce pineapple juice

1 ounce fresh orange juice

½ ounce fresh lime juice

¼ ounce pomegranate syrup (page 5)

1 barspoon cane syrup

2 dashes Angostura bitters

Crushed ice

1 thin orange slice, for garnish

1 thin pineapple slice, for garnish

1 lime wedge, for garnish

Pinch of freshly grated nutmeg, for garnish

Combine the rums, pineapple juice, orange juice, lime juice, pomegranate syrup, cane syrup, and bitters in a shaker. Pour into a tall glass filled two-thirds of the way with crushed ice. Add a straw and top with more crushed ice. Garnish with the orange slice, pineapple slice, and lime wedge and sprinkle with the nutmeg.

TRINIDAD AND TOBAGO

Trinidad and Tobago has only been a fully independent republic since 1976. Yet the southernmost island nation in the Caribbean has played an indispensable role in global cocktail culture for far longer—1876 to be exact, when the hallowed House of Angostura moved its base of operations to Port of Spain, Trinidad, primarily to manufacture its world-renowned bitters. Originally sold and marketed as a medicinal tonic, the still-secret blend of gentian, herbs, and spices is a crucial component of countless iconic drinks, a timeless hodgepodge of ingredients and flavors that beautifully mimics Trinidad and Tobago's population and its one-of-a-kind, post-colonial mix of African, Indian, and European influences.

Angostura bitters, as you'd expect, also play a role in Trinidad and Tobago's most iconic and enduring cocktail, the Queen's Park Swizzle. It was first served in the early twentieth century at Port of Spain's uber-swanky Queen's Park Hotel, the premier digs for visiting celebrities, politicians, and British royalty, where it quickly became the hotel bar's signature drink. Tall, regal, minty, and almost supernaturally refreshing, the multilayered, mojito-like QPS (as it's affectionately called by brevity-loving bartenders) was once described by tiki iconoclast Victor "Trader Vic" Bergeron as being "the most delightful form of anesthesia given out today," and it's easy to see—and taste—why. If you're still not convinced, whip up one of your own. Or head to one of the thousands of bars around the world that still serve this red, white, and green and utterly icy classic, a testament to a liquid legacy that reaches far beyond the drink's namesake hotel, which, sadly, was demolished in 1996.

Due to their powerful botanical properties, Angostura bitters are often used sparingly as a seasoning to enhance a drink's primary flavors—the cocktail equivalent of salt and pepper. That line of thinking was gleefully disregarded by Giuseppe González when he concocted the Trinidad Sour at Brooklyn's Clover Club in the late 2000s. Featuring an unheard-of ounce and a half of bitters as its base spirit, this bloodred eschewer of conventional wisdom tastes intensely rich, savory, nutty, and slightly sour, yet somehow remains well-balanced. It's a complex, sassy, and not-so-subtle introduction to Trinidad and Tobago's uniquely herbal and spicy terroir that everyone should try at least once—or several dozen times.

Queen's Park Swizzle

Makes 1 drink

2 ounces aged rum, such as Angostura 7 Year

1 ounce fresh lime juice

¾ ounce simple syrup (page 5)

6 to 8 mint leaves

1 sugar cube

Crushed ice

8 dashes Angostura bitters

1 mint sprig, for garnish

Muddle the rum, lime juice, simple syrup, mint leaves, and sugar cube in a Collins glass. Fill the glass two-thirds of the way with crushed ice. Add the bitters and stir briefly with a swizzle stick. Fill the glass to the top with crushed ice. Garnish with the mint sprig.

Trinidad Sour

Makes 1 drink

1½ ounces Angostura bitters

1 ounce orgeat

¾ ounce fresh lemon juice

½ ounce rye whiskey

Combine all the ingredients in an ice-filled shaker. Shake vigorously and then strain into a coupe.

Trinidad and Tobago / Queen's Park Swizzle (page 233)

UNITED STATES

H. L. Mencken once noted, "The cocktail is a uniquely American invention, and it is the only American invention as perfect as the sonnet." While that isn't entirely accurate—beverages that combined alcohol with other ingredients existed long before any of the Founding Fathers' grandparents—no country has been more inextricably linked to the mixed-drink phenomenon. The US has remained at the forefront of global cocktail culture since the first mention of the word "cock-tail" in *The Balance, and Columbian Repository*, a Hudson, New York tabloid. This boozy hegemony extended through the so-called golden age of cocktails, when celebrated American bartenders like Jerry Thomas (author of 1862's *Bar-Tender's Guide*, the world's first drinks book) were inventing still-beloved classics at an astounding rate, to the equally innovative gin-soaked Prohibition and post-Prohibition eras, to the still-ongoing modern cocktail renaissance that began in the late 1990s.

But to discover the true origins of American mixology, you'd have to go much farther back in time, long before anyone was arguing about the proper etiquette for serving punch, before the creation of signature native spirits like bourbon or rye whiskey, before the idea of "America" even existed. Creative boozing began in earnest in the early 1600s with the settlement of New England by perma-buzzed English Puritans, whose love for multiple daily helpings of beer, brandy, and the earliest rums imported from the Caribbean led to the creation of the flip (see page 236). Unlike the modern shaken version, this colonial-era tavern nightcap was served hot. A mixture of mulled ale, rum or brandy, spices like nutmeg, and fresh eggs, it was first warmed over a fire, then transferred back and forth between two jugs until silky smooth, then poured into mugs, and heated once more by inserting a scalding fireplace poker called a flipdog or toddy rod directly into the drink. Which sounds like a lot of work. But it's not like there was much else to do in the 1600s when the sun went down, besides contemplating a lifetime of backbreaking labor and the likelihood of dying early from disease or an animal attack.

After several decades of trying—unsuccessfully—to grow decent grapes for winemaking, early colonial hooch producers like Scottish-born William Laird turned to another introduced crop that had taken nicely to the North American soil—the apple. First distilled in 1698 in Monmouth County, New Jersey, Laird's apple brandy, which he named Applejack, became an immediate sensation and is considered America's original spirit. Though its popularity decreased over the centuries due to the rise of other domestic and imported liquors, the potent "Jersey Lightning" was a favorite of US presidents George Washington, Abraham Lincoln, and Franklin Roosevelt, and is still produced by the Laird family today. It's also the base in several cocktails dating back to the golden age, the most well-known being the Jack Rose (page 236), which appeared at the turn of the twentieth century. Subtly fruity, tart, and mildly sweet, with an always-fashionable rosy hue, it's no surprise that many call this New Jersey's finest entry in the cocktail pantheon.

In the late eighteenth and early nineteenth centuries, a new homegrown spirit—whiskey—began to tantalize the now-independent American palate. The barrel-aged grain-based liquor (and especially its two most notable varieties, bourbon and rye) became the tipple of choice for millions, gradually replacing rum and brandy in the great triumvirate of famous early American beverages: the Old-Fashioned (page 237), whose recipe closely follows the original 1806 cocktail definition ("A stimulating liquor, composed of spirits of any kind, sugar, water, and bitters"); the Sazerac (page 237), a similarly powerful antebellum New Orleans sipper fortified by absinthe and local creole-style bitters; and the Mint Julep (page 237), a decadently minty and icy tonic that's served in an elegant silver cup and has been heavily associated with the southern United States—and specifically the Kentucky Derby—since at least the 1770s.

By the late nineteenth century, the saloon was an essential part of American social life. Knowledgeable bartenders from Brooklyn to Los Angeles were armed with a plethora of exotic spirits, liqueurs, vermouths, and bitters, as well as a growing selection of cocktail-centric literature from which to draw inspiration and throngs of thirsty patrons willing to try whatever potation happened to slide their way. But things weren't all roses and rickeys. The temperance movement had also been gaining steam for decades, led by radical buzzkills like Kansas's Carrie Nation, who would walk into bars and smash innocent bottles with a hatchet for fun.

Then in 1919 the unthinkable happened. The passage of the Eighteenth Amendment would prohibit the production, sale, and transportation of alcohol everywhere in the US until 1932. However, as the nickname "Roaring Twenties" suggests, the following decade-plus was anything but sobriety-filled, with cocktails becoming even more popular as a less harsh method for consuming questionable black market booze. For many speakeasy regulars, gin was the spirit of choice. It served as the base in dozens of iconic 1920s cocktails invented by drink-slingers working in "American-style" bars in London and Paris—such as the Bee's Knees, White Lady, and Hanky-Panky—that surreptitiously made their way across the Atlantic like so many crates of bootlegged hooch. One cocktail that didn't have to travel nearly as far is the Last Word (page 239), a 100% American sipper concocted at the Detroit Athletic Club shortly before the enactment of the Eighteenth Amendment. Sweet, sour, herbal, and impeccably balanced, this altogether perfect nightcap fell into obscurity for close to nine decades before returning to its rightful perch in the rafters of cocktail royalty.

The mid to late-twentieth-century American drinking scene gifted imbibers with a handful of distinctive—and some might say, tasty—tipples that have since become household names, like the Moscow Mule, White Russian, and cosmopolitan. Nevertheless, this era has been described by modern cocktail historians, whether fairly or not, as somewhat of a dark age, filled with unnecessarily aggressive and unbalanced happy-hour hazards (the Long Island Iced Tea); saccharine, neon-hued monstrosities (the Appletini); and enough crudely concocted shooters to fill a frat house.

That changed in the early 2000s, when a coterie of cocktail historians and nightlife veterans at now-hallowed dens like New York's Milk & Honey, Pegu Club, and Angel's Share reintroduced a more serious, mindful approach to drink-making that had all but disappeared in the previous decades. Emphasizing traditional techniques, fresh ingredients, high-quality booze, and a respect for classic recipes, visionaries like Sasha Petraske, Dale DeGroff, and Audrey Saunders reintroduced hundreds of long-forgotten drinks from the golden age and Prohibition eras, created their own celebrated variations, and laid the foundation for the diverse and growing cocktail culture that we know and love today.

The most talked-about "modern classic" to have emerged from our current epoch is the Penicillin (page 239), the brainchild of Australian expat Sam Ross, which made its debut at Milk & Honey in 2005 and has since appeared on hundreds of bar menus around the world. Described by Ross as a Whiskey Sour variation utilizing the amazing qualities of smoky Islay Scotch, it's about as idealistically American as it gets: created by a successful immigrant, utilizing global ingredients in a way that still nods to long-standing domestic traditions, with an overall experience that feels both balanced and slightly decadent.

Colonial Hot-Ale Flip

Makes 1 drink

1½ ounces dark rum
1 tablespoon molasses
1 large egg
8 ounces dark beer, such as brown ale, porter, or stout
Pinch of freshly grated nutmeg, for garnish

Pour the rum and molasses into a pint glass. Crack the egg into a second pint glass and beat well with a fork until the white and yolk of the egg are completely combined.

Warm the beer in a medium saucepan over low heat until it begins to froth; don't let it come to a boil. Pour the beer into the pint glass with the rum and molasses, then pour the mixture into the pint glass containing the egg. Continue to pour the drink back and forth between the pint glasses until smooth and well blended. Pour the drink into a mug and garnish with the nutmeg.

Jack Rose

Makes 1 drink

2 ounces applejack
¾ ounce fresh lime juice
¾ ounce grenadine

Combine all the ingredients in an ice-filled shaker. Shake vigorously and then strain into a coupe.

CONTRARY TO WIDESPREAD belief, most of the apples planted by the legendary missionary John "Johnny Appleseed" Chapman were too sour to eat, but made excellent cider, and even better brandy. According to author Michael Pollan, Chapman—the "American Dionysus"—was almost single-handedly responsible for applejack's early popularity through-out the fledgling United States.

Old-Fashioned

Makes 1 drink

1 white sugar cube

4 dashes Angostura bitters

2 ounces American whiskey of choice

1 lemon twist, for garnish

1 orange twist, for garnish

Drop the sugar cube into a rocks glass. Douse the cube with the bitters, then muddle. Add the whiskey and ice and stir with a long-handled spoon for 5 or 6 seconds. Place the lemon and orange twists in the glass beside the ice.

Sazerac

Makes 1 drink

Crushed ice

¼ ounce absinthe

1 sugar cube

4 dashes Peychaud's bitters

2 ounces rye whiskey

1 lemon twist, for garnish

Fill a rocks glass with crushed ice and add the absinthe; set aside. Put the sugar cube in a mixing glass and douse it with the bitters. Muddle, then add the whiskey and fill the mixing glass with cracked ice. Stir with a long-handled spoon for 25 seconds. Discard the ice and absinthe in the rocks glass, then strain the contents of the mixing glass into the rocks glass. Garnish with the lemon twist.

Mint Julep

Makes 1 drink

Handful of mint leaves, plus 1 sprig for garnish

2½ ounces bourbon

¼ ounce simple syrup (page 5)

1 sugar cube

Crushed ice

Gently squeeze the mint leaves in your hand (to release their fragrance) and drop them into a traditional silver julep cup. Add the bourbon, simple syrup, and sugar cube to the cup. Muddle lightly to break up the sugar cube (but not to bruise the mint) and fill the cup two-thirds of the way with crushed ice. Stir with a swizzle stick, then add a straw and top with more crushed ice. Garnish with the mint sprig.

Mint Julep

Last Word

Makes 1 drink

¾ ounce gin

¾ ounce green Chartreuse

¾ ounce maraschino liqueur

¾ ounce fresh lime juice

1 brandied cherry, for garnish

Combine the gin, Chartreuse, maraschino liqueur, and lime juice in an ice-filled shaker. Shake vigorously and then strain into a coupe. Garnish with the brandied cherry.

Penicillin

Makes 1 drink

2 ounces blended Scotch, such as Monkey Shoulder

¾ ounce fresh lemon juice

⅜ ounce ginger syrup (page 5)

⅜ ounce honey syrup (page 5)

¼ ounce Islay Scotch, such as Bowmore 12 Year

1 piece candied ginger, for garnish

Combine the blended Scotch, lemon juice, ginger syrup, and honey syrup in an ice-filled shaker. Shake vigorously and then strain into a double rocks glass over ice. Float the Islay Scotch on top by pouring it over the back of a spoon into the glass. Skewer the piece of candied ginger with toothpicks and place it on the rim of the glass.

PROHIBITION in the United States could be quite a nuisance for American drinkers, but the thirteen-year era had far darker aspects than most people today realize. One of these was the "chemist's war," where federal officials ordered the widespread poisoning of the industrial alcohols that bootleggers frequently stole to make their hooch, in the hopes of scaring people away from illicit booze. Described by 1920s New York City medical examiner Charles Norris as a "national experiment in extermination," the nationwide program directly caused at least 10,000 deaths, including twenty-three Manhattan partygoers on Christmas 1926, one of whom hallucinated that he was being chased by a baseball-bat-wielding Santa Claus before succumbing to the government-approved toxins.

Penicillin

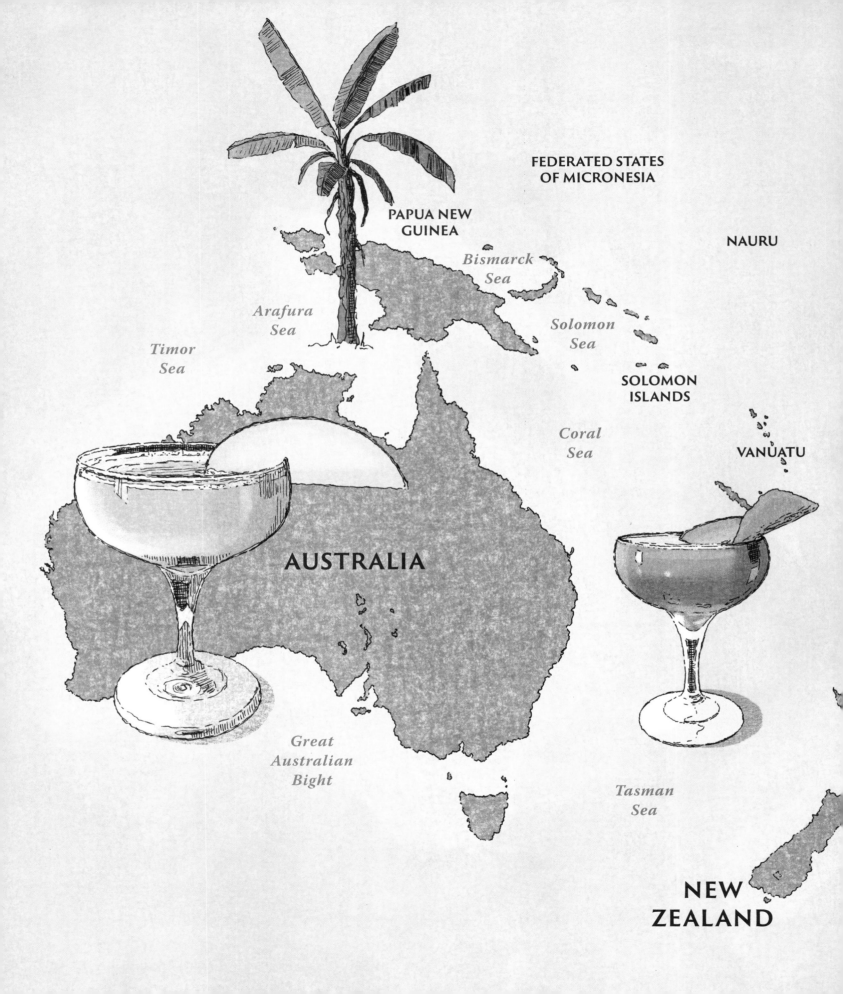

SAMOA

FRENCH
POLYNESIA

FIJI

COOK
ISLANDS

*South
Pacific
Ocean*

OCEANIA

AUSTRALIA

Many of modern Australia's settled coastal areas—especially its urban centers—are plentiful with posh, first-world conveniences, including copious food and drink options, countless entertainment, sports, and music events, access to top-notch healthcare, and, in the largest cities Sydney and Melbourne, one of the world's premier cocktail scenes. But for much of the country's 65,000-year history of human habitation (and even today in much of its violently rugged interior), the land Down Under was a notoriously treacherous place to live, rife with poisonous critters and inhospitable weather, an environment that required an uncommon amount of strength—and perhaps a bit of craziness—to survive.

Both the Aboriginal peoples and Australia's first British settlers—many of whom had been longtime guests of their country's penal system—were no strangers to hardship. The latter group, if the country's earliest printed food writing is to be believed, was also quite fond of some truly brain-bending libations. Appearing in *The English and Australian Cookery Book* (1864), the pleasantly named Blow My Skull is attributed to notorious boozer lieutenant governor Thomas Davey and calls for sugar, lime, one pint of porter or ale, one pint of rum, and half a pint of brandy. Ostensibly intended as a communal punch, it was said that Davey would consume it at the barbecues he frequently hosted, keeping his composure while his less tolerant guests stumbled around utterly plastered. The following single-serving adaptation has slightly milder aspirations, though it still delivers a liver-jarring punch worthy of one of the planet's roughest landmasses.

The current crop of Australian bartenders are no slouches when it comes to both classic cocktails and the modern standbys. You won't have to look long for a respectable old-fashioned, White Lady, or Porn Star Martini in any of the country's bigger towns. But if you really want to rachet things up, check out Sydney or Melbourne. In these modern drinks meccas, globally recognized bars maintain a great respect for European, American, and Asian cocktail traditions while pushing the envelope in fresh and exciting ways. That trend began in the 1980s, with drink-slingers like Jean-Paul Bourguignon at Melbourne's Mietta Restaurant. His signature creation, the Japanese Slipper, is still one of the most popular cocktails using Midori, a honeydew-melon liqueur made by Japanese distiller Suntory. It's fun, fruity, irreverent, and blessedly easy to shake up, even in the most remote corners of the outback.

Blow My Skull
Makes 1 drink

1 ounce aged rum
1 ounce brandy
8 ounces dark beer, such as a brown ale, porter, or stout
1 ounce fresh lime juice
¾ ounce simple syrup (page 5)
1 lime wedge, for garnish

Pour the rum and brandy into a heat-resistant pint glass. Combine the beer, lime juice, simple syrup, and 4 ounces of water in a medium saucepan and heat over medium heat until it begins to froth; don't let it come to a boil. Pour the beer mixture into the pint glass with the rum and brandy. Perch the lime wedge on the rim of the glass.

Japanese Slipper
Makes 1 drink

1 ounce Midori
1 ounce Cointreau
1 ounce fresh lemon juice
1 honeydew melon slice, for garnish

Combine the Midori, Cointreau, and lemon juice in an ice-filled shaker. Shake vigorously and then strain into a coupe. Perch the honeydew melon slice on the rim of the glass.

ONE OF THE MOST widely practiced Australian drinking traditions is known as "shouting," though it has nothing to do with raising one's voice. When a group of "shouters" gets together, it basically means that they take turns buying rounds.

Japanese Slipper

FEDERATED STATES OF MICRONESIA

A confederation of 607 islands spread across 1,700 miles of the equatorial Pacific, the Federated States of Micronesia was, for centuries, visited—and subjugated—by hard-boozing Spanish, German, Japanese, and American colonizers until gaining full independence in 1979. Yet, for most native inhabitants, the opportunity to enjoy a stiff beverage has only existed since 1959, when a long-standing ban on alcohol sales was finally lifted.

Rather than impinging on thousands of years of culture, drinking has been fully integrated into local societal customs. Beer and liquor are consumed almost exclusively by men aged eighteen to around thirty-five, as part of the concept of an extended adolescence, wherein rowdiness, poor decision-making, and all manner of hooligan-like behavior is permitted with little to no consequences. Once the decade-plus of frat-dogging finally ends, most of these ne'er-do-wells put down their bottles and assume the responsibilities of adulthood, like marriage and supporting a family.

Due to their country's extensive trade relationship with the United States, Micronesia's weekend warriors have access to an impressive selection of favorite American party favors like tequila. Which happens to be the main attraction in the Milk Maid, a delightfully silky sipper from bartender Elizabeth Weiss that was first served at New York's Lantern's Keep. Dosed with coconut syrup and cream—a foil for the coconut milk that's essential to just about all of Oceania's far-flung culinary cultures—the drink also features locally cultivated fruits like lime and cucumber for a velvety island voyage that's as indulgent as a thirty-year-old Micronesian teenager.

Milk Maid

Makes 1 drink

2 ounces tequila

¾ ounce fresh lime juice

¾ ounce coconut syrup, such as Wildly Organic Coconut Syrup

½ ounce heavy cream

5 thin cucumber slices

Pinch of sea salt

Combine the tequila, lime juice, coconut syrup, cream, 3 cucumber slices, and salt in an ice-filled shaker. Shake vigorously and strain into a double rocks glass over ice. Perch the remaining 2 cucumber slices on the rim of the glass.

FIJI

If you've seen the classic 1998 Jim Carrey drama *The Truman Show*, you may remember the main character's unrequited obsession with Fiji, which he considers the ultimate paradisiacal destination. Turns out that in this case, reality and fiction are one and the same. The 333-island archipelago—87 percent of the population lives on Viti Levu and Vanua Levu, the two largest ones—has a wealth of brilliant coral reefs, untouched lagoons, super lush mountainous forests, and some of the best locally produced rums found anywhere in the Pacific. The country's oldest (and until recently, only) distillery, Rum Co. of Fiji, has been exporting several award-winning brands since 1980, harvesting sugarcane that grows in nutrient-rich volcanic soil, using pure local water. After filtering the product through coconut shell carbon, the rum matures in ex-bourbon oak barrels.

Many of Rum Co. of Fiji's best-sellers—especially the dark and spiced varieties—have more than enough personality to be enjoyed on their own or on the rocks (as does the lovely Bati Banana 2 Year), but they also work amazingly in just about any tropically oriented beverage. The Bula, one of whose many versions was first served at the 2021 Arizona Tiki Oasis bartending seminar, is one such mind-erasing mixture. Its name means "welcome" in Fijian, and there's nothing that's uninviting about the following adaptation, which highlights dark rum alongside sultry warm-weather bedfellows guava and passion fruit. Even if, like Truman Burbank, you find yourself hopelessly stuck in your hometown, you can still whip up one of these and escape to Fiji one sip—or slightly larger quaff—at a time.

Bula

Makes 1 drink

2 ounces guava nectar

1½ ounces Fijian dark rum, such as Rum Co. of Fiji 2 Year Old Bati Premium Dark Rum

1 ounce fresh orange juice

¼ ounce passion fruit syrup, such as Liber & Co. Tropical Passionfruit Syrup

5 dashes tiki bitters, such as Bittermens 'Elemakule Tiki Bitters

Crushed ice

1 thin orange slice, for garnish

Combine the guava nectar, rum, orange juice, passion fruit syrup, and bitters in a shaker. Pour into a tall glass filled two-thirds of the way with crushed ice. Add a straw and top with more crushed ice. Garnish with the orange slice.

FIJI IS ONE of the only places in the world where the rum-making process is done entirely by hand, from the cutting of the sugarcane to the operation of the stills to putting labels on the bottles.

Fiji / Bula (page 245)

KIRIBATI

More so than some of their Pacific neighbors, the residents of Kiribati's thirty-two widely dispersed atolls adhere to a mostly traditional lifestyle, even after centuries of British colonial rule. The islands' unique forms of dancing, folk music, dueling, and martial arts are still widely practiced, as is the harvesting of sap (toddy) from the coconut palm tree to make karewe, the local palm wine. Boys are taught from a very early age how to climb and properly cut trees, as both the unrefined sap and the fermented alcoholic beverage are major sources of household income and a vital part of Kiribati's culinary and social scenes.

That's not to say that Kiribatians are immune to change, as is evident in the significant numbers of chickens being raised across the islands. Once virtually unheard of, poultry and eggs are now working their way into the traditionally seafood-and-coconut-based local diet, with great success. This new Kiribati meets the old in the Coconut Fizz, a foamy, sparkling, and blissfully straightforward concoction with only four delicious, time-tested ingredients: rum, coconut water, egg white, and soda. This low-calorie, low-ABV take on the piña colada is a rare treat for health-conscious vacationers, and it's also perhaps the closest one can get to experiencing the flavors of Kiribati, albeit in spirits form.

Coconut Fizz

Makes 1 drink

4 ounces coconut water
1 ounce white rum
1 egg white
Club soda, to top

Combine the coconut water, rum, and egg white in a shaker. Shake without ice for 5 or 6 seconds to emulsify the egg white, then add ice and shake vigorously. Strain into a tall glass filled with ice. Top with club soda.

MARSHALL ISLANDS

It probably goes without saying, but if you're in the mood for a raucous, cosmopolitan party scene, the Marshall Islands are not your jam. Virtually all the former United States territory's limited nightlife—consisting of little more than half a dozen nightclubs and a few karaoke-friendly hostel bars—is concentrated in the capital city of Majuro, with many outlying islands still enforcing total alcohol prohibition. Those interested in experiencing the local flavors of the 70-square-mile archipelago would be better off kicking back on one of thousands of tranquil beaches and sampling indigenous crops like pandanus, breadfruit, cassava, and noni, an evergreen tree whose fruit is high in potassium, vitamins C and A, and other immune-friendly ingredients.

A noni shake, a detoxifying blend of that fruit plus mango, banana, pineapple, and almond milk, might be in the cards if you somehow manage to sneak onto Bikini Atoll, the remote, uninhabited sliver of land and coral reefs that was the site of twenty-three nuclear tests by the United States between 1946 and 1958. This still-radioactive area is the inspiration for a cocktail of the same name, which first appeared on Frederic Yarm's *Cocktail Virgin* blog in 2011. Featuring many of the same elements as the classic mai tai, as well as modern tropical liver punchers like the Nuclear Daiquiri and the H Bomb, the Bikini Atoll ramps up the alcohol content to atomic levels with the addition of Wray & Nephew rum and green Chartreuse (125.5 proof and 110 proof, respectively). Have more than one of these funky, herbaceous, and dangerously drinkable tiki time bombs and your insides may become pickled enough to withstand nuclear fallout.

Bikini Atoll

Makes 1 drink

1 ounce Wray & Nephew Rum, or comparable overproof rum

½ ounce green Chartreuse

½ ounce falernum, such as John D. Taylor's Velvet Falernum

½ ounce curaçao or comparable orange liqueur

½ ounce fresh lime juice

½ ounce orgeat

Crushed ice

1 mint sprig, for garnish

Combine the rum, Chartreuse, falernum, curaçao, lime juice, and orgeat in a shaker. Pour into a tall glass filled two-thirds of the way with crushed ice. Add a straw, then top with more crushed ice. Garnish with the mint sprig.

THE MOST FREQUENTLY spoken Marshallese word—used for "hello," "goodbye," "love," and to compliment a perfectly crafted cocktail—is *iakwe*. In English it means "you are a rainbow," which is quite a lovely way to be greeted.

NAURU

As the smallest island nation and the smallest country in the world that isn't a city-state, with a population of less than 10,000, Nauru is a speck on the international radar. But this former British Protectorate still packs plenty of character into its eight square miles. Thanks to a phosphate mining boom in the twentieth century, Nauruans were exposed to the greater international community, creating a fascinating fusion of tradition and modernity unlike any of its neighboring islands. Fueling a lively—if understandably compact—nightlife scene, Nauru's restaurants serve locally inspired seafood and coconut-based dishes alongside Chinese, British, American, and even German meals. Iced coffee, the islanders' de facto national beverage, flows freely wherever drinks are sold.

When Nauruans are in the mood for something a little stronger, they choose from a widely available selection of imported spirits like rum, gin, tequila, and whiskey. The latter is also one of the main attractions in the Coffee Pineapple Old-Fashioned, a pleasantly caffeinated sipper adapted from a recipe by bartender Heather Wibbels. This boozy eye-opener pairs bourbon's rich notes of oak and vanilla and coffee liqueur's inherent bitterness with the sweetness and slight acidity of pineapple—one of the island's few locally cultivated fruits—for a finish that's unapologetically boozy but still as smooth as the backside of a palm leaf. A rare combination of both tropical and global flavors that, like tiny Nauru, is brimming with surprises.

Coffee Pineapple Old-Fashioned

Makes 1 drink

1½ ounces bourbon

¾ ounce coffee liqueur

½ ounce Pineapple Syrup (see page 14)

2 dashes chocolate bitters

1 pineapple spear, for garnish

Combine the bourbon, coffee liqueur, pineapple syrup, and bitters in an old-fashioned glass. Add ice and stir with a long-handled spoon for 5 or 6 seconds. Place the pineapple spear in the glass beside the ice.

NEW ZEALAND

What's under Down Under? That would be New Zealand, one of the world's southernmost countries and perhaps the most gorgeous at any latitude. The filming location of the *Lord of the Rings* movies is an outdoor enthusiast's nirvana, with top-notch ski resorts, mesmerizing hiking trails, unbelievably clear lakes, and countless opportunities for golf, bungee jumping, or simply breathing in the cleanest air in the Southern Hemisphere. And you'll be able to do it all mostly unbothered, as New Zealand is also one of the least densely populated places on the planet. But that doesn't mean it's difficult to get your drink on. Stereotypically jovial New Zealanders have an acute fondness for just about any spirit, exemplified by the impressive number of artisanal whiskeys, rums, and gins currently being distilled in the island nation.

New Zealand's gin industry, in particular, is enjoying its moment in the sun, both abroad and in the bevy of world-class watering holes in cities like Auckland and Wellington. One of the best-known small-batch distilleries, Waiwera, is also responsible for the Kiwi Smash, a liquid shoutout to the flightless bird beloved by all New Zealanders—who affectionately refer to themselves as Kiwis—and the eponymous fruit, which, although native to China, is still a frequently slurped snack. And when muddled into a mixture of local gin, lemon, basil, and manuka honey (a strong, florid, earthy, and unusually viscous sweetener prized for its host of health benefits), that snack becomes a buffet of insatiably sippable summertime flavors.

New Zealand's professional rum slingers are no slouches either, tweaking trodden classics to suit their spirit of choice. Such is the Te Anaka (page 252) from bartender James Crinson. Reminiscent of iconoclasts like the Bee's Knees and the Honeysuckle, its cascading layers of honey-sweetened froth, white rum, and fino sherry might stir your nature-loving spirit to Kiwi-level adventures. Or, more likely, have you fantasizing about them while sipping a few rounds by the pool.

Kiwi Smash

Makes 1 drink

½ kiwifruit, peeled, plus 1 thin slice for garnish

3 fresh basil leaves, plus 1 basil sprig for garnish

2 ounces New Zealand gin, such as Mahurangi

¾ ounce honey syrup (page 5), preferably made with manuka honey

½ ounce fresh lemon juice

Muddle the peeled kiwifruit and basil leaves in a shaker. Add the gin, honey syrup, lemon juice, and ice. Shake vigorously and then strain into a double rocks glass over cracked ice. Place the basil sprig and kiwifruit slice in the glass beside the ice.

Te Anaka

Makes 1 drink

1½ ounces white rum

¾ ounce fresh lemon juice

¾ ounce honey syrup (page 5)

½ ounce fino sherry

1 egg white

1 lemon wedge, for garnish

Combine the rum, lemon juice, honey syrup, sherry, and egg white in a shaker. Shake without ice for 5 or 6 seconds to emulsify the egg white, then add ice and shake vigorously. Strain into a coupe or sour glass. Perch the lemon wedge on the rim of the glass.

THERE'S A SOLID case that the award for most disgusting shot ever served at a bar should go to Steven Drummond, co-owner of the Green Man Pub in Wellington and inventor of the Hoihoi Tatea. This custard-like shooter—a blend of horse semen from a local stallion farm and apple flavoring—was created in 2011 as an entry in a local food and drink contest and was served for several months at the Green Man, though it apparently never caught on with customers. Hard to tell why.

PALAU

Tiny Palau is often overshadowed by its much larger and well-known Asian neighbors like the Philippines and Indonesia. And that's a shame, because this 177-square-mile, 18,000-person archipelago boasts a fascinating cultural and political history, as well as hundreds of pristine volcanic islands, magical forests, and mesmerizing turquoise lagoons. Organized along strict tribal and matrilineal lines—the annual Palau Women's Conference is the de facto cultural authority—modern Palauan society is a unique hodgepodge of Micronesian, Asian, and Western influences, thanks to colonization attempts by the likes of Spain, Germany, Japan, and, after some epic World War II battles, the United States, from whom Palau gained full independence in 1994.

The traditional beverage of choice here, as with most Pacific Island nations, is kava, a mildly sedating brew made from the roots of the, um, kava plant that's used in a myriad of social and religious ceremonies. However, if you're making your way through Palau's surprisingly extensive bar scene—a by-product of decades of American occupation—you're far more likely to encounter a wide array of classic tiki drinks, like the Kava Cocktail. Created by the legendary Victor "Trader Vic" Bergeron in the early 1940s, this multi-rum, sweet-and-sour team-up doesn't contain any actual kava, though like its namesake it packs a Pacific-size tidal wave of flavor that will calm the nerves and have you thinking tropical thoughts in no time. And if you want to experience the communal aspects of a kava ceremony, be sure to make enough for your friends.

Kava Cocktail

Makes 1 drink

1½ ounces white rum

1 ounce pineapple juice

¾ ounce fresh lemon juice

½ ounce gold rum

¼ ounce cane syrup

¼ ounce pomegranate syrup (page 5)

Crushed ice

1 pineapple wedge, for garnish

1 brandied cherry, for garnish

Combine the white rum, pineapple juice, lemon juice, gold rum, cane syrup, and pomegranate syrup in a shaker. Pour into a tall glass or tiki mug filled two-thirds of the way with crushed ice. Add a straw and top with more crushed ice. Garnish with the pineapple wedge and brandied cherry.

KAVA'S CALMING, soothing effects differ greatly from other substances like alcohol or cannabis, which can make you feel intoxicated and unbalanced. Instead, kava provides relaxation and balance without the risk of losing control. It's a mental state users of the plant describe as being rooted, or grounded in the present moment.

PAPUA NEW GUINEA

Thanks to centuries of aggressive exploration—and, more recently, Google Earth—there aren't many places left on the planet that are a complete mystery to humanity. That's not the case with Papua New Guinea. The country that comprises the eastern half of the island of New Guinea still has mountainous areas that are so inaccessible no person has ever stepped foot there—and maybe never will. Home to an estimated 5 percent of the entire planet's biodiversity, it's one of the few places where new species of plants and animals are being discovered all the time, with a population that's almost as diverse. Papuans speak around 800 different languages, making it by far the most linguistically complex nation in the world. But there's one love language just about everyone in this remote corner of Oceania speaks—the desire for a tall, frosty glass of beer.

Outside of the capital Port Moresby, liquor is almost nonexistent. However, imported bottles and local brews like Niugini Ice and South Pacific Lager have penetrated the deepest Papuan jungles, where tribes have been existing as hunter-gatherers for more than 40,000 years. And while the Michelada—a Mexican drink that, in its most basic form, contains light beer, lime juice, hot sauce, and salt—doesn't have quite as long a history, originating in the 1960s, it's a great starting point for any zesty, hops-related cocktail. The Melanesian Michelada embellishes its lager and hot sauce base with spices commonly used in Papuan cooking like turmeric, cardamom, and dried chiles for a fiery blend that will fortify you before any Papuan-like journey into the unknown. Or revive you when you wake up after facing the darkness and barely making it back.

Melanesian Michelada

Makes 1 drink

Sea salt, for rimming the glass
1 lime wedge, for rimming the glass
Cracked ice 1 ounce fresh lime juice
¾ ounce Worcestershire sauce
¾ ounce hot sauce, such as Cholula
Pinch of ground turmeric
Pinch of ground cardamom
Pinch of chili powder
1 (12-ounce) can or bottle beer, such as South Pacific Lager

Spread some salt over a small plate. Run the lime wedge around the rim of a tall glass, then dip the rim into the salt to coat. Fill the glass two-thirds of the way with cracked ice and set aside. Combine the lime juice, Worcestershire, hot sauce, turmeric, cardamom, and chili powder in a shaker. Stir with a long-handled spoon until the spices are fully dissolved. Pour half the contents of the shaker into the prepared glass and fill nearly to the top with beer. Taste and add more of the lime juice mixture if desired.

SAMOA

Known as "the Cradle of Polynesia," Samoa's two main islands, Savai'i and Upolu, have played a central role in the cultural, linguistic, and artistic development of the Western Pacific region for thousands of years. Polynesian languages, religions, styles of clothing, dance, and visual art all have distinctly Samoan roots. And though Samoa's native people (*tagata Sāmoa* in their native tongue) didn't invent sailing, they're still considered some of the most prolific—and proficient—oceanic travelers, so much so that the first Europeans to visit the archipelago named it the Navigator Islands, marveling in their diaries at the uncanny ability of the Polynesians to read the night sky like a compass.

Odes to Samoan seafaring prowess also exist in liquid form, the most famous of these being the Samoan Fog Cutter. The dizzying mélange of three different liquors, a heavy dose of citrus, almond syrup, and a sherry float was first served by bartending legend Victor "Trader Vic" Bergeron at his Oakland, California, restaurant in the 1940s and appeared in recipe form in his 1947 *Bartender's Guide.* "Fog Cutter, hell," the always-crusty tiki mastermind writes about the cocktail's purported ability to clear a drinker's sight and mind. "After two of these, you won't even see the stuff." Anyone who's attempted to navigate a few city blocks, let alone a boat, after a few too many tiki-strength libations will have to begrudgingly agree.

Samoan Fog Cutter

Makes 1 drink

1½ ounces light rum

1 ounce cognac

1 ounce fresh orange juice

½ ounce London dry gin

½ ounce fresh lemon juice

½ ounce orgeat

Crushed ice

½ ounce oloroso sherry

1 mint sprig, for garnish

Combine the rum, cognac, orange juice, gin, lemon juice, and orgeat in a shaker. Pour into a tall glass filled two-thirds of the way with crushed ice. Float the sherry on top by pouring it over the back of a spoon into the glass. Add a straw and top with more crushed ice. Garnish with the mint sprig.

SAMOANS LIKE to nurse their hangovers—or simply refresh themselves—with a rather unexpected beverage for the tropics: hot chocolate, or *koko Samoa* as it's known locally. A major part of Samoan culinary culture, it's thought to have been introduced through contact with South America around 700 CE.

SOLOMON ISLANDS

With a territory spanning more than 930 miles from its easternmost to westernmost points—roughly the same as the distance between Italy and Belarus—the Solomon Islands contain an extremely wide variety of cultures and geographic features that range from towering mountains and rain forests to low-lying atolls and coral reefs. And while English is technically the official language on each of the country's 347 inhabited islands, only 1 to 2 percent of the population uses it regularly. Instead, most residents speak at least one of 120 indigenous languages and dialects, depending on tribal affiliation. One thing most Solomon Islanders do share is a love for drinking kava, with each island having its own customs and traditions for consuming the mildly psychoactive brew.

If you're looking for a quick buzz and don't have the patience to sit through a kava ceremony (which can last hours or even days), there are plenty of accessibly boozy beverages to be found at tourist-friendly bars, especially on larger islands like Guadalcanal and Choiseul. Like the Solomon Island Cocktail, a drink of unknown origin that's been popping up in tiki circles for decades. Its base of gin and cherry liqueur—perhaps a reminder of the country's British and French colonial eras—is unique among tropical potations but works exceedingly well with more conventional tiki ingredients like pineapple and passion fruit to thrust you headfirst on the path toward Pacific-inspired bliss.

Solomon Island Cocktail

Makes 1 drink

1½ ounces gin

1 ounce fresh pineapple juice

½ ounce cherry brandy or comparable cherry liqueur, such as Cherry Heering

½ ounce Cointreau

½ ounce fresh lime juice

½ ounce passion fruit syrup, such as Liber & Co. Tropical Passionfruit Syrup

Crushed ice

1 thin orange slice, for garnish

1 brandied cherry, for garnish

Combine the gin, pineapple juice, cherry brandy, Cointreau, lime juice, and passion fruit syrup in a shaker. Pour into a tall glass filled two-thirds of the way with crushed ice. Add a straw and top with more crushed ice. Garnish with the orange slice and brandied cherry.

TONGA

Despite its relatively small size and remote location (then again, what isn't remote in Oceania?), Tonga stands out from its neighboring countries in numerous ways. The only Pacific island country never to have been colonized by a foreign power, it's retained most of its authentic culture in the form of elaborate, gender-segregated kava ceremonies and traditional arts like basket-making, bone-carving, and fine weaving, all under the auspices of a still-powerful monarchy that's lasted for more than 1,000 years. Tonga is also the birthplace of 'otai, a luscious, juicy blend of water, shredded coconut meat, sugar, and a variety of grated fruits, most commonly watermelon. Unlike kava, which only men are allowed to consume, Tongans of all stripes partake of the eminently refreshing beverage that can now be found on just about every Polynesian archipelago.

If you're of a certain noble mindset, you recognize that no tantalizing mixture of coconut and tropical fruit is complete without some boozy embellishment. Hence the 'Otai Colada, wherein your favorite clear spirit—white rum, tequila, vodka, and gin are all tasty options—adds a welcome kick to the sweet and nutty milieu. Tongans prefer their 'otai chunky enough to eat with a spoon, but this recipe is totally flexible. Add as much water as you need for your desired consistency. Prefer mango over pineapple? Want to use both? Neither? It's all good. And for those who are particularly chunk-averse, feel free to blend it up. If you're drinking the embodiment of an idyllic Pacific vacation, you might as well act like you're on one and do it your way.

'Otai Colada

Makes 1 drink

3 ounces full-fat coconut milk

2 ounces clear spirit of choice

2 to 4 watermelon chunks

2 to 4 pineapple chunks

Cane syrup (if using unsweetened coconut milk; optional)

¾ cup cracked ice

Combine all the ingredients in a blender and blend until smooth. Pour into a double rocks glass or large wineglass and add a straw.

ALTHOUGH ONLY men are allowed to drink kava, women have an important role in the traditional Tongan kava ceremony, as only they can offer a required blessing to the beverage before consumption.

TUVALU

Europe is famous for its pocket-size countries, but only two of its microstates—Monaco and Vatican City—as well as neighboring Pacific state Nauru, are smaller than Tuvalu. The remote Commonwealth realm is the home of nearly 12,000 citizens living on just 10 square miles of atolls and narrow reef islands, with a maximum elevation of 15 feet. As sea levels rise, the archipelago is in real danger of disappearing into the ocean. Which is why, in 2022, the government announced that it would be creating a digital copy of the entire country in the Metaverse, in order to indefinitely preserve Tuvalu's history and Polynesian culture.

Obviously, natural resources here are thin. The one exception is the coconut palm, which grows abundantly and provides Tuvaluans with a plant-based food source to supplement their seafood-heavy diet, as well as red toddy, a sweet sap collected from the tree that's fermented to make the country's only native alcoholic beverage, kao. For a boozier, crisper, yet similarly straightforward take on coconut-inspired bliss, there are few drinks as refreshing as the Agua de Coco, which originally appeared in Charles H. Baker Jr.'s *South American Gentleman's Companion* (1951). While the inclusion of rum and citrus might break with Tuvalu's coconut-only tradition, they're exactly the kind of imported ingredients that you're likely to find in Tuvalu's sparse handful of bars and restaurants.

Agua de Coco

Makes 1 drink

2 ounces light rum

1½ ounces coconut water

½ ounce fresh lime juice

½ ounce simple syrup (page 5)

Club soda, to top

1 lime wedge, for garnish

1 mint sprig, for garnish

Combine the rum, coconut water, lime juice, and simple syrup in a shaker. Add 1 or 2 ice pebbles, shake briefly, and pour into a Collins glass filled with ice. Top with club soda. Perch the lime wedge on the rim of the glass and place the mint sprig in the glass beside the ice.

VANUATU

If you've heard of Vanuatu, it might be because of the archipelago's freaky history of cannibalism. The first British missionaries to visit in 1839 were swiftly captured and roasted and stories of people eating each other were reported as recently as 1969, with living Ni-Vans (the common name for the country's citizens) still able to recall the recipe—apparently three to five hours is the ideal cooking time for human. These days there's only good times on the menu, as visitors to the islands are welcome to enjoy countless natural delights, some of the best scuba diving and volcano viewing in the world, and the strongest kava found anywhere in the Pacific, which is freely consumed without any of the gender- or age-based restrictions that are common elsewhere in the region.

But beware: First-time users of kava have been known to suffer some serious gut-crippling side effects. So if you find yourself in Vanuatu's party capital Port Vila, you might want to stick to the familiar tropical tipples that can be scavenged at just about every one of the city's surprisingly plentiful selection of watering holes. Like the aptly named Chill Bar & Restaurant, whose signature cocktail, the not-so-accurately-named Bikini Martini, is a bona fide tiki treasure. Its dry gin base (which, okay, does jive with the whole martini thing) is a nice contrast to super fruity elements like blue curaçao, peach schnapps, and pineapple juice. So easy-sipping that, like today's Ni-Vans, you'll forget about any questionable past life choices.

Bikini Martini

Makes 1 drink

2 ounces dry gin

¾ ounce blue curaçao

¼ ounce peach schnapps

¼ ounce fresh lemon juice

1 orange twist, for garnish

Combine the gin, blue curaçao, peach schnapps, and lemon juice in an ice-filled shaker. Shake vigorously and then strain into a coupe. Place the orange twist in the glass.

IN VANUATU, the legal drinking age is 18, but it is rarely enforced. Anyone can purchase alcohol as identification is not required. It can be quite shocking for visitors to go to places like bars and nightclubs and see children as young as 12 knocking back a drink.

Caribbean Sea

VENEZUELA

COLOMBIA

ECUADOR

PERU

BRAZIL

BOLIVIA

PARAGUAY

CHILE

South
Pacific
Ocean

URUGUAY

ARGENTINA

SOUTH AMERICA

South Atlantic Ocean

ARGENTINA

When someone mentions Argentina, several things might come to mind. Tango, the Andes, prized beef cattle raised by skilled gauchos, Patagonia's otherworldly terrain, Italian amari. Okay, probably not the latter. But these bitter, aromatic spirits have been a huge part of the local culture since the early nineteenth and twentieth centuries, when Europeans, often hailing from the Apennine Peninsula, immigrated to Argentina in droves. Today, stepping into a Buenos Aires bar still often feels closer to Florence or Naples than the Southern Hemisphere.

Many Argentines love a good Negroni, but there is one amaro-based concoction that reigns supreme: Fernet con Coca, also known as the Fernando, which is comprised of Fernet-Branca, an Italian digestivo made from a proprietary blend of herbs like myrrh, saffron, chamomile, and gentian, and Coca-Cola. First whipped up by students in the college town of Córdoba in the 1980s, the drink has become so popular that Argentina currently consumes 75 percent of all fernet produced globally and is home to the only Fernet-Branca distillery outside Milan. Though somewhat of an acquired taste when taken straight—just ask any novice bartender who's been persuaded to shoot copious amounts of the pitch-black stuff with palate-abusing veterans—Fernet's astringently bittersweet, minty, and licorice-like notes mingle exceptionally well with Coke's sweet and spicy overtones, creating a tonic that's ideal for both getting the party started and recovering from it the next day.

If fernet's intense flavor just isn't your thing, not to worry. Argentina is also a wine lover's paradise, producing some of the best Malbecs in the world, as well as dozens of other delightful reds and whites. One of these, New Age White, a bright, slightly sweet blend of Torrontés and sauvignon blanc, is often served over ice with lime juice, a mixture known as a tincho. My San Rafael Spritz, named for the region where the wine is produced, is a souped-up version of this popular cooler—minty, summery, sparkling, and featuring Latin America's omnipresent sugarcane-based spirit, aguardiente.

Fernet con Coca

Makes 1 drink

2 ounces Fernet-Branca
Coca-Cola, to top
1 lemon wedge, for garnish

Pour the fernet into a Collins glass filled with ice. Top with Coca-Cola. Perch the lemon wedge on the rim of the glass.

San Rafael Spritz

Makes 1 drink

1 ounce aguardiente
1 ounce fresh lime juice
¼ ounce cane syrup
Small handful of mint leaves
4 ounces semisweet white wine (New Age White, if you can get it)
Club soda, to top
1 lime wedge, for garnish

Combine the aguardiente, lime juice, cane syrup, and mint in a shaker. Gently muddle and then add the wine. Pour into a large wineglass filled with cracked ice. Top with club soda. Place the lime wedge in the glass.

Fernet con Coca

BOLIVIA

What you choose to call something can be as important as how you make it. That's certainly the case with singani, Bolivia's longtime national spirit. Named for a word in the indigenous Aymara language that describes a species of local plant, the clear, grape-based brandy shares many physical characteristics and a similar historical timeline with the pisco that's produced in neighboring Peru and Chile. Yet, because of its distinct appellation, it's never been embroiled in any fierce domain controversy like the one that exists between those two countries.

Like pisco, it was first distilled by wine-loving Spanish monks in the early sixteenth century but differentiates from its liquid cousin in that it must be made only with white Muscat of Alexandria grapes grown in specific regions of Bolivia at altitudes above 5,250 feet, with aging taking place exclusively in neutral casks for a minimum of six months. The result is quite enticing—floral, slightly sweet, and mildly peppery, with a soft, smooth mouthfeel that rivals the best eaus-de-vie.

As you'd imagine, it's also an outstanding starting point for a variety of mixed drinks. Many of these resemble creamy, citrusy Pisco Sours, but for something a bit warmer that's also indisputably Bolivian, try the Té con Té. The Toddy riff made with singani, black tea, cinnamon, and a pinch of lime has been served for centuries in villages in the Andes Mountains—where altitudes routinely soar close to 20,000 feet—as a throat-soothing, revitalizing potion. It also makes a great summertime refresher when served chilled. However you choose to enjoy it, just be sure not to call it pisco.

Té con Té

Makes 1 drink

4 ounces water

1 teaspoon loose black tea leaves

1 cinnamon stick

2 ounces singani

1 lime wedge, for garnish

Combine the water, tea, and cinnamon stick in a small pot and heat over medium heat for 3 to 5 minutes, being careful not to let the mixture boil. Strain into a warmed mug. Pour the singani into the mug and stir briefly to combine the mixture. Perch the lime wedge on the rim of the mug.

LONG BEFORE the invention of singani, Bolivians were infusing their teas with another mind-altering ingredient: coca leaves. Notorious for being the natural source of cocaine, the relatively mild plant is especially popular in the Andes as an energy booster and a method for combating altitude sickness.

BRAZIL

Brazil is a truly colossal country, South America's largest by several million square miles. And from the deepest reaches of the Amazon Basin to the seemingly endless Atlantic coastline, one spirit—cachaça—captures the country's heart and soul like no other. Production began way back in the early 1500s, when Portuguese merchants bearing sugarcane plantings and pot stills from Madeira arrived on the shores of what they called the New World. Made from fermented cane juice and distilled like Martinique's rhum agricole and Haiti's clairin, the fruity, aromatic liquor has been experiencing a major glow-up the past few decades. Artisanal and industrial cachaça producers—who churn out well over a billion liters of hooch annually—now harness the unique properties of barrels made of indigenous Brazilian woods like Amburana, Cabreúva, and Brazil nut tree, creating an impressive range of characteristics among the nearly 1 million liters bottled each year.

Even before cachaça's epic surge in global relevance, American drinkers—who now import more than 100,000 cases annually—were familiar with Brazil's national cocktail, the caipirinha. A simple, incredibly tasty blend of cachaça, sugar, and muddled lime, it was purportedly invented near the city of São Paulo around 1918 as a remedy for the common cold. Once the original recipe—which called for garlic, honey, and lemon—was scrapped for the modern version, the drink spread quickly around the world, serving as a perfectly citrusy and sweet introduction to cachaça's exceptionally aromatic flavor profile.

Shockingly, it's possible—or so I've heard—that you may eventually grow bored of caipirinhas and go in search of slightly more complex cachaça-based cocktails. Look no further than the Batida (page 268), which means "shaken" or "milkshake" in Portuguese. First appearing on Liquor.com, the following adapted recipe combines passion fruit syrup, coconut milk, and fresh lime juice for a result that's bright, creamy, beachy, impeccably balanced, and—like the caipirinha, an authentically Brazilian treasure.

Caipirinha

Makes 1 drink

2 ounces cachaça

5 lime wedges

¾ ounce simple syrup (page 5)

1 sugar cube

Combine all the ingredients in a shaker. Muddle thoroughly and fill the shaker with cracked ice. Shake 5 or 6 times and pour the contents of the shaker into a double rocks glass.

Batida

Makes 1 drink

2 ounces cachaça

1 ounce passion fruit syrup, such as Liber & Co. Tropical
   Passionfruit Syrup

½ ounce full-fat coconut milk

½ ounce fresh lime juice

¾ cup crushed ice

1 pineapple leaf, for garnish

Pinch of freshly grated nutmeg, for garnish

Combine the cachaça, passion fruit syrup, coconut milk, and lime juice in a blender with the crushed ice and blend until smooth. Pour into a double rocks glass and add a straw. Place the pineapple leaf in the glass and sprinkle with the nutmeg.

ALTHOUGH IT CONTINUES to increase in popularity outside of its country of origin, most cachaça never leaves Brazil. According to recent reports, Brazilians consume around 1.5 *billion* liters of cachaça per year, while the rest of the world only consumes about 15 million liters.

CHILE

With the second longest coastline in Latin America after Brazil (roughly the same as the distance between Maine and California), serpentine Chile stretches thousands of miles from the southernmost reaches of Patagonia to the dry northern desert border with longtime adversary Peru. Across all that varying landscape, the spirit of choice is pisco, the brandy-like semisweet grape distillate that was introduced in the sixteenth century by Spanish colonizers.

As the centuries-long dispute between Chile and Peru over the fragrant liquor's origins and who is even allowed to call it pisco continues to rage with no end in sight, it's clear that the spirit is a deep source of pride and patriotism for Chileans. And for good reason. Their versions of the sacred hooch, unlike Peruvian varieties, is often aged in wood, can be made from fourteen different varietals, doesn't need to be distilled to proof, and can be distilled multiple times, resulting in what grape lovers describe as a uniquely floral and fruity bouquet.

That flavor profile is most frequently enjoyed in Chile's national cocktail, the Pisco Sour, whose birthplace is—no surprise—another source of contention between Peru and Chile. But if you're looking for a drama-free drink that's 100% Chilean, try the Serena Libre, which originated in the 1990s in the northern city of La Serena. A bright, succulent combination of pisco and papaya—which happens to be one of La Serena's biggest exports and an unofficial cultural symbol of the town—it's bursting with vitamin C, a must-have especially if you're planning on trekking across the Andes, which comprise much of Chile's eastern border.

Serena Libre

Makes 1 drink

1½ ounces Chilean pisco
1½ ounces papaya juice
½ ounce fresh lime juice
¼ ounce cane syrup
Club soda, to top
1 lime wedge, for garnish

Combine the pisco, papaya juice, lime juice, and cane syrup in a shaker. Add 1 or 2 ice pebbles, shake briefly, and pour into an ice-filled Collins glass. Top with club soda. Perch the lime wedge on the rim of the glass.

COLOMBIA

There's a popular Colombian saying that loosely translates to "Those who are sad can't even have fun when they're drunk." Luckily, it's hard to feel downtrodden for long in one of South America's most vibrant countries, which boasts a colorful mixture of Amerindian, African, European, and Asian cultural influences and a people who exude passion in everything they do. That enthusiasm extends to the local aguardiente, which is markedly unlike any other cane-derived liquor. That difference is mostly attributed to the infusion of anise from Spain, as well as a variety of indigenous herbs and cinnamon, giving it strong ouzo vibes, but with only about half of the Greek spirit's potency. Government-run distilleries in every Colombian state produce their own variations, meaning that visitors can sample up to nine distinct versions of the national hooch.

Wherever you travel in Colombia (or if you happen to catch their national baseball team playing in international competitions like the World Baseball Classic), you'll notice its citizens' palpable love for their country. The patriotism is personified in the national drink, the Colombia Cocktail. Steady-handed bartenders can perfectly layer the concoction's boozy and fruity components to emulate the blue, yellow, and red of the Colombian flag. But even if you prefer to shake or blend yours into a palate-stimulating Pollack painting, the silky, sweet, and melodious fusion of blue curaçao, orange, lemon, and grenadine, jacked up with Colombian aguardiente's unique herbaceous accents, it will still check all the boxes as a one-of-a-kind tropical treasure.

Colombia Cocktail

Makes 1 drink

2 ounces aguardiente or vodka

¾ ounce fresh lemon juice

½ ounce fresh orange juice

½ ounce grenadine

1 ounce blue curaçao

Combine the aguardiente, lemon juice, and orange juice in an ice-filled shaker. Shake vigorously and then strain into a rocks glass. Slowly pour the grenadine over the back of a spoon into the glass, then repeat the same process with the curaçao. This will create red, blue, and yellow layers, so the cocktail is striped with the colors of the Colombian flag.

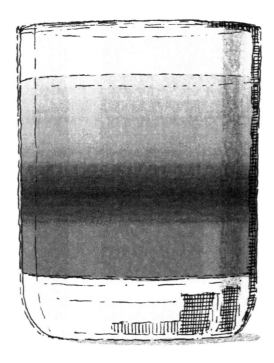

COLOMBIA'S WORKERS have plenty of opportunities for guilt-free aguardiente drinking sessions, thanks to eighteen government-sanctioned holidays throughout the year (usually occurring on Mondays), the most of any country besides India.

ECUADOR

Human rights are obviously important. But what about all the other living things that share the planet with us? Ecuador's got their back, becoming the first country to officially recognize the right of nature to flourish. And that's of particular importance in an equatorial country that has more biodiversity per square mile than anywhere on the planet—including 15 percent of all known bird species. That commitment to extreme environmentalism is also why Ecuador's aguardiente is considered some of the purest in South America. Production methods may differ slightly depending on where the sugarcane-derived firewater is distilled, with regional variations ranging from a paltry 10% ABV to a brain-bruising 70% or more. What these disparate liquors share, unlike their equivalents in neighboring countries like Colombia, is that they're mostly unflavored, stripping them down to an essential form that's remained unchanged for 500 years.

Dominated by Amazon rainforest—and, lately, an increasing number of oil fields—Ecuador's southern regions stay fairly sweltering. But the capital, Quito, despite being built almost directly on top of the equator, is also more than 9,000 feet above sea level, so nights tend to get chilly in this thin-air metropolis. Quiteños like to warm up with the country's favorite cocktail, the Canelazo, and its fruitier spinoff, the Naranjillazo. Slight variations exist throughout Ecuador, but all of them in their simplest form feature the local aguardiente mixed with hot water, cinnamon, an unrefined whole cane sugar called panela, and, in the Naranjillazo, juice concentrate from the tangy naranjilla fruit. Tangential to the hot toddy and no less potent or delicious, there's nothing finer for appreciating nature at its most brisk. Go ahead, you've earned that right.

Canelazo

Makes 6 drinks

6 cups water

1 cup sugar or grated panela

8 cinnamon sticks

9 ounces aguardiente

Combine the water, sugar, and cinnamon sticks in a medium saucepan. Bring to a boil, reduce the heat to low, and simmer for 30 to 40 minutes. (Alternatively, simply boil the mixture for 10 to 15 minutes.) Remove from the heat, add the aguardiente, and pour into large mugs. Serve immediately.

Naranjillazo

Makes 6 drinks

4 cups water

2 cups naranjilla concentrate or Goya naranjilla fruit pulp

1¼ cups sugar or grated panela

8 cinnamon sticks

9 ounces aguardiente

Combine the water, naranjilla concentrate, sugar, and cinnamon sticks in a medium saucepan. Bring to a boil, reduce the heat to low, and simmer for 30 to 40 minutes. (Alternatively, simply boil the mixture for 10 to 15 minutes.) Remove from the heat, add the aguardiente, and pour into large mugs. Serve immediately.

EVEN THE MOST adventurous drinkers have been known to balk at chicha, Ecuador's indigenous cassava-based alcohol. That's because this super-starchy oatmeal-like brew—a popular ceremonial beverage throughout the Amazon region—is made using human saliva, which accelerates the fermentation process.

GUYANA

The only English-speaking country in South America, sparsely populated and deeply forested Guyana is best known for its remarkable biodiversity, though this small nation's centuries-old contributions to rum culture deserve just as much attention as its flora and fauna. Since the 1850s, when the British introduced distillation practices to their sugarcane-rich colony, Guyanese rum—called Demerara rum after the river along which it's produced—has been considered one of the finest spirits in the world. The unique terroir of the Guyanese coast, as well as the use of wooden stills, creates a flavorful and aromatic bouquet found nowhere else, resulting in deep, rich rums with lots of earthy, smoky notes that give them a unique complexity.

One of the most recognizable Demerara rums today is Lemon Hart 151, which, as its name suggests, weighs in at a diabolical 151 proof. It's mostly used sparingly—as an accent in tiki drinks, as the means of ignition in fiery shooters like the Flaming Buzzard, or as a mystery shot that evil bartenders foist upon their unsuspecting coworkers. El Dorado 12 Year, from legendary Demerara Distillers Ltd., is a much more palatable introduction to the Guyanese good life. Its notes of vanilla, burnt sugar, and baking spices shine through in Martin Cate's Kaieteur Swizzle, adapted from his 2016 book *Smuggler's Cove: Exotic Cocktails, Rum, and the Cult of Tiki.* This outrageously smooth offering of maple, almond, citrus, and bitters, named for Guyana's most famous waterfall, is so good, you won't be able to get it down your own gullet fast enough.

Kaieteur Swizzle

Makes 1 drink

2 ounces blended aged rum, such as El Dorado 12 Year

¾ ounce fresh lime juice

½ ounce pure maple syrup

½ ounce falernum, such as John D. Taylor's Velvet Falernum

Crushed ice

2 dashes Angostura bitters

1 lime wedge, for garnish

1 mint sprig, for garnish

Combine the rum, lime juice, maple syrup, and falernum in a shaker. Pour into a tall glass filled two-thirds of the way with crushed ice. Add the bitters and stir briefly with a swizzle stick. Add a straw and fill the glass to the top with crushed ice. Garnish with the lime wedge and mint sprig.

PARAGUAY

Frequently overlooked by travelers headed to South America's trendier destinations, landlocked Paraguay is the continent's least-visited country. That doesn't mean you should write off this land of massive waterfalls, wildlife-filled wetlands, and spectacular rock formations. Especially if you fancy a scrumptious, energy-inducing beverage. Paraguay's national drink, tereré, is a zesty infusion of yerba mate, cold water, and a rejuvenating blend of medicinal herbs like saffron, verbena, mint, and *ajenjo* (wormwood). It's been brewed by the indigenous Guarani people for centuries and is considered a cultural icon, with its own holiday celebrated each year on the last Saturday of February.

While it doesn't share the same prestige, the country's local liquor, caña—a distillate of fermented sugarcane juice and honey that's similar to Brazilian cachaça—is still the go-to for Paraguayans who prefer to get turned up in a boozier manner. Mixing caña and tereré isn't really a thing—though you're more than welcome to try it. Instead, Paraguay's drink-makers blend their domestic spirit with juice from native fruits, with the passion fruit taking precedence. But not just any passion fruit. *Passiflora edulis*, or purple passion fruit (*maracuyà* to the locals), is prized for its aroma, intense citrusy notes, and juicy texture and is a staple in cosmetic fragrances, desserts, and cocktails like the Paraguay Passion. The drink's bold and summery blend of caña, maracuyà, orange liqueur, and fresh lime serves as both a delightful refresher and a good reminder that sometimes the least-traveled roads (and flavors) can be the most worthwhile.

Paraguay Passion

Makes 1 drink

2 ounces passion fruit nectar

1½ ounces caña (if unavailable, use cachaça)

½ ounce Cointreau

½ ounce fresh lime juice

2 dashes Angostura bitters

1 thin orange slice, for garnish

Combine the passion fruit nectar, caña, Cointreau, lime juice, and bitters in an ice-filled shaker. Shake vigorously and then strain into a double rocks glass over ice. Perch the orange slice on the rim of the glass.

THE MAJORITY of caña production can be traced to Paraguay's Guairá region, where nearly 60 percent of the heavily indigenous population is involved in the sugarcane industry.

PERU

Chileans won't want to read this, but in the centuries-long debate over where pisco originated and who should even be allowed to call the grape-based liquor by that name, the pro-Peru camp may have the most convincing arguments. The first written mention of the word *pisco*—which means "bird" in the local Quechua language—dates to 1764, referring to both the spirit and its purported birthplace, the town of Pisco, an important trading port from which its namesake hooch has been exported since at least 1572. A nineteenth-century report in the Austrian newspaper *Wiener Zeitung* confirmed that while Chileans were distilling their version of pisco in much higher quantities, Peruvians produced it first.

Rivalries aside, today's Peruvian piscos, fermented from the must of eight specific grape varieties and distilled a single time using traditional artisanal methods—often in pot stills—are lauded for their purity, smoothness, floral notes, and fiery palate. That intensity can be at least partially attributed to the fact that all pisco produced in the country must be bottled at proof (or the strength at which it leaves the still), without water or any other additives, which preserves the grapes' natural flavors. Aside from the Pisco Sour, Peru's national cocktail, there are many authentically Peruvian beverages that highlight the country's biggest source of boozy pride, like the Chicha Sour. Featuring chicha morada, a juice made from Andean purple corn and spices that's been consumed for centuries, most notably during the Incan Empire, it's prized for its tanginess, its high levels of antioxidants and other nutrients, and the cleanest grape-based buzz south of the equator.

FEELING HUNGOVER? Tired? Asthmatic? Impotent? If you're in Peru, try some of the local frog juice. Used as a cure for countless bodily ailments, this sludgy mix of native ingredients like maca, coca leaves, chia, and, yes, cooked frog meat has been slurped for centuries by the country's indigenous peoples. When blended well, the drink is said to have a pleasantly earthy and malty flavor, with hardly a hint of its namesake amphibian.

Chicha Sour

Makes 1 drink

2 ounces Peruvian pisco

1 ounce unsweetened chicha morada

¾ ounce simple syrup (page 5)

½ ounce fresh lime juice

1 egg white

Combine all the ingredients in a shaker. Shake without ice for 5 or 6 seconds to emulsify the egg white, then add ice and shake vigorously. Strain into a stemmed cocktail glass.

SURINAME

The history of colonization in South America—particularly its early years—is often described as a two-horse race between Spain and Portugal to gobble up the continent's land and resources. But that doesn't mean other European powers weren't trying to sink their teeth in. One of these, the Netherlands, founded Suriname in the seventeenth century as a key West Indian trading post. Dutch is still the official language in South America's smallest country (the only place outside of Europe where that's the case), which is also one of its most diverse. Creole, Indonesian, Amerindian, and Chinese ethnic communities contribute to Suriname's ultra-rich cultural mixture and the seemingly endless festivities held year-round. Not surprisingly, rum has long been the Surinamese partier's favor of choice, as its capital Paramaribo's location on the Caribbean Sea means that distillation occurred here early and often.

What's a little bit more surprising are the massive numbers of Surinamese who can trace their heritage to the Indonesian island of Java, another former Dutch colony. Their unmistakable presence has ensured that holidays like Javanese Arrival Day will always be celebrated and that refreshing culinary staples like Rose Dawet feature heavily in Suriname's restaurant scene. The thick and luscious drink marries vegetal and fragrant lemongrass, silky-smooth coconut milk, and lots of rosy notes for a complex, can't-miss cooler. Like most beverages, its flavors—and more importantly, fun quotient—is amplified with the inclusion of alcohol, in this case locally distilled Black Cat rum, which has been enticing sugarcane lovers and molasses mavens since the 1970s.

Rose Dawet

Makes 1 drink

4 ounces full-fat unsweetened coconut milk

2 ounces Surinamese rum, such as Black Cat White Rum

¾ ounce Lemongrass-Rose Syrup (recipe follows)

1 tablespoon young coconut meat

In a blender, crush 2 or 3 small ice cubes. Add the coconut milk, rum, and lemongrass-rose syrup and blend until thoroughly combined. Place the coconut meat in the bottom of a tall glass. Pour the contents of the blender into the glass.

Lemongrass-Rose Syrup

Makes 1½ cups

1½ cups water

2 lemongrass stalks

1 cup sugar

Rose paste or rose water

Combine the water and lemongrass in a small saucepan (cut the stalks to fit the pan, if needed) and bring to a boil. Add the sugar and cook, stirring, until the sugar has fully dissolved. Remove from the heat and discard the lemongrass. Let cool completely, then add rose paste to taste and stir to combine. Store in an airtight glass container in the refrigerator for up to 1 week.

THE WORLD'S strongest commercially available rum is Marienburg overproof white rum from the Suriname Alcoholic Beverages (SAB) company, which is sold at an eye-popping 90% ABV, with some special batches reaching 94%. That doesn't stop Suriname's gnarliest drinkers from enjoying it in the traditional way, as a straight shot with only a bit of water for a chaser.

URUGUAY

Statistically speaking, the answer to the question "Where's the beef?" is, emphatically, Uruguay. Tucked between Brazil and Argentina on South America's southeastern coast, the continent's smallest Spanish-speaking country consumes more beef per capita than any other nation on Earth. Nearly 60 percent of Uruguay's land is used for cattle farming, with beef also being its main export. During long days on the range, the country's many *gauchos*, or cowboys, stay energized with mate, a traditional tea made from the caffeine-rich leaves of the yerba mate plant that's wildly popular throughout the region. But after work, they prefer an icy glass of grappamiel, the national beverage and a great source of pride for booze-loving Uruguayans.

A blend of grappa—a potent grape-based pomace brandy that was first brought to South America by waves of Italian immigrants in the late nineteenth and early twentieth centuries—plus grain alcohol, honey, and water, it's most often served chilled or on the rocks, and can be infused with a wide range of flavor additives like chocolate, almond, and chamomile. Grappamiel's sweet and delicate bouquet has also been featured in cocktails like the Rosa Negroni, a signature drink from the Basta Spirit beverage company in the city of Canelones. Grappamiel and Cynar perform a perfectly bittersweet candombe (Uruguay's national folk dance) alongside a crisp blast of grapefruit. You don't need to be a cattle rancher to thoroughly enjoy this complex, refreshing—and, thankfully, meat-free—sipper.

Rosa Negroni

Makes 1 drink

1 ounce grappamiel, such as Rosa Negra

1 ounce Cynar

1 ounce fresh grapefruit juice

1 grapefruit twist, for garnish

Combine the grappamiel, Cynar, and grapefruit juice in a shaker. Shake vigorously and then strain into a double rocks glass over ice. Place the grapefruit twist in the glass beside the ice.

URUGUAYANS ARE ALSO exceptionally fond of Scotch. In 1981, they began making Dunbar, one of the first blended whiskies produced in South America, a mixture of imported barley from Scotland and local spring water that's aged in Uruguayan oak barrels for five years.

VENEZUELA

Named for national icon Simón Bolívar, Venezuela's currency gets less respect than its revolutionary hero. The bolivar has seen wild inflation rates of up to 1,000,000 percent in recent years in this oil-rich socialist republic where gas is cheaper than water. Luckily, Venezuelans have plenty of distractions to take their minds off the economy, including a seemingly endless bucket list of one-of-a-kind beaches, mountains, jungles, and even deserts. And some of the smoothest rums in the world. The Caribbean-facing nation's flagship distillery, Santa Teresa, was established in 1796 as a sugarcane, cacao, and coffee plantation, which later transitioned to rum production under the leadership of German immigrant Gustav Julius Vollmer, whose descendants continue to run the globally expanding family business.

Many of Santa Teresa's rums, like 1796 Solera and Claro, are prized as bases in spirit-forward, old-fashioned-style tipples or straightforward, daiquiri-like citrus sippers. But all of these varieties do more than a little justice to Venezuela's national cocktail, the Guarapita, an enchanting mix of local spirit, passion fruit, orange juice, muddle lime, and grenadine. Shaken up for decades at every Venezuelan rum joint—reputable or otherwise—it's consumed in volume each year during the country's extravagant July 5 holiday celebrating its independence from the Spanish crown. It's also the usual first drink Venezuelan teenagers experience when they come of legal boozing age. And what an introduction it is.

SANTA TERESA, besides making excellent rums, is all about helping the local community. In 2003, when a group of gang members broke into the distillery, owner Alberto Vollmer offered them the unusual choice of either being reported to the police or working for him at the company. The men took the latter option, which led to the creation of Project Alcatraz, an initiative that provides rehabilitation and outreach programs to thousands of former criminals and local at-risk youth.

Guarapita

Makes 1 drink

2 ounces Santa Teresa 1796 aged rum

½ ounce passion fruit syrup, such as Liber & Co. Tropical Passionfruit Syrup

¼ ounce pomegranate syrup (page 5)

4 lime wedges

3 or 4 mint leaves, plus 1 sprig for garnish

3 thin orange slices

Combine the rum, passion fruit syrup, pomegranate syrup, lime wedges, mint leaves, and 2 orange slices in a shaker. Muddle thoroughly and fill the shaker with cracked ice. Shake a few times and then pour the contents of the shaker into a double rocks glass. Garnish with the mint sprig and remaining orange slice.

ACKNOWLEDGMENTS

Immense, endless thanks to all the generous souls who made the journey of writing this book a greater joy than I ever thought it could be:

My inimitable agent, Rica Allannic, for her unflinching guidance and support.

The brilliant team at Union Square & Co.—especially my editor, Caitlin Leffel, for her incredible insight and enthusiasm—Amanda Englander, Gavin Motnyk, Ivy McFadden, and Kevin Iwano, as well as copyeditor Donna Wright and Marcella Lopez of Writing Diversely.

The gracious and talented Zoë Barker, for the gorgeous illustrations and maps that bring these pages to life.

Håvard Lund and the other artists in residence at the Arctic Hideaway, for providing an unbelievably epic environment in which to work and think, and all the sauna sessions, elk sausages, midnight hikes, and cold plunges I could handle.

Everyone in the LB bartending family—past and present—who has taught and inspired me and had my (increasingly cranky) back for nearly two decades in the industry. Especially Luis Gil, Vito Dieterle, Alex Mendoza, Michael Timmons, Travis Hernandez, Jackson Hernandez, Grace McCabe, Evan Rubin, Christopher Covey, Oscar Gil, Jose Gil, Lucinda Sterling, Sofia Present, Brody Robinson, Ethan Sugar, Carolyn Gil, Matthew Linzmeier, Courtney McKamey, Lauren Schell, Ben Schwartz, Matty Clark, Sam Ross, and Sasha Petraske. As well as the dozens of bartenders from every (habitable) continent whose creations appear in this book and make it a truly global affair.

And my parents, for encouraging my obsession with far-off places and giving me the courage to go out and explore them.

Japan / Improved Yokohama Cocktail (page 99)

INDEX

Page numbers in *italic* indicate illustrations.

Basotho Gin, 48

Batavia arrack, 94

Batida, 267, 268

Becher, Josef, 154

Becherovka, 115, 154

beef consommé, 106

beer, 39
    dark, 236, 242
    German, 161
    Mesopotamian, 96
    Nepalese, 113
    Papua New Guinea, 253
    Slovenian, 191
    stout, 200

Belarus, 147

Belfast Buck, 197, 200

Belgian jenever, 148

Belgium, 148

Belize, 207

Bénédictine, 99, 121, 126, 177

Benin, 11

Bergeron, Victor, "Trader Vic," 233, 253, 257

bhang lassi, 84

Bhutan, 85

Biancaniello, Matthew, 107

Bikini Atoll, 248

Bikini Martini, 261

Bissap Syrup, 4, 43, 64, 72

Bittermens Xocolatl Mole bitters, 88

Bitter Queens Shanghai Shirley Five-Spice bitters, 88

bitters
    Bittermens Xocolatl Mole bitters, 88
    Bitter Queens Shanghai Shirley Five-Spice bitters, 88
    chocolate, 19, 231, 249
    mint, 194
    orange, 112, 143, 166
    Peychaud's, 54, 237
    tiki, 244

Black Balsam Currant, 169

Black Balsam liqueur, 169

Black Belgian, 148

blackberries, 55, 192, 198

blackberry liqueur, 25

blackcurrant liqueur, 158

Black Latvian Cocktail, 169

Black Panther, 69

black rum, 66, 88, 116

blackstrap rum, 109, 206

black tea, 57, 67, 119, 145, 266

blanche Armagnac, 143

blanc vermouth, 143, 201, 213

Blossom Caresser, 178

Blow My Skull, 242

blueberries, 169

Blushed Arak, 98

Bohemian Mixology (Melia), 194

Bolívar, Simón, 277

Bolivia, 266

Bolkiah, Hassanal (Sultan), 86

Boon, Ngiam Tong, 121

Boozy Mango and Makrut Lime Lassi, 91

borovička, 190

Bosnia and Herzegovina, 150

Boston shaker set, 2

Botswana, 12

boukha, 73

Bourbon Banana Flip, 62

Bourguignon, Jean-Paul, 242

de Bouve, Franciscus Sylvius, 148

Bradsell, Dick, 197

Bramble, 197, 198

brandied cherry, 90, 150, 161, 198, 205, 212, 239

brandy, 8, 57, 67, 68, 90, 103, 189, 190, 242
    apple, 103, 235
    Armenian, 81
    cherry, 258
    Cypriot, 153
    Moldovan, 176
    pear, 94

    plum, 150, 178, 186

    pomace, 167, 276

    raki, 131, 142

Brandy Laban, 60

Bravo, Guillermo, 94

Brazil, 267–68

brem, 94

Brennivín, 1, 165

Brunei, 86

Bubbly Afghan Cherry, 80

Bula, 245, *246*

Bulgaria, 151

Burkina Faso, 14

Burnt Almond Cocktail, 50

Burundi, 15

Bushmills, 197, 200

buttermilk, 91

C

Cabo Verde, 16

cachaça, 47, 63, 130, 185, 267, 268

Caesar, 209

Café con Leche, Arabian-Style, 116

Caffé Lolita, 51

Caipirinha, 1, 47, 130, 267

Calabash Cocktail, 217

Cambodia, 87

Cambodian Coley, 87

Caméléon, 11

Cameroon, 17, *18*

Cameroon's Kick, 17, *18*

Campari, 77, 109, 168, 193, 218

caña, 273

Canada, 209–10

cana de cajeu, 44

Canadian rye whisky, 35

Canelazo, 271

Cane Spirit Rothschild (CSR), 229

cane syrup, 101, 219, 223, 232, 253, 259, 264, 269

cannabis extract, 84

Cantrell, Thomas, 197

Caperitif, 35